# Turkish Intelligence and the Cold War

# Turkish Intelligence and the Cold War

*The Turkish Secret Service, the US and the UK*

Egemen Bezci

**I.B. TAURIS**
LONDON • NEW YORK • OXFORD • NEW DELHI • SYDNEY

I.B. TAURIS
Bloomsbury Publishing Plc
50 Bedford Square, London, WC1B 3DP, UK
1385 Broadway, New York, NY 10018, USA
29 Earlsfort Terrace, Dublin 2, Ireland

BLOOMSBURY, I.B. TAURIS and the Diana logo are trademarks of
Bloomsbury Publishing Plc

Copyright © Egemen Bezci 2020

First published in Great Britain 2020
Paperback edition published 2021

Egemen B. Bezci has asserted his right under the Copyright, Designs and Patents Act, 1988, to be identified as Author of this work.

For legal purposes the Acknowledgements on p. ix constitute an extension of this copyright page.

Cover design by Charlotte Daniels

All rights reserved. No part of this publication may be reproduced or transmitted in any form or by any means, electronic or mechanical, including photocopying, recording, or any information storage or retrieval system, without prior permission in writing from the publishers.

Bloomsbury Publishing Plc does not have any control over, or responsibility for, any third-party websites referred to or in this book. All internet addresses given in this book were correct at the time of going to press. The author and publisher regret any inconvenience caused if addresses have changed or sites have ceased to exist, but can accept no responsibility for any such changes.

A catalogue record for this book is available from the British Library.

A catalogue record for this book is available from the Library of Congress.

ISBN: HB: 978-1-7883-1325-4
PB: 978-0-7556-3649-5
ePDF: 978-1-7867-3609-3
eBook: 978-1-7867-2603-2

Typeset by Integra Software Services Pvt. Ltd.

To find out more about our authors and books visit www.bloomsbury.com and sign up for our newsletters.

# Contents

| | |
|---|---|
| Acknowledgements | ix |
| List of Abbreviations | xi |
| Introduction: Dark Origins of the Turkish-British-American Alliance | 1 |
| Intelligence diplomacy | 3 |
| Secrecy and the study of intelligence | 9 |
| Organization | 20 |
| Note on sources | 22 |
| Notes | 25 |
| 1 Machinery in Comparison | 31 |
|    Gearing the machinery | 32 |
|    The American intelligence community | 35 |
|    British intelligence community | 38 |
|    The Turkish intelligence community | 42 |
|    From intelligence to policy making | 51 |
|    Conclusion | 56 |
|    Notes | 56 |
| 2 Historical Background, 1923–45 | 63 |
|    Early steps | 65 |
|    The interwar years | 68 |
|    Turkey and the powers, 1939–41 | 72 |
|    Wartime clandestine cooperation | 75 |
|    An element of distrust | 82 |
|    Conclusion | 89 |
|    Notes | 90 |

| | | |
|---|---|---|
| 3 | **(Dis)Trusting Your Allies: NATO and CENTO** | 97 |
| | Intelligence Security and Confidence Building | 101 |
| |     Reds in the Ranks | 103 |
| |     NATO | 104 |
| |     Baghdad Pact | 109 |
| | Military Intelligence | 113 |
| |     NATO | 113 |
| |     Baghdad Pact | 123 |
| | Conclusion | 128 |
| | Notes | 129 |
| 4 | **Spies, Atoms and Signals** | 137 |
| | Human intelligence and smuggling of agents | 141 |
| | Running errands in Bulgaria | 146 |
| | Signals: Listening to the atoms | 151 |
| | The Turks' trial with atoms | 158 |
| | Conclusion | 167 |
| | Notes | 168 |
| 5 | **Counter-Subversion: Our Common 'Enemies'** | 175 |
| | Intelligence-made enemies: Communists and Kurds | 176 |
| | Do Kurds have no friends but the mountains? | 181 |
| | Convincing allies | 186 |
| | Our common enemy | 193 |
| | Radio debacle | 199 |
| | Conclusion | 201 |
| | Notes | 202 |
| 6 | **Covert Action: The Turks' Hidden Hand in Syria** | 211 |
| | Making sense of Turkish covert operations | 211 |
| | Turkey's struggle for Syria | 216 |
| | Early approaches | 218 |
| | Beginning of the coups | 223 |
| | Back in Aleppo | 224 |
| | Ankara does not give up | 230 |

|   |   |
|---|---|
| Alliance in discord | 233 |
| Last try | 237 |
| The coup against itself | 242 |
| Conclusion | 245 |
| Notes | 246 |
| Conclusion: Keeping up with the Alliance | 255 |
| Contributions and further investigation | 261 |
| Notes | 267 |
| Bibliography | 269 |
| Index | 288 |

# Acknowledgements

Writing a book is a tiresome, long and intensive process. It is not just about contributing to the field, but is also about building a narrative that reflects onto tangible research outputs. This is a reciprocal process which has also changed my intellectual trajectory (hopefully in a positive way) and produced this book. There are so many important people who have contributed immensely to this process, and without their help this book would not have been possible.

My PhD supervisors and examiners Professor John W. Young, Professor Richard J. Aldrich, Dr Rory Cormac and Dr Louise Kettle deserve most of the credit for this. Without their critical questions, guidance, and support this book would not have been possible. Also, they were always readily available to answer all my questions, and patiently listen to my frustrations along the way. I am indebted to them. The late Dr Chikara Hashimoto was an amazing human being, a scholar and a friend. Our lengthy conversations were of huge importance in helping me to formulate my questions, and build my narrative. Also I would like to thank Professor James Warhola and Professor Paul Holman, who were kind enough to offer their comments on this project, although we live in different continents.

There are many other people, without whose generous friendship I would not have been able to tackle the difficulties of finishing this book. Stefanos Apostolou, Gina Rekka and Steven Parfitt have been great friends in Nottingham. Their friendship and our valuable conversations mean a great deal to me. Nicholas Borroz in Washington, DC opened his house to me during my visit to the National Archives and posed very critical questions to improve the narrative of this book. Marie Flick and her lovely family kindly welcomed me into their family during my trip to the Presidential Archives in Missouri and Kansas.

Also, I would like to extend my appreciation to Dr Paul T. Levin and the Stockholm University Institute for Turkish Studies staff who did their best to provide me with a comfortable academic environment to complete this book.

I would also like to thank the editorial team of Taylor and Francis for letting me reprint the revised excerpts in this book from my previously published articles in the *Journal of Intelligence History* (2016), and *Middle Eastern Studies* (2016).

Finally, this book would not have been possible without the generous financial support of the University of Nottingham Graduate School, Truman Presidential Library and Archives, Eisenhower Presidential Library and Archives, University of Nottingham School of Humanities, Swedish Institute Research Grant, Royal Swedish Academy of Sciences and University of Nottingham Vice-Chancellor Research Excellence Scholarship.

I would also like to thank audiences in the conferences which I have attended. Their questions helped me to produce a stronger book by spotting various conceptual weaknesses during the earlier stages of my research. Lastly, I would like to thank my editor Mr. Tomasz Hoskins for his kindness in believing in this book project. Still, all errors and mistakes in this book solely belong to me.

# List of Abbreviations

| | |
|---|---|
| AFTAC | Air Force Technical Applications Center |
| ASA | Army Security Agency |
| CENTO | Central Treaty Organization |
| CHP | Republican People's Party |
| CIA | Central Intelligence Agency |
| COMINT | Communications Intelligence |
| EKSA | European Kurdish Students Association |
| ELINT | Electronic Intelligence |
| GC&CS | Government Code and Cypher School |
| GCHQ | Government Communications Headquarters |
| GRU | Main Intelligence Agency |
| HUMINT | Human Intelligence |
| JIC | Joint Intelligence Committee |
| JUSMATT | Joint United States Military Mission for Aid to Turkey |
| KGB | Committee for State Security |
| MAH | Millî Emniyet Hizmeti (National Security Service) |
| MGB | Ministry for State Security |
| MI5 | Security Service |
| MI6 | Secret Intelligence Service |
| MSYK | National Defence High Commission |

| | |
|---|---|
| NATIS | NATO Information Service |
| NATO | North Atlantic Treaty Organization |
| NIE | National Intelligence Estimates |
| NKGB | The People's Commissariat for State Security |
| NRO | National Reconnaissance Office |
| NSA | National Security Agency |
| NSC | National Security Council |
| NKVD | People's Commissariat for Internal Affairs |
| OSS | Office of Strategic Services |
| PSB | Psychological Strategy Board |
| SHAPE | Supreme Headquarters Allied Powers Europe |
| SIGINT | Signals Intelligence |
| SOFA | Status of Forces Agreement |
| SSU | Strategic Services Unit |
| TGS | Turkish General Staff |
| TKP | Communist Party of Turkey |
| TUSLOG | The United States Logistics Group |

# Introduction: Dark Origins of the Turkish-British-American Alliance

This book examines the hitherto unexplored history of Turkish secret intelligence cooperation with the United States and the United Kingdom during the early Cold War. Located at the intersection between comparative politics, international history and security studies, it shows that our understanding of the Cold War as a binary rivalry between the Western and Eastern blocs is too simple an approach and obscures the specific characteristics of intelligence cooperation between the various allies. The question is whether there can be an examination of Turkish-Western relations during the early Cold War that transcends the context of binary rivalry between East and West. Turkish decision makers used secret intelligence liaison during the early years of the Cold War to deceive and manipulate their Western partners to obtain their commitment to Turkish strategic imperatives which were not necessarily aligned with the Cold War context. This caused the Turkish-Western Alliance to be built on distrust at its inception. Shedding light on the missing dimension of the origins and development of Turkish secret intelligence during the early Cold War transforms our understanding of Turkey as an ally on NATO's Southern Flank during the crucial early period in the history of the Cold War.

There are various ways to demonstrate Ankara's distrust of her Western Allies. The literature on Turkish Foreign Policy argues that during the early Cold War, Ankara pursued an inward and passive foreign policy while widely employing a cautious approach with a strong Western commitment during the Cold War's bipolar world order.[1] Moreover, incidents such as US President Lyndon Johnson's letter of 5 June 1964, which warned Turkey not to expect US protection should the Soviets intervene as a result of a possible Turkish intervention in the ethnic conflict between Greeks and Turks in Cyprus, and the US arms embargo on Turkey following Turkish intervention in Cyprus in July 1974, proved that Ankara had compelling reasons to be wary of her Western Allies.[2] Therefore, this research demonstrates that in the Cold War origins of the Turkey-Western Alliance, each side showed considerable distrust of the other. Such distrust pushed Ankara to treat engagement with the West as an episodic and tactical relationship rather than as a strategic alliance. Short-term goals stemming from concrete external threats and an agenda imposed by domestic political challenges helped shape Turkey's attitude to her Western Allies.

The book also seeks to enhance our understanding of intelligence cooperation more broadly by developing a model called intelligence diplomacy. This model explores a vital, if little understood, aspect of contemporary international relations given the prevalence of transnational threats today. Intelligence diplomacy is the conduct of diplomacy to reflect an understanding obtained by intelligence activities. Intelligence diplomacy involves negotiations and the use of different aspects of joint intelligence activities and is mostly synchronized between diplomats and specialized intelligence officers. Moreover, while such efforts often result in overlap between diplomats and intelligence liaison efforts, there is an indication that the acts of intelligence services vary from the instructions of their foreign ministries. More specifically, the book argues that a pragmatic approach allows states to seek new means of influence by conducting intelligence diplomacy in order to influence crucial areas such as nuclear weapons, and to exploit cooperation in pursuit of their own national strategic imperatives. Therefore, it is important to explain initially what is meant by the term 'intelligence diplomacy' in this work.

## Intelligence diplomacy

Intelligence diplomacy aims to bridge the gap between intelligence cooperation and conventional diplomacy. Diplomacy is a form of artful communication between states, or through their designated agents, to conduct foreign policy without resorting to force, law or propaganda.[3] Intelligence cooperation, however, includes a variety of tools distinct from diplomacy where the use of force (such as in covert action) or propaganda is rather frequent. The distinction between intelligence cooperation and diplomacy can be identified by the nature of the conduct. Diplomacy is a medium of state behaviour in which the exchange between agents and structures must be confined within the limits of international law; thus, there is an international audience for this exchange.[4] In intelligence cooperation, however, either the means to execute an action, or the action itself, is highly secretive and not necessarily confined by international law. Therefore, intelligence diplomacy emerges as a useful concept to cover the grey area between intelligence cooperation and conventional diplomacy.

Intelligence diplomacy is not a novel concept. Sir Stephen Lander, former Director-General of Britain's Security Service, MI5, defines the term as 'the recognition by governments that there are relationships and understanding in their intelligence communities which can be used diplomatically'.[5] Lander argues that the conduct of intelligence diplomacy increasingly became a phenomenon in the post–Cold War era. Intelligence diplomacy has become more prominent since the disappearance of the Soviet threat, as the main enemy, has facilitated more channels and manoeuvre arenas for minor states to operate. However, this argument is a product of a Cold War historiography that undermines the agency of the minor states, and falls short of explaining certain characteristics of intelligence cooperation.

While the examination of intelligence diplomacy in the academic literature has been slim, the majority of existing studies focus on the topic as a part of intelligence liaison, referring to cooperation between intelligence services in either multilateral or bilateral agreements by employing theoretical conclusions from international relations.[6] Also, attention is paid in the academic world to the study of intelligence cooperation with a particular focus on the field of counterterrorism.[7] Both streams in the literature are limited since they overlook the diplomatic ramifications of the intelligence cooperation.[8]

Recently, a remarkable contribution was made to the field by Chikara Hashimoto, who provided an analytical account of British intelligence liaisons in the Middle East during the Cold War.[9] Although Hashimoto creates an analytical framework to demonstrate how intelligence liaison can also be used as a method of diplomatic influence in the Middle East, he encountered a methodological hurdle due to the fact that he did not exploit the archives of the regional governments, a hurdle that means his conclusions do not quite reveal the asymmetrical nature of intelligence diplomacy. In particular, Hashimoto's work does not thoroughly investigate how local governments exploited intelligence liaison as a leverage against their Western partners. It is important to take into account local particularities such as historical lessons or domestic considerations and not to discard facts for the sake of the narrative.

Particularly in the Turkish context, the spectre of the Ottoman past has haunted the memories of Turkish intelligence officers and shaped intelligence diplomacy as well. There are two important internal army studies reflecting this: The first is by Captain Sadi Koçaş (who became the deputy prime minister following the 1971 military intervention) whose *Intelligence Requirements for the Third World War* of 1959 argued that during the Gallipoli campaign in 1915, the lack of proper intelligence and the failure of the German General Otto Liman von Sander's counter strategy against the Allied amphibious operations cost the lives of 200,000 Turkish soldiers.[10] This episode, showing how trusting a Western power could lead to catastrophe, was still extant in Turkish officers' minds decades later. Also, Kocaş further revealed their thinking that the Soviet Union, as a non-democratic state, was not bound by democratic procedures and the rule of law; thus, its intelligence apparatus was more vigorous, even ruthless, in its operations. At the end of the study, he hinted that the Turks did not believe that the Western secret intelligence services were ready for the coming Third World War, which some Turkish officers saw as inevitable.[11] This insight from the Turkish secret intelligence perspective illustrates that the existence of a shared perception does not necessarily facilitate trust and efficient intelligence cooperation. Previous experience, and also the perception of partners' good will and capabilities, as well as the regime type of the countries involved, plays a significant role in intelligence cooperation. In this particular case of Turkish intelligence, although they saw a Third World War with the Soviets as inevitable, the imminence of a major conflict did not necessarily make Ankara trust its Western Allies.

Another illustrative internal study was written by Brigadier General İbrahim Ethem Tiryakioğlu, a former head of the Turkish Military's Intelligence School, as a response to rising Parliamentary enquiries in the mid-1960s regarding Turkish intelligence cooperation with foreign powers. His insight revealed that the weaker partners in intelligence cooperation are always concerned at being a 'stooge' or 'regional pawn' of the stronger partner in the alliance. To describe this, he used a Turkish idiom, *El verirken Kol Kaptırmak*, which translates as 'give someone an inch and he'll take a yard'.[12] And he warns that intelligence cooperation should always be coordinated with the foreign ministry, to have a synchronized approach among the institutions, and that there can never be a long-term strategic-level intelligence cooperation that would risk the minor country being reduced to a mere stooge. Thus, he adds intelligence cooperation could only be on an ad hoc basis and on a tactical level.[13] This insight illustrates that the weaker partner in an intelligence cooperation alliance is aware of the dangers of being over-exploited by the powerful partner, and at the end being 'the errand boy' in the alliance. Thus, intelligence diplomacy necessitates a mechanism of self-protection through political leverage in order not to fall under the total hegemony of the powerful partner in the alliance. This is mainly done by using intelligence diplomacy as a political leverage mechanism.

Intelligence diplomacy also works as a means of exerting political influence on the behaviour of partners in the realms of diplomacy, the military and internal security.[14] Such a leverage mechanism is well embedded in the intelligence liaison process, one of the main pillars of intelligence diplomacy. Neutral Turkey as a weaker state, for instance, provided the British with intelligence on German Abwehr agents in the Middle Eastern theatre in the Second World War, and hoped to receive economic and military aid in return.[15] Similarly, assisting foreign security services through intelligence liaison can be a means of implementing foreign policy. The methods used to increase a friendly state's capacity-building can be used as a leverage mechanism in intelligence liaison, and this trade-off between military aid and intelligence gathering also constitutes an element of intelligence diplomacy. For instance, the assessment of the Soviet threat during the post-war era remained the ultimate task for the Turkish intelligence community. However, the Turkish intelligence community lacked technical capacities, methods and training for both acquiring a broad range of intelligence on the Soviet Union and conducting espionage and counter-espionage missions at home and abroad. Therefore, the Turkish intelligence community underwent a series of capacity-building initiatives via the country's mutual security arrangements with the United States and the United Kingdom. For instance, the Anglo-US alliance established several Signal Intelligence (SIGINT) posts to monitor Soviet activities.[16]

Western aid to increase Turkey's SIGINT capabilities reached such a point that a British agent, who took part in these capacity-building arrangements, remarked that 'Turkey's Black Sea coasts were prominent destinations for us during the Cold War before the country's Mediterranean coasts became a tourist destination.'[17] He was referring to a vast network of undercover British Government Communications Headquarters (GCHQ) and American National Security Agency (NSA) bases set up along Turkey's Black Sea coast to spy on the Soviets. As the asymmetrical partner in the intelligence liaison process, Turkey both benefited from building up its capacity and was able to exploit the existence of crucial SIGINT sites on its territory as diplomatic leverage to gain further Western commitment and economic aid for the country. For their part, the United States and the United Kingdom also used the existence of these sites for diplomatic purposes, in particular to make sure that Turkish foreign policy aligned with British and American aims in the region.

Similar methods and practices used in intelligence diplomacy during the Second World War and Cold War can also be found in contemporary counter-insurgency campaigns, where providing security training to local authorities has been essential for keeping incumbent regimes in power.[18] Lander noted that operational collaboration takes place 'where there is a pressing shared need that goes beyond the capacity or capability of one country to address'.[19] This was particularly obvious for Turkish intelligence diplomacy during the Cold War, as counter-subversion units in both the Central Treaty Organization (CENTO) and North Atlantic Treaty Organization (NATO) focused on communist activities in the region, and Ankara needed both training and an enhanced intelligence collection capacity to suppress the Kurdish nationalist movement in the country. Thus, the Turks used intelligence diplomacy to widen the intelligence liaison from a one-sided flow into a comprehensive mechanism designed to convince their Western partners to collaborate against the Kurdish movement.

Intelligence diplomacy also functioned as a supplement to conventional diplomatic relations. These are often termed 'clandestine diplomacy' or 'back-channels'.[20] Depending on the political situation in a country, an intelligence liaison channel often works as a substitute for conventional diplomacy.[21] A recent work on the roles of Central Intelligence Agency (CIA) officers in the Middle East shows that intelligence officers maintained a closer link with Gamal Abdul Nasser, the Egyptian President, and had more influence over him than the US Ambassador in Egypt.[22] Recently in the Turkish case, Turkey's current spymaster Hakan Fidan has been visiting Washington, Baghdad and Moscow among others to engage in diplomatic affairs.[23] Yet, it is not exceptional for Ankara to use its spies to conduct diplomatic missions. As will be shown in this book, during the early Cold War Turkey's intelligence officers regularly conducted intelligence diplomacy, and mostly acted independently from the instructions of the Turkish Foreign Office.

The role of intelligence diplomacy as a generator of influence is identified in the academic literature as part of special political action (a form of 'covert action'), and is more specifically referred to alongside 'agents of influence', whose task is to 'influence directly government policy rather than to collect information' in the intelligence liaison process.[24] However, intelligence diplomacy is both a tool for intelligence collection and an agent of influence. In this context, the subjects of diplomacy and special political action certainly overlap.[25] Additionally, looking at intelligence diplomacy as a means of exercising influence on the policy of a foreign government also raises the question of the distinction between conventional diplomacy (conducted by a diplomatic service) and secret diplomacy (by an intelligence service). Conventional diplomacy and intelligence diplomacy usually overlap when both countries engage in joint covert action, since both countries try to shape joint plans in line with their own strategic goals. However, there is a danger in this overlap since it may backfire due to tactical level differences between the countries. Moreover, negativity created at the tactical level may easily spread into the strategic dimension of diplomatic relations due to the blurred lines between intelligence and conventional diplomacy.

This is particularly true for Turkish intelligence diplomacy. The Turkish intelligence service remains among the essential tools for the country's foreign policy and security planning.[26] Foreign policy and security planning are derived from the assessment of threats and risks that the country confronts.[27] Efficiently devising a country's intelligence community as an additional influence generator is a vital task for pursuing a coherent foreign policy as a weak state and for providing intelligence to the policy makers. Blurring the lines between secret intelligence and conventional diplomacy, while examining Turkey's relations with her Western friends, requires a comprehensive archival study to reveal the characteristics of Turkish intelligence diplomacy through empirical episodes from the early–Cold War era. However, due to the secret nature of intelligence activities, it will be useful first to examine the methodological hurdles that arise when conducting an academic enquiry into state secrets.

## Secrecy and the study of intelligence

The study of secret intelligence serves to further our analysis of national security and foreign policies. Any account of foreign policy and national security that fails to consider the role of secret intelligence 'is bound to be incomplete'.[28] Intelligence studies in recent decades have devoted significant attention to the topic, but most scholarly work has been produced in the Anglo-American sphere and deals with the intelligence organizations and activities of American and British governments.[29] The large-scale declassification of American and British archival material accelerated the production of scholarly works in the field, whilst the lack of extensive declassification outside of this sphere traditionally made a comparative approach to the study of intelligence difficult. Particularly in the last decade, partial declassification of archives in NATO, Germany, other continental European countries, as well as a few Middle Eastern countries such as Israel, has enabled some valuable efforts to broaden intelligence studies in a comparative way.[30] In Turkey, however, engagement with the field of intelligence studies has largely been absent. Turkish archives on intelligence-related matters have not yet been extensively declassified. Thus, the historiography of its foreign and security policy has been left without the all-important secret intelligence dimension.

Moreover, a comparative analysis of the secret intelligence machinery of the United States, the United Kingdom and Turkey reveals that, in the Turkish case, secret intelligence was more a tool for gaining political power and protecting the incumbent regime. It should be noted that in the Turkish case, the intelligence service does not completely serve as the secret police of an authoritarian regime. Literature discussing the role of intelligence in non-democratic regimes argues that, in such regimes, the intelligence apparatus acts as a secret police with a primary focus on oppressing domestic political dissidence, protecting the party and leader, and furthermore maintaining their political power within the system.[31] However, Turkish intelligence fits into practitioner-turned scholar from South Africa, MA van den Berg's typology of intelligence services in hybrid regimes.[32] Hybrid regimes, as referred to by Thomas Carothers:

> Have entered a political gray zone. They have some attributes of democratic political life, including at least limited political space for opposition parties and independent civil society, as well as regular elections and democratic constitutions. Yet they suffer from serious democratic deficits, often including poor representation of citizens' interests, low levels of political participation beyond voting, frequent abuse of the law by government officials, elections of uncertain legitimacy, and very low levels of public confidence in state institutions, and persistently poor institutional performance by the state.[33]

According to van den Berg, intelligence services of the hybrid regimes can be categorized as a Political Intelligence Service.[34] The term 'Political Intelligence Service' is a perfect fit for the Turkish intelligence service:

> [It] contains elements of both a democracy and authoritarian regime. In short, such intelligence practices are less democratic and more supportive to the political party in power which leads to a situation of politicised intelligence. More so, the focus of intelligence is more on the protection of the political regime and specifically the power elite, rather than the constitution and the welfare of the people. These services are continuously restructured and legislation amended to suit the needs of the power elite and to ensure that they remain in power. Intelligence is vulnerable to be misused as a tool against any opposition.[35]

In the Turkish case too, secret intelligence was less important for informing policy decisions with a clear set of intelligence targets and priorities, and to develop the capabilities that Turkey needed to meet the challenges of the Cold War. As the US National Security Council observed in 1960, 'Turkey's political problem has been one of tyranny by an unchecked majority, and what the Turkish political system requires is an appropriate set of institutional checks and balances on pure majority rule.'[36] Turkey, thus, fits into the definition of a hybrid regime, where there is an unconsolidated democracy based on charismatic political leadership which derives its legitimacy from elections. Turkey's intelligence community has become politicized, and vulnerable to political influences due to lack of accountability. However, in contrast to totalitarian and authoritarian regimes, in these hybrid regimes political exposure of the security services may also backfire, as was the case in Turkey in 1960. The National Security Council explained the reason for the 27 May 1960 coup d'état as follows: 'Growing indications that Menderes [the ousted Prime Minister] was preparing to use the army and the security forces to crush his opponents led a group of military officers, despite aloofness of the military from politics since the time of Atatürk, to carry out the May 1960 coup.'[37] This book contributes to literature on the politicization of the intelligence services by exploring a case study from Turkey. The Turkish case not only contributes to the literature on political intelligence services in hybrid regimes, but also demonstrates how the politicization on one side of the intelligence diplomacy affects the characteristics of the whole relationship.

Secret intelligence, while essential for a comprehensive study of national security and foreign policy, is also covered with a thick veil of secrecy due to the nature of the work itself. In the Anglo-American sphere, the issue of secrecy before the large-scale declassification efforts did not prevent scholars, former officials or journalists from contributing to the field.[38] In the Turkish case, however, the lack of memoirs from intelligence officers and the lack of specialized journalists working on security affairs have placed limits on the information available to scholars.[39] Academics have refrained from focusing on secret intelligence issues in this highly secretive and politicized realm, such that the official government approach has been to police the past rather than keep the record intact and inform the public. To illustrate the point, the Turkish National Intelligence Agency published a brief but official history covering its early period until 1965, which is simply a dull government pamphlet, without any substantial contribution to the literature.[40]

This book covers secret intelligence activities, as coordinated between the United Kingdom, the United States and Turkey, particularly against the Soviet Union, during the early–Cold War era between 1945 and 1960. Attention is also devoted, initially, to the interwar years and the Second World War in order to trace the origins of modern Turkey's secret intelligence apparatus and its role in security affairs and foreign policy more generally. During the era of the Cold War, the secrecy that shrouded intelligence work could never be lifted; there was a concern not to reveal essential methods, sources or details of the capacities of Western intelligence services against their Cold War adversary. Hulnick demonstrates a particular example of CIA secrecy by noting that, when the agency was established in 1947, 'the law creating the agency was suitably vague, so much so that early leaders of the CIA wondered from time to time about the limits of their charter'.[41]

After the end of the Cold War, secrecy over the CIA's activities was perceived as less necessary, and the agency made a partial attempt to establish a balance between secrecy and a degree of openness, while not hampering its activities.[42] This partial attempt to expose the agency to public scrutiny enabled students of secret intelligence to conduct research on the declassified materials of the early–Cold War period. This was true not just for the CIA but, albeit to a limited extent, for other parts of the US intelligence community, such as the NSA and the National Reconnaissance Office (NRO).[43] Earlier activities of the NSA fall within the scope of this book whereas those of the NRO, founded only in 1961, do not. It is also important to note that the Army Security Agency (ASA), responsible for SIGINT activities, falls within the scope of this research since the records suggest that this agency engaged in cooperation with Turkey while it was under the supervision of the NSA and CIA. Traces of ASA's activities can be found in the relevant archives and recently surfacing memoirs of former officers. There is also recent scholarship that suggests that the Drug Enforcement Agency engaged in high levels of cooperation during the Cold War against transnational drug and smuggling cartels. However, since crime is police work, which did not necessarily have a substantial effect on strategic intelligence and diplomacy matters, it will not form a part of this book.[44]

In contrast to the partial openness in the American example, both the British and Turkish secret intelligence services, mainly the Secret Intelligence Service (MI6), and the National Security Service (MAH),[45] still throw a thick veil of secrecy over the activities they undertook during the Cold War era. There may be a 'special relationship' between the US and British intelligence agencies, but in terms of their obsession with secrecy and keeping the intelligence service records sealed it is the Turks and British who share a similar attitude, summarized thus by wartime intelligence officer turned author Malcolm Muggeridge:

> Secrecy is essential to intelligence as vestments and incense to a Mass, or darkness to a spiritualist seance, and must at all costs be maintained, quite irrespective of whether or not it serves any purpose.[46]

The very issue of secrecy, as Joshua Rovner points out, may lead to a politicization of the intelligence by the decision makers, through knitting a layer of secrecy into the formulation of foreign and national security policy.[47] The politicization of intelligence behind closed doors creates what Rovner calls a 'pathologic relation' between the policy making and intelligence communities. Due to the secrecy and lack of public scrutiny of intelligence matters, the realm of intelligence is open to more politicization. Thus, the politicization could lead to a pathological relationship between decision makers and the intelligence community resulting in the manipulation of intelligence products to reflect policy preferences. These policy preferences are not necessarily based on a consensus on national security matters but may also reflect the political leader's domestic concern to gain more public support.

Therefore, it is crucial to address this issue at the outset. How did this perceived or accepted understanding of 'secret intelligence' shape institutions, the attitudes of intelligence consumers and producers, as well as intelligence activities themselves? Michael Herman, intelligence practitioner-turned-scholar, argues that 'before the emergence of private newspapers and press freedom, governments tended to see all information as their property, secret to some extent; the distinction between information in the public domain and classified official information is a modern one'.[48] Similarly, in analysing the American example, Thomas Troy points out that 'by the end of the eighteenth century, when our National Intelligencer was established, the private newsletter was being dwarfed by the rise of the modern newspaper'.[49]

Thus, the study of intelligence is crucially linked to the secret characteristics of the work itself. However, when the definition of secrecy has changed through the creation of a distinction between public and classified official information, a specialized institution has been required to acquire this 'necessary information' for policy formation, and to keep such information secret. Therefore, the development of national secret intelligence services as a government institution emerged due to a perceived need to handle the collection of secret information, to implement special skills for this process, and also to avoid the danger of duplication of efforts where there were different intelligence consumer institutions within the government.[50]

Modern conceptualization of secret intelligence refers to three particular aspects of the process: 'a kind of secret knowledge', a 'type of organization that produces that knowledge' and 'the activity pursued by that organization'.[51] In the Anglo-American sphere, secret intelligence is mainly crafted for the following aims: (1) to avoid strategic surprises, (2) to provide long-term expertise, (3) to support the policy process, and (4) to maintain the secrecy of information, needs and methods.[52] In all these areas, secret intelligence may be defined as 'information that meets the stated and understood needs of policy makers and [that] has been collected, processed and narrowed to meet those needs'.[53] However, every nation employs a different, though not necessarily unique, approach to it. There is evidence that policy makers who may not be especially interested in processed intelligence may nonetheless have a tendency to see raw intelligence as a base from which their policies derive. In the Turkish case, it has been particularly true, as the heavily politicized realm of the security institutions exploit the intelligence apparatus for domestic political gains, aided by the lack of accountability of the intelligence services. Raw intelligence provides more opportunities for manipulation and exploitation due to room for 'interpreting' its precise meaning. For instance, Turkey's first spymaster, Colonel Şükrü Ali Öğel, resigned from his post in 1941 because decision makers did not value his intelligence assessments, and because Prime Minister Refik Saydam tended to use the MAH for the surveillance of domestic political dissidents, instead of focusing on the urgent need to collect foreign intelligence during the Second World War.[54] Although this example is from the war years, the characteristics of the Turkish conceptualization of intelligence have survived long after the war, partly because there has not been any reform since then to implement a mechanism to oversee the relationship between the intelligence apparatus and policy makers.

The above conceptualization of secret intelligence has traditionally been associated with defence and foreign policy formation. However, when new methods of information collection and communication were introduced, particularly during the Second World War, other sources of secret information gathering such as Signals Intelligence, or 'non-communications' emissions such as radars, also became significant. As Aldrich states, 'With the onset of the Cold War, SIGINT seemed equally important for a dangerous new era of nuclear confrontation'.[55] Hence, this new growing and prominent aspect of secret intelligence gathering also required its own institutionalization beside the traditional human-intensive clandestine services. The later introduction of covert satellite missions also falls within the scope of this book. The CORONA mission launched by the United States in 1958 is especially noteworthy, in that it aimed to realize a comprehensive image of the United States' main Cold War adversary, the Soviet Union. Such technological advances could themselves create differences between intelligence services. As discussed in this book, both the British and the Americans felt that Ankara's perspective on intelligence failed to adapt to new methods of intelligence gathering, instead tending to prioritize its conventional approach of relying on human agents.

The departmentalization of secret intelligence activities increased over the course of the Cold War, partly due to these new technologies. However, the finished intelligence or 'end-product' collected by the single-source or all-source agencies was still presented to policy makers through a single process, such as the National Intelligence Estimates in the United States, the Joint Intelligence Committee (JIC) in the United Kingdom or the National Security High Commission in Turkey. Over the years these specialized collation and assessment bodies became, as Johnson calls them, 'the Domino's Pizza of information delivery to high-level officials'. They developed a distinct sense of collating information and established a skilled process of rapid processing and distribution of the information through reports and briefings.[56] Ultimately, the secret information collection process within modern governments could be summarized as the gathering and analysing of political, social, biographic, economic and security-related information on state or non-state actors, without the target's cooperation or knowledge, and mostly through covert means to penetrate the target's organized secrecy.[57]

The term 'intelligence', while referring to secret government activities for the collection of information, also refers to two other aspects of intelligence, which are operational rather than solely focusing on secret information collection. These are *covert operations* and *security intelligence*. During the Cold War, countries typically experienced the development of subversive activities in the domestic arena, which were connected with the foreign adversary in the eyes of their political elites and thus acquired a dual significance.[58] Security intelligence, which mainly focuses on domestic targets, took on a transnational nature because of the subversive activities encouraged by the Cold War. According to Herman, security intelligence can have some purely domestic targets as well as overseas ones, but even the domestic ones are 'foreign' in the sense of being outsiders, with an 'otherness' rejecting or threatening the state or society in some special way. The practice of security intelligence on domestic targets, embedded with other domestic concerns, left countries such as Turkey without a necessary oversight mechanism on security affairs, leading in turn to the politicization of intelligence and a tendency to characterize political dissidents as 'outsiders'. This tended to make intelligence more about 'them' and 'us', rather than about gaining deeper self-knowledge from which to construct a more genuinely secure polity.[59] In authoritarian countries, such as Turkey between 1945 and 1960, there was no debate based on professional consideration in the intelligence process – collection, processing and production. As Bar-Joseph argues, the intelligence process is geared from the start to meet the mindset or political needs of the leader, even in the most crucial matters.[60] In the Turkish experience, a poisonous politicization of the intelligence process resulted in catastrophic incidents, such as the anti-Greek pogroms of 6–7 September 1955, or in fiascos such as Turkey's Syria policy, which brought the two countries to the brink of war in 1957. These incidents and their relation to the politicization of intelligence will be further analysed in this book.

Herman's explanation sheds light on two important dimensions of the nature of secret intelligence during the Cold War. Initially, since the nature of subversive activities during the Cold War had a transnational element, the security intelligence institutions of the various governments also sought cooperation from their allies in the overseas arena. For instance, within the Central Treaty Organization (CENTO), a Western alliance centred on the Middle East during the Cold War, there was a counter-subversion mechanism of intelligence sharing among the member states' head of security intelligence agencies. A similar mechanism was implemented by the NATO Special Committee to exchange information on designated communist activities in Europe. One of the advantages of intelligence pooling via CENTO was that members shared their knowledge of communist activities, which enabled the member states to obtain a wider picture of the local threats posed by international Communism. These discussions were highly important, not only to the British and the Americans who sought to gain an insight into the hidden, underground activities of communist movements in the region, but also to the security services of the regional powers themselves, in terms of their abilities to counter internal threats which potentially undermined the stability of their respective governments.

The subjects of information exchange included, for instance, the strength and activities of the Communist Parties in each signatory to the Treaty; propaganda broadcasts by the various radio stations of the Eastern Bloc countries, aiming to instigate subversive activities in the region; and any scheduled communist-sponsored international meetings.[61] The exchanged information also included a list of known communist members in the region; a 'watch list' containing forthcoming communist and relevant non-communist meetings; and actions needed to be taken by the relevant authorities to combat them. These actions, for instance, involved making recommendations to their own authorities to refuse any applications by any individuals for exit visas in order to participate in the events.[62]

However, such cooperation between the security intelligence services was also a highly risky process since informers were most of the time the only means of gathering information on subversive movements.[63] Thus, sharing secret intelligence on subversive elements even among allies could risk the exposure of sources and methods of intelligence gathering concerning subversive movements. As we will see in this book, the forming of multilateral intelligence mechanisms also required crafting an intelligence sharing mechanism that could undertake the essential tasks of preventing subversive activities in the region, as well as keeping a tight veil of secrecy over the nation's intelligence capabilities and methods. Thus, in terms of intelligence sharing, bilateral mechanisms between the United Kingdom, the United States and Turkey, or between Turkey and Middle Eastern countries, were preferred over the lengthy bureaucratic processes needed at the multilateral level. Countries also found it more convenient and effective to cooperate bilaterally to prevent any leakage or exposing their weaknesses and strengths in a multilateral setting.

The domestic security focus on subversive movements during the Cold War blurred the distinction between domestic and foreign secret intelligence activities since the foe – the subversive element – was perceived to be an outsider to the domestic political order. This blurring also lifted the intelligence services out of the realm of mere secret information collection, and into the realm of covert action and clandestine diplomacy. As we will see later in this book, differences in the organization of the secret intelligence services further complicated matters. The CIA and MI6 were tasked with foreign intelligence operations and their powers and responsibilities were directed against 'enemy' targets. However, their Turkish counterpart 'the MAH' was tasked with both external and internal aspects of intelligence, and thus its power and responsibilities frequently overlapped in domestic and foreign arenas.

Aldrich states that intelligence activities also include 'operations to influence the world by unseen means', or covert action.[64] While the limits of covert action vary according to each country's approaches, it generally includes propaganda, sabotage, subversion and covert support to non-state actors. According to Scott, 'Notwithstanding the fact that different tasks are performed by different organizations, since 1945 Western intelligence services have nevertheless used the same organizations and the same group of people to perform different tasks'.[65] In the literature there are studies to analyse such orchestrated covert action tasks within NATO, particularly focusing on stay-behind covert networks.[66] However, so long as records of the NATO Special Committee and the NATO 'Working Group on Civil Organization in Time of War' remain sealed, it is difficult to draw an accurate picture of NATO covert actions during the Cold War. Moreover, if any record of such covert action still exists, it would also be in the member country's Top-Secret registries, which are currently hidden from public scrutiny.

Eugene Poteat, a former senior intelligence officer himself, states that 'all intelligence services are used for propaganda and perception management'.[67] However, the extent of covert action, including propaganda and perception management in domestic affairs, remains subject to each nation's approach to the issue. In the United States, covert action distinctly falls under the secret intelligence operations undertaken abroad; however, it could be argued that the 'various British government activities in Northern Ireland, for example, appear to have fallen within otherwise accepted definitions of covert action'.[68] Moreover, the Turkish intelligence service's activities against its Kurdish minority would be considered as examples of covert action on the domestic scene. Thus, it is crucial to analyse each institutional structure in the United States, the United Kingdom and Turkey, with regard to their respective uses of and approaches to intelligence by employing a multi-archival methodology to encompass the multifaceted nature of secret intelligence.

## Organization

This book follows a thematic focus rather than a linear narrative. The first chapter is dedicated to a comparison of the secret intelligence machineries of the respective countries, namely the United Kingdom, the United States and Turkey. Further details are provided on the relationship between the intelligence mechanisms and the countries' decision makers, so that the role of secret intelligence in the decision-making process will be revealed. This chapter provides a historical survey of the intelligence apparatus in these countries, in order to highlight the changing structure and roles of the intelligence service due to the Cold War security structure. This historical survey also reveals to what extent the secret intelligence services of the United States, the United Kingdom and Turkey established multilateral and bilateral intelligence cooperation mechanisms with each other, in accordance with their assigned missions and roles. The second chapter focuses on wartime secret intelligence cooperation between Turkey and the West. It is shown in this chapter that there were compelling reasons for Turkey to remain neutral until the very end of the war. It also, however, reveals that being neutral did not prevent Ankara from actively engaging in intelligence diplomacy both to further gain material benefits and to stave off increasing pressure from the Soviet Union.

The third chapter is devoted to multilateral intelligence cooperation within the major Cold War alliances, namely NATO and CENTO. In particular, issues concerning NATO include attempts to standardize intelligence services, the aims of the respective countries regarding intelligence cooperation within NATO and particularly the attempts to develop the intelligence capabilities of Turkey. Special attention is devoted to KGB/NKVD attempts to infiltrate NATO, and the role of Turkey in counter-espionage missions against Soviet agents. Moreover, this chapter reveals the distrust and manipulation among the members of the alliances, and how Turkey took advantage of these frictions within the alliances by using intelligence diplomacy to gain further security commitments and aid for its own strategic goals.

The fourth chapter is dedicated to nuclear intelligence. As one of the most crucial issues in the Cold War era, gathering information on the Soviet Union's nuclear programme and capabilities formed a major part of Turkish secret intelligence activities. As a small Western ally, but adjacent to the Soviet Union, it is crucial to investigate how much information the Turks gathered on Soviet nuclear capabilities. In this chapter it will be argued that the Turks also played an important role in discovering the extent of Soviet nuclear capabilities, while at the same time these capabilities shaped Turkish threat perceptions during the era. This chapter will also discuss the fact that while intelligence sharing between the United Kingdom, the United States and Turkey was crucial, all parties shared intelligence that suited their own national focus rather than that of the alliance as a whole.

The fifth chapter focuses on the joint anti-subversion activities of the United States, the United Kingdom and Turkey. Soviet subversive activities in the region posed a serious concern for regional countries and for the Western Alliance. The Soviets reached out to minority groups in the region, such as Kurds and Armenians, even as they helped Communist/Socialist Parties and organizations to infiltrate the state apparatus and conduct subversive activities. This chapter examines the

Soviet-supported subversion activities in the region and argues that although Soviet subversion was a common threat to all, the intelligence sharing on these activities between Turkey, the United States and the United Kingdom, as well as the other regional countries, did not represent full-scale cooperation. The intelligence cooperation between these countries was based on each nation's strategic imperatives, and this led to the withholding of intelligence in most cases.

The sixth chapter will reveal cooperation and policies regarding joint covert operations in Syria, namely the Turkish role in the Operation Straggle in Syria. This case shows that there was a certain degree of cooperation in these covert operations, but while they were dominated by American and British intelligence, the Turks still considered this region as their 'imperial backyard' and sought opportunities through these covert actions to expand their influence on this particular region. It also examines whether the individual approaches of these countries reflect a common policy in Cold War rivalry, or each country's pursuit of their own policies under a larger security umbrella.

The concluding chapter draws from historical examples from the Cold War period, and points out that attitudes regarding Turkish intelligence diplomacy which originated in the early–Cold War period also shaped foreign policies and intelligence cooperation for the rest of the Cold War, and were also maintained beyond the post–Cold War era.

## Note on sources

Although there are methodological difficulties for a historical study of secret intelligence cooperation, time-consuming and patient archival research can give fruitful results. This book does not intend to solely employ a strong Turkish or Western voice in its sources, and draws on a wide range of archives. Thus, archival sources from Turkey, the United Kingdom, the United States, Poland and NATO are the primary basis for this research. In particular, the Turkish State Archive's Republic period Council of Ministers and Prime Minister's Office series includes detailed documents on the era. Turkish parliamentary records, the Turkish military archives (ATASE), are also helpful in this regard. Several of these archives are open to researchers, subject to permission from the authorities. The primary contribution of these archives based in Turkey is that they demonstrate both the inner workings of the security establishment and the attitude of the political leadership concerning intelligence and foreign policy. Both these archives are going through an ongoing cataloguing process which results in restricted access to documents, especially those covering the late 1950s. However, I was able to gain access to a considerable number of intelligence estimates, memorandums and correspondence. Moreover, as Aldrich points out, circumventing methodological hurdles due to the still ongoing secrecy surrounding the Cold War secret intelligence archives (which is particularly tight in the Turkish case), I had to 'invest some time [and money] in the organic process of growing [my] own records'.[69] I chased down auction houses, antique shops and even sometimes garage sales to obtain the private papers of former practitioners. Since there was a tendency among Turkish officials to take a copy of the documents home (they did not perceive it as public property but rather as a report they had written), an ample number of official reports appeared among these papers and greatly contributed to my research.

In addition to the Turkish archives, the declassified CIA records are open to research through the CIA Records Search Tool (CREST). The US National Archives and Records Administration's State Department Central Decimal Files, Records of the National Security Agency/Central Security Service contains relevant documents for this research. Recently the NSA worked closely with the National Archives, thus making it available for researching through the documents dealing with the early–Cold War era. Besides the National Archives, the personal papers and official papers in the Truman and Eisenhower Libraries, and the Library of Congress include valuable materials.

The NATO archives are also going through a declassification process. The released materials particularly include relevant documents on the standardization of secret intelligence, intelligence sharing under the NATO structure and the intelligence capacity-building in the member countries. NATO's Military and the Defence Committee series contains particularly useful documents pertaining to this study. However, NATO's intelligence documents undergo a rather slower pace of declassification vis-à-vis other relevant archives. Therefore, NATO archives serve instead as a substantial source for that era. Joint Intelligence Committee records, Ministry of Defence Records, Foreign Office Records and the records of the Security Service in the British National Archives also include primary documents pertaining to this research and there were some materials in the Churchill Archive Centre in Cambridge. The archives in the United Kingdom, the United States and NATO not only complement the Turkish sources by providing an insight into the attitude of Western intelligence, but they are also essential as regards reflecting the asymmetrical nature of Turkish-Western intelligence diplomacy. Also, a comparative assessment of national archives in relation to the NATO archives demonstrates the prevalence of distrust amongst allies in a multilateral setting.

In addition to the Western and Turkish archives, Poland's Institute of National Remembrance recently released Polish archives on Soviet secret intelligence operations in Turkey during the Cold War, and this has helped researchers to provide a Soviet perspective on Turkish-Western intelligence cooperation.

The CENTO archives, Turkish Ministry of Foreign Affairs archives and the Turkish Intelligence archives, however, remain mostly closed to public access. Similarly, the NATO, CIA and British Security Service archives offer only a limited access to their intelligence operations in cooperation with the Turkish intelligence service. As a substitute for the limited archival material on particular dimensions of secret intelligence cooperation, the private collections of published memoirs and interviews with ministers, officers and diplomats have been exploited to shed light on events.

However, as Philip Davies argues, 'arbitrarily mixing and matching the versions of events emerging from reported evidence is simply not a viable approach' to producing a reliable conclusion in research on secret intelligence activities.[70] As Davies suggests, in order to have a reliable source of data for intelligence research, this book employs a triangulation method, using multiple primary and published secondary sources, corroborating the information within and between these various sources.[71] In doing so, this book also integrates information from previously unexplored archives, not least in Turkey, to complement or challenge conclusions in previously published research.

## Notes

1   See M. Aydin, 'Determinants of Turkish Foreign Policy: Changing Patterns and Conjectures during the Cold War', *Middle Eastern Studies*, 36:1 (2000), 103–139.
2   M. Mufti, 'Daring and Caution in Turkish Foreign Policy', *Middle East Journal*, 52:1 (1998), 40–42.
3   G. R. Berridge, *Diplomacy: Theory and Practice* (Bansington, 2010).
4   I. Hurd, 'Law and the Practice of Diplomacy', *International Journal*, 66:3 (2011), 581–581.
5   S. Lander, 'International Intelligence Cooperation: An Inside Perspective', *Cambridge Review of International Affairs*, 17:3 (2004), 482.
6   See J. Walsh, *The International Politics of Intelligence Sharing* (New York, 2010); S. Chesterman, *Shared Secrets* (New South Wales, Australia, 2006); J. Sims, 'Foreign Intelligence Liaison: Devils, Deals, and Details', *International Journal of Intelligence and Counterintelligence*, 19:2 (2006), 195–217; A. Svendsen, 'Connecting Intelligence and Theory: Intelligence Liaison and International Relations', *Intelligence and National Security*, 24:5 (2009), 700–729; R. Bock, 'Anglo-Soviet Intelligence Cooperation, 1941–45: Normative Insights from the Dyadic Democratic Peace Literature', *Intelligence and National Security*, 30:6 (2015), 890–912.
7   See R. Aldrich, 'Transatlantic Intelligence and Security Cooperation', *International Affairs*, 80:4 (2004), 731–753; M. Rudner, 'Hunters and Gatherers: The Intelligence Coalition against Islamic Terrorism', *International Journal of Intelligence and Counterintelligence*, 17:2 (2004), 193–230; D. Reveron, 'Old Allies, New Friends: Intelligence-Sharing

in the War on Terror', *Orbis*, 50:3 (2006), 453–468; S. Lefebvre, 'The Difficulties and Dilemmas of International Intelligence Cooperation', *International Journal of Intelligence and Counterintelligence*, 16:4 (2003), 527–542.

8   In this book, the terms 'intelligence liaison' and 'intelligence cooperation' are used interchangeably. Both terms refer to a wide range of activities including joint operations and training assistance. For a seminal work on intelligence liaison, see H. B. Westerfield, 'America and the World of Intelligence Liaison', *Intelligence and National Security*, 11:3 (1996), 523–560. Intelligence diplomacy refers to the use of intelligence cooperation as a tool in conventional diplomacy. In this book, the term intelligence diplomacy is used particularly to describe the Western–Turkish intelligence liaison.

9   C. Hashimoto, *British Intelligence, Counter-Subversion, and 'Informal Empire' in the Middle East, 1949-63*, unpublished PhD thesis (Aberystwyth University, 2014).

10  MKB: S. Kocaş, ' Üçüncü Dünya Harbinin İstihbarat İhtiyacı,' *Kara Kuvvetleri Dergisi*, 1959.

11  Ibid.

12  MKB: İ. Ethem Tiryakioğlu, 'Yabancı İstihbarat ve Güvenlik Örgütleriyle Koordinasyon ve İşbirliği,' *Silahlı Kuvvetler Dergisi*, 1980.

13  Ibid.

14  M. Herman, *Intelligence Power in Peace and War* (Cambridge, 1996), 212–217, c.f. A recent study highlights how minor states in East Africa use intelligence and security cooperation as a leverage in other realms of diplomatic relations with the United States, see S. O. Odinga, *Looking for Leverage: Strategic Resources, Contentious Bargaining, and US-African Security Cooperation*, unpublished thesis (City University of New York, 2016).

15  E. Bezci, 'Turkish Intelligence Diplomacy during the Second World War', *Journal of Intelligence History*, 15:2 (2016), 80–95.

16  M. Gunter, 'United States-Turkish Intelligence Liaison since World War II', *Journal of Intelligence History*, 3:1 (2003), 33–46.

17  Interview conducted in Athens, Greece, 14 July 2013.

18  See P. Rich and I. Duyvesteyn, *The Routledge Handbook of Insurgency and Counterinsurgency* (London, 2012).

19  Lander, 'International Intelligence Cooperation', 492.
20  Ibid.
21  Ibid., 536–539, 543–545. Also see L. Scott, 'Secret Intelligence, Covert Action and Clandestine Diplomacy', *Intelligence and National Security*, 19:2 (2004), 322–341.
22  H. Wilford, *America's Great Game* (New York, 2013), 195, 201.
23  See 'Top Turkish Officials in Baghdad to Defuse Tension over Troop Deployment', *Hurriyet Daily News*, 10 December 2015; 'Top Soldier, Intel Chief Talk Syria in Moscow', *Hurriyet Daily News*, 2 November 2016.
24  A. N. Shulsky and G. J. Schmitt, *Silent Warfare: Understanding the World of Intelligence*, 3rd ed. (Dulles, VA, 2002), 78–80.
25  On the role of liaison or clandestine diplomacy in the form of clandestine actions or covert action in general, cf. Scott, 'Secret Intelligence, Covert Action and Clandestine Diplomacy'.
26  Mufti, 'Daring and Caution in Turkish Foreign Policy', 42.
27  D. Strachan-Morris, 'Threat and Risk: What Is the Difference and Why Does It Matter?' *Intelligence and National Security*, 27:2 (2012), 172–186.
28  C. Andrew, *Secret Service: The Making of the British Intelligence Community* (London, 1985), xvi.
29  For a detailed historiography in Anglo-American sphere, see C. Moran and C. Murphy, *Intelligence Studies in Britain and the US: Historiography since 1945* (Edinburgh, 2013).
30  For instance, the establishment of the Journal of Intelligence History in 2001 has immensely contributed on this direction to expand the intelligence studies outside of Anglo-American sphere.
31  See L. Hutton, Looking beneath the Cloak: An Analysis of Intelligence Governance in South Africa (Pretoria, 2007); H. Born and M. Caparini, Democratic Control of Intelligence Services: Containing Rogue Elephants (Farnham, 2007); T. C. Bruneau and S. C. Boraz, eds., Reforming Intelligence: Obstacles to Democratic Control and Effectiveness (Austin, TX, 2007); F. C. Matei and T. C. Bruneau, 'Policy Makers and Intelligence Reform in the New Democracies', *International Journal of Intelligence and Counterintelligence*, 24:4 (2011), 656–691.
32  M.A. van den Berg, *The Intelligence Regime in South Africa (1994–2014): An Analytical Perspective*, unpublished thesis (North-West University, 2014).

33 T. Carothers, 'The End of the Transition Paradigm', *Journal of Democracy*, 13:1 (2002), 9.
34 Van den Berg, *The Intelligence Regime in South Africa (1994–2014): An Analytical Perspective*, 76.
35 Ibid., 75.
36 Eisenhower Presidential Library and Archives: White House, Office of the Special Assistant for National Security Affairs: Records, 1952–61: NSC Series Policy Paper Subseries: Box 29: 'US Policy on Turkey', 5 October 1960.
37 Ibid.
38 See C. Moran, *Classified: Secrecy and the State in Modern Britain* (Cambridge, 2012).
39 There have been some exceptions in journalistic work, in a highly politicized realm they either praise or defame the Turkish Intelligence organizations. See T. Özkan, *Milli İstihbarat Teşkilatı-MİT (Mit'in Gizli Tarihi)* (Istanbul, 2015); M. Eymür, *Analiz: bir MİT mensubu'nun anıları* (Istanbul, 1991); E. Hiçyılmaz, *Teşkilât-ı Mahsusa'dan MİT'e* (Ankara, 1990).
40 E. İlter, *Milli İstihbarat Teşkilatı Tarihçesi* (Ankara, 2002).
41 A. S. Hulnick, 'Openness: Being Public about Secret Intelligence', *International Journal of Intelligence and Counterintelligence*, 12:4 (1999), 466.
42 D. D. Gries, 'Opening Up Secret Intelligence', *Orbis*, 37:3 (1993), 366.
43 M. Warner, 'Sources and Methods for the Study of Intelligence', in L. K. Johnson, ed., *Handbook of Intelligence Studies* (London, 2007), 24.
44 R. Gingeras. *Heroin, Organized Crime, and the Making of Modern Turkey* (Oxford, 2014).
45 Renamed as MİT (National Intelligence Agency) after a vast intelligence reform introduced in 1965.
46 M. Muggeridge, *Chronicles of Wasted Time* (New York, 1974), 123, qtd. in Hulnick, 'Openness: Being Public about Secret Intelligence', 464.
47 J. Rovner, *Fixing the Facts: National Security and the Politics of Intelligence* (Ithaca, NY, 2011).
48 Herman, *Intelligence Power in Peace and War*, 11.
49 T. F. Troy, 'The "Correct" Definition of Intelligence,' *International Journal of Intelligence and Counter Intelligence*, 5:4 (1991), 435.

50 Herman, *Intelligence Power in Peace and War*, 25.
51 Ibid., 1–2.
52 M. Lowenthal, *Intelligence: From Secrets to Policy* (London, 2011), 2–4.
53 Ibid., 2.; Also, Micheal Warner draws attention to the debate surrounding the definition of secret intelligence, yet also his attempts falls within the Anglo-American sphere of intelligence studies. See M. Warner, 'Wanted: A Definition of "Intelligence"', in C. Andrew, R. Aldrich, and W. Wark, eds., *Secret Intelligence: A Reader* (London, 2010), 3–12.
54 Ş. Â. Ögel, 'Millî Emniyet Hizmeti Nasıl Kuruldu?' *Türk Kültürü*, 128 (1973), 605–607.
55 R. Aldrich, *GCHQ: The Uncensored Story of Britain's Most Secret Intelligence Agency* (London, 2010), 5.
56 L. K. Johnson, 'Preface to a Theory of Strategic Intelligence', *International Journal of Intelligence and Counterintelligence*, 16:4 (2003), 648.
57 Herman, *Intelligence Power in Peace and War*, 81.
58 The most famous cases are McCarthyism in the United States, and 1951 Communist Trials in Turkey. See. Özdemir and A. F. Sendil, 'The Turkish Left as an Image between Reality and Perception in the Cold War: Approach of Democrat Party towards Leftist Movements', *Cumhuriyet Tarihi Arastirmalari Dergisi*, 12:23 (2016), 332; and E. Schrecker, *Many Are the Crimes: McCarthyism in America* (Princeton, 1998).
59 Herman, *Intelligence Power in Peace and War*, 34.
60 U. Bar-Joseph, 'The Politicization of Intelligence: A Comparative Study', *International Journal of Intelligence and Counterintelligence*, 26:2 (2013), 347–348.
61 TNA: FO 371/127861: VB1692/9: 'Report by the Turkish Delegation on Communist Activities in Turkey', 23 May 1957.
62 TNA: FO 371/149746: EB1691/2/G: 'Draft Report of the UK Contribution to the CENTO Liaison Committee Papers by MI5, "Special Study 1: The Iraq Communist Party"', 3 March 1960. TNA: FO 1110/1353: PR146/20: 'Monthly Report on the CSO (January) by Peter Joy of FO', 5 February 1960.
63 Herman, *Intelligence Power in Peace and War*, 65.
64 Aldrich, *GCHQ: The Uncensored Story of Britain's Most Secret Intelligence Agency*, 5.
65 Scott, 'Secret Intelligence, Covert Action and Clandestine Diplomacy', 323.

66 For a detailed study, see D. Ganser. *NATO's Secret Armies: Operation Gladio and Terrorism in Western Europe* (London, 2005).
67 E. Poteat, 'The Use and Abuse of Intelligence: An Intelligence Provider's Perspective', *Diplomacy and Statecraft*, 11:2 (2000), 14.
68 Scott, 'Secret Intelligence, Covert Action and Clandestine Diplomacy', 324.
69 R. Aldrich '"Grow Your Own": Cold War Intelligence and History Supermarkets', *Intelligence and National Security*, 17:1 (2002), 149.
70 P. Davies, 'Spies as Informants: Triangulation and the Interpretation of Elite Interview Data in the Study of the Intelligence and Security Services', *Politics*, 21:1 (2001), 78.
71 Ibid.

# 1

# Machinery in Comparison

Any historical research on the Turkish-Western intelligence relationship during the early Cold War depends on a sound understanding of the organizational and functional roles of the intelligence communities in the respective countries. It is important to have an insight into the machinery because of two important and interlinked dimensions. Ryan Bock, deriving his lesson from the study of Anglo-Soviet intelligence cooperation during the Second World War, argues that the regime type of the countries shapes the depth of intelligence cooperation.[1] It is particularly true for a study of Turkish-Western intelligence diplomacy, since intelligence cooperation between Turkey and her Western partners during the early Cold War was a far from smooth process, even though all perceived the same target as the source of threat, the Soviet Union.

In order to reveal how the regime type shaped the intelligence cooperation, it is imperative to conduct a comparative analysis of Turkey, the United States and the United Kingdom. As Glenn P. Hastedt asked the same question more than two decades ago, it is important to define 'what is to be compared' for a comparative study of secret intelligence.[2] How does the definition of intelligence differ between Turkey, the United States and the United Kingdom? How are institutions shaped? What is the relationship between the intelligence service and policy makers? What is the legal framework in each country? If these questions are not answered properly, 'then one's analysis could produce misleading comparisons between dissimilar intelligence organisations'.[3] The paucity of previous historical or organizational research on the intelligence services outside of the

Anglosphere makes the study of the Turkish case particularly original in the field.[4] Moreover, Damien Van Puyvelde and Sean Curtis's recent qualitative study on the intelligence literature, analysing the field's two flagship journals, *Intelligence and National Security* and the *International Journal of Intelligence and Counterintelligence*, revealed that intelligence studies are indeed not diverse.[5] Their findings suggest that the field is dominated by Anglo-American male researchers who work on Western-centric topics.[6] Due to the dearth of accumulated knowledge on the topic, particularly on Turkish intelligence, which is outside of Europe but part of the Western Alliance, a comprehensive research on the topic needs a detailed understanding of the differences in the intelligence culture. As Richard Aldrich and John Kasuku point out, 'Comprehension of what intelligence culture might be will have value only when it is derived from close observation of real behaviour and when we have enough substantive data to undertake meaningful comparisons.'[7] Therefore, it is essential to provide an analytical framework of comparison on the Cold War origins of the American, Turkish and British intelligence communities. By doing so, both the characteristics of intelligence diplomacy will be better understood, and a new path will be opened in intelligence studies out of the Anglo-American-dominated literature.

## Gearing the machinery

In the Anglo-American sphere, different departmental institutions and independent intelligence organizations usually conduct single-source intelligence collections according to their specialization, such as using human assets abroad or electronic and signal sources such as radar, signal interceptions or satellites to gather intelligence. Usually, however, all intelligence is analysed and processed in a multi-sourced institution to provide a finished result for policy makers. Moreover, the duties and powers of these institutions are stated in a legal framework, with the limits of their powers and responsibilities in the domestic political arena clearly drawn, so that they do not jeopardize the domestic political processes of their countries. On either side of the Atlantic, though, the meaning of intelligence varies. In the United States, the term 'intelligence' refers to a broader concept in government, covering the clandestine collection of information as well as the analysis of this information. In the UK, however, the assessment process was not a part of the intelligence picture until the formation of the JIC. More precisely, 'in the United States "information" is a component of "intelligence" while in the UK, "intelligence" is a particular type of information'.[8] In the Turkish context, the equivalent of the word intelligence is İstihbarat. İstihbarat, a word derived from Arabic, means actively gathering 'unknown news', and there is an element of intrigue that the word itself connotes. In contrast to the Anglo-American experience, a look at the Turkish intelligence community suggests that such a division of labour does not exist and that a clear distinction of the duties and responsibilities regarding which department does what to gather information is not stated.

The reports prepared by MAH and the Turkish military during the Second World War suggest that in Ankara there was a constant debate among military and civilian organizations about the role of the country's intelligence agency in peacetime activities. An internal army briefing from 1944, prepared by one Major Kılıç, suggested that intelligence focusing solely on military-war time preparedness was not enough for Turkey's needs. The briefing suggested that other aspects of intelligence, such as establishing permanent agents abroad, acquiring psychological warfare techniques, being aware of the increasing importance of SIGINT activities and dealing with possible defectors/refugees were new areas that the intelligence community should prioritize.[9] The briefing also mentions the importance of undercover human assets abroad to assist the work of military attachés. However, the briefing clearly reflects a military point of view and, given Turkey's position during the war era, its priorities reflect the desire to protect

Turkish security at home, rather than planning offensive espionage/intelligence missions abroad. Lastly, as we will see in Chapter 2, during the Second World War Turkey was a target of both Axis and Allied intelligence operations. Moreover, the poor security of information – in particular, problems with adequately securing the channels of Turkish military and civilian communication from outside interception – resulted in major leaks from Turkish agencies. Thus, the briefing warned that Turkish officers should tightly adhere to secrecy guidelines and not compromise confidential information by communicating via non-secure channels.

However, in another briefing prepared by MAH, the Turkish civilian secret intelligence service, on strategic intelligence techniques and methods, in 1945, special emphasis was given to possible operations abroad.[10] This difference between the two agencies does not reflect a division of labour among the organizations, but rather reflects different attitudes among various agencies within the Turkish intelligence community. The army was traditionally hesitant about risky operations, whereas the secret intelligence agency has been more prone to risky behaviour and more aligned towards clandestine operations. As we will see in Chapter 6, which deals with an empirical case study concerning covert operations in Syria, the interplay between the military and civilian branches of the Turkish intelligence community not only conducted operations, but also influenced Turkish decision makers when it came to diplomatic and intelligence cooperation too. As a negative consequence of this inter-departmental rivalry, both MAH and the military focused on creating their own intelligence assessments to gain greater influence over policy makers. However, since the Turkish policy makers were rather more interested in intelligence concerning domestic dissidents who might challenge their power, both the MAH and the military intelligence's gendarmerie branches diverted their energy and attention to 'tailing' a small handful of communists in Turkey.[11] As a result, the necessary attention to capacity-building in foreign intelligence activities was hampered.

## The American intelligence community

In the American experience, especially due to rising tensions between the Americans and Soviets after the Potsdam Conference of July–August 1945, the perceived need for a centralized American foreign intelligence agency became a pressing issue.[12] The wartime intelligence organization, the Office of Strategic Services (OSS), is described as having 'demonstrated ... the usefulness of a central body to process materials from every source of information. Its experiences indicated that a single authority ought to have charge of collecting secret information outside of the United States'.[13] However, it was a wartime agency, to be liquidated by September 1945. Thus, the OSS spymaster General Bill Donovan drafted a plan for creating a new intelligence agency to 'take over the valuable assets created by OSS and aid the nation in the organization and maintenance of peace'.[14]

The closure of the OSS seriously compromised American clandestine intelligence capabilities in the early post-war period. The Strategic Services Unit (SSU), its much-reduced successor, was hard pressed to maintain established collection programmes, let alone embark on new operations. To supplement its collection efforts, SSU relied to a significant extent on liaison with friendly European intelligence services who shared some of the results of their espionage against Soviet targets.[15] Not surprisingly, Britain's MI6 was the major partner, but smaller services, particularly the Danish, Italian, Turkish and Swedish services, also helped the Americans.

During this transition in Washington from a wartime to a permanent peacetime intelligence agency, intense debate surrounded Donovan's plan to establish a centralized intelligence apparatus directly reporting to the president. Criticisms of the plan emerged mostly from the State Department and the military, who believed that a 'single intelligence agency could not manage the complex array of civilian and military departments'.[16] Upon the dissolution of the OSS, aside from the powers vested in the SSU, some duties were split between the State Department (under the Research and Analysis Branch) and the War Department (including the employment of Special Forces). But President Harry Truman agreed to a proposal from the Joint Chief of Staff (1181/5) that he should form a centralized body, in January 1946, to coordinate national intelligence activities, known as the Central Intelligence Group.[17] It was recognized that the coordination of peacetime strategic intelligence activities could not be achieved via cooperation between departmental one-source intelligence agencies. Moreover, Truman was convinced that 'strategic intelligence requires knowledge of economic, social and political forces within the structure of a nation that are not so readily ascertainable in swift reconnaissance as in deliberate research'.[18]

However, in order to fulfil such a duty, the Central Intelligence Group required more capabilities and resources: as originally constituted, it operated without its own funds and personnel. Hoyt Vandenberg, who led the Central Intelligence Group between June 1946 and May 1947, was 'certain that the Central Intelligence Group could not meet its primary obligation to produce strategic intelligence unless it had better arrangements for collecting the raw materials for such intelligence'.[19] Moreover, Vandenberg considered that 'in order to produce strategic intelligence efficiently, the group should have independent funds that could be spent as desired without dependence upon or accountability to some other agencies'.[20]

The Central Intelligence Agency (CIA) was officially created as a new independent national intelligence body in the September 1947 National Security Act. It is important to note that, since its formation, the CIA has been an organisation engaged in both intelligence gathering and covert action. During the course of the Cold War, a direct confrontation with the nuclear-capable Soviet Union was unthinkable. Almost every president used the agency to conduct secret wars, mostly in peripheral countries between the Western and Eastern blocs, since it was almost impossible to carry out overt or covert operations behind the Iron Curtain.[21] The operational branches of the CIA became the heart of the agency. As a senior CIA officer, Milton Bearden, states: 'The CIA is the DO [Directorate of Operations]. The rest of it, the analysis, etc. is just the RAND Corporation or the Brookings Institution with razor wire around it.'²² Therefore, the CIA emerged more as an operation-oriented intelligence agency, with an almost military attitude to fighting the Cold War. But there have been clashes between the operational and analysis branches of the agency, and it is important to note that the necessity of a specialized agency to prepare valuable policy-related intelligence analysis has been an essential part of the decision-making process, and may be more important than the operational branch of the Agency. After all, when Truman abolished the OSS, 'he discovered that the conflicting intelligence reports flowing across his desk left him confused and irritable – and monumentally uninformed. Characteristically, he announced one morning that he wanted, as soon as possible, somebody, some outfit, that can make sense out of all this stuff.'²³

In order to fine-tune relations between the operational and analysis branches of the agency, the head of the CIA is responsible for the entire national intelligence and for drafting the National Intelligence Estimates (NIEs) as an end product of the multi-source intelligence collection.²⁴ The deputy head of the agency leads the directorate of operations, which is responsible for the clandestine collection of the intelligence as well as for covert action. These two different tasks of the agency created an ambiguity in its early years regarding its place in the bureaucracy.²⁵

For the CIA was not the only player within that bureaucracy: the emergence of new nuclear threats and the Soviet programme on developing a thermo-nuclear bomb gave birth to the America's most secret intelligence agency, the National Security Agency (NSA). Truman issued a Top Secret memorandum on 24 October 1952 on 'Communications Intelligence Activities' that formed the NSA as another central national intelligence agency. It was held responsible for the clandestine collection of signals intelligence, which was divided into two categories, namely Communications Intelligence (COMINT) and Electronic Intelligence (ELINT) activities. Briefly, COMINT refers to the interception of communications such as radio/phone communications, whereas ELINT refers to the tracking of non-communications intelligence such as missile tests and submarine movements. In particular, the United States Army Security Agency (ASA) had been operating under the supervision of the NSA in its foreign bases. In American SIGINT bases in Turkey (coded TUSLOG), the ASA became the first point of contact between Turkish Military Intelligence and the Americans.

## British intelligence community

British secret intelligence agencies pursued a different path from the Americans, mainly because the origins of a sophisticated British intelligence community predated the Second World War. MI5, MI6 and the signals intelligence agency, Government Communications Headquarters (GCHQ, previously the Government Communications and Cypher School), acted as the main bodies for intelligence collection, domestic security and covert action due to the respective division of labour among them, while the Special Branch of the London Metropolitan Police acted in some ways as a political police force, directed against subversive activities. However, the role of the London Metropolitan Police as a political police force is well defined, as opposed to that of its Turkish counterpart. Moreover, it has not engaged in intelligence liaison activities with the Turks, and, even if it has, its records are currently sealed, thus, it is beyond the scope of this research to know whether such cooperation has existed or not.[26]

In parallel with its Turkish counterpart, the necessity for a foreign intelligence agency in the British context emerged at the beginning of the twentieth century, as British policy makers perceived their interests as threatened by rising German belligerency. Headed by Commander Mansfield Cumming, the Secret Intelligence Bureau was formed in October 1909 as an embryonic form of MI6 and MI5.[27] The agency became a prominent part of the British government during the First and Second World Wars. After the Second World War, the Secret Intelligence Service had to adapt not only to the emerging Soviet threat, but also to the economic restrictions that Britain faced due to its virtual bankruptcy.[28] Thus, British policy makers considered how they might align the Secret Intelligence Service with these post-war necessities.

The debate surrounding this issue mostly revolved around covert action. The Ministry of Defence wanted to establish control of the Secret Intelligence Service. Although the leadership of the Secret Intelligence Service has traditionally come from a military background, the service remained under the purview of the Foreign Office. Links between the Secret Intelligence Service and the Foreign Office took place through the Permanent Undersecretary (the Office's senior civil servant) and a lower level liaison official.[29] It was made clear that 'on matters considering the Foreign Office no action should be taken except after consultation with the Foreign Office'.[30] The subordination of MI6 to the Foreign Office seems to have caused the former to be more cautious when dealing with issues of covert action, and human intelligence-based espionage activities.[31] As a result, 'not a single SIS career agent has been killed in action since the Second World War'.[32] However, as Rory Cormac suggests, following the joint CIA–MI6 fiasco to oust Albania's Enver Hoxha in the late 1940s, MI6 did not stop engaging in covert action.[33] On the contrary, by the end of 1949, a highly secretive Official Committee on Communism (Overseas) was formed in Whitehall to implement covert action plans behind the Iron Curtain. Cormac argues that these operations were adopted in a 'pinprick' approach where they were less provocative and smaller in scale compared with the earlier experiences.[34] While all branches of intelligence have been used, particularly on covert action, the line between Special Forces and MI6 could blur. Cormac points out: 'Intelligence and Special Forces actors have long been seen as a useful means of resolving this divide between ideational constructions of the global role and the material reality of decline.'[35]

The post-war structure of British intelligence tried to avoid an overlap between the responsibilities and powers of MI6 and MI5 in terms of counter-intelligence. MI5 was supposedly only responsible for the 'defence of the realm' in British territory (the Empire, as well as the UK itself), while the collection of secret intelligence in foreign territories, including counter-intelligence, was the responsibility of MI6. But MI5 also took part in the security inspections in NATO and CENTO registries and recent scholarship analysing its role in foreign territories has opened further debate on the topic.[36] The post-war organization of MI6 is a rather less contentious issue. It had four branches. The Requirements Branch was responsible for determining intelligence targets and assessing production of the intelligence as well as assisting the Production Branch. The Production Branch was responsible for obtaining secret intelligence, in other words producing the raw intelligence. The two other branches, Finance and Administration, assisted the core intelligence activities of the Service by providing administrative support.[37] Also, after the Second World War, SOE was dissolved into MI6, thus increasing its covert action capabilities, particularly in the War Planning Department.[38]

The domestic intelligence service, MI5, was formed alongside MI6 from within the Secret Security Bureau due to the same German threat in the early twentieth century. While sharing the same office with Cummings, MI5's first chief, Vernon Kell, who also came from a military background, took the initial steps towards establishing a domestic counter-espionage service.[39] By the 1920s, when Soviet subversion activities increased due to the Comintern's increased interest in British socialism, MI5 was also tasked with counter-subversion as well. Thus, these two core missions of counter-espionage and counter-subversion also constituted the security service's main branches. However, although MI6's and MI5's roles were divided into domestic and foreign territories, before the Second World War there was an overlap where MI6 was running agents within the UK as well. The reason for MI6 to run agents within the country was due to their claim that MI5 was incapable of efficiently running agents and discovering the Comintern's domestic connections.[40]

Indeed, this ambiguity between the respective roles of MI6 and MI5 was carried into the post-war years. Clement Attlee, Prime Minister between 1945 and 1951, established a close relationship with the Director General of the Service, Sir Percy Sillitoe, who came from a police background, rather than the military or Oxbridge establishments. Sillitoe even informed Attlee about the possibility of subversive elements among MPs or the families of MPs.[41] MI5's role was only made explicit by the Churchill government in 1952, through the Maxwell Fyfe Directive:

> The Security Service is part of the Defence Forces of the country. Its task is the Defence of the Realm as a whole, from external and internal dangers arising from attempts of espionage and sabotage, or from actions of persons and organizations whether directed from within or without the country, which may be judged to be subversive of the state.[42]

The Security Service was directly responsible to the Home Secretary, Maxwell Fyfe, yet there was no clear definition of what was meant by the term 'subversive of the state'. In practice, the Director General was left to his own judgement on the matter.[43] However, the level of politicization was not even close to what it became in their Turkish counterpart, the MAH.

In addition to MI5 and MI6, the GCHQ was tasked with the SIGINT intelligence collection that proved essential during the Second World War (then named GC&CS), particularly in breaking the German communication codes known as ULTRA. GCHQ also intercepted Turkish diplomatic communications during the war to assess the likely course of Turkish policy.[44] It is important to note that the SIGINT provided by GCHQ comprised a large portion of the intelligence that Britain collected during the Cold War. Nuclear weapons development, as well as the new conventional and unconventional weapons, required a system for intercepting enemy codes so as not to experience a nuclear Pearl Harbor. Over the course of its development, '[GCHQ] has commanded more staff than the Security Service (MI5) and the Secret Intelligence Service (MI6) combined, and has enjoyed the lion's share of Britain's secret service budget'.[45]

The origins of GCHQ can be traced back to the end of the First World War, when the Government Communications and Cypher

School (GC&CS) was established. Since its early years, GCHQ was often led by people from a naval background. It should be noted that in the Cold War years it followed the same track as MI6 and MI5 in operating against the Soviet Union, as directed by the JIC. GCHQ, like MI6, has remained under the responsibility of the Foreign Office from the beginning. Beside its clandestine SIGINT collection responsibility, GCHQ acts to assure the information and communication security of the army and the government. Thus, GCHQ more closely resembles its American counterpart, the NSA, than the Turkish SIGINT agency, which was directly responsible to the military chief of staff. Moreover, the Turkish SIGINT capabilities were only developed after the Americans turned over the control of TUSLOG bases to the Turks, and provided technical instruction to the Turkish officers regarding how to operate them.

## The Turkish intelligence community

The creation of a nationalized intelligence agency in Turkey, in terms of its organization as well as its duties and structure, followed a very different path to the United States and United Kingdom examples. Initially, an intelligence branch already existed within the Turkish General Staff (Erkan-ı Umumiye Riyaseti), and was responsible for gathering military tactical intelligence. The difference between Turkish military intelligence and its American and British military counterparts predated the creation of their respective civilian services, with the Turkish body conducting counter-espionage in a broad sense of the term. The overarching role of Turkish military intelligence originated in the fact that its gendarmerie forces had acted as a paramilitary domestic unit since Ottoman times. However, the country's founding leader, Mustafa Kemal, widely known as Atatürk, ordered the foundation of a civilian and centralized secret intelligence agency. Atatürk was particularly worried about the activities of foreign states, particularly Soviet Russia, and the subversive actions by minorities such as Kurds,

Armenians and Greeks, and also by domestic political groups such as the communists. Activities of the former Ottoman dynasty against the newly established Turkish republic appear to have concerned him as well. Thus, by 6 January 1926, modern Turkey's first centralized intelligence agency, the National Security Service (MAH) was founded by a top secret memorandum.

Following its foundation, the initial organizational and tactical instructions followed advice from a German military officer, Walter Nicolai. Nicolai's responsibility was to consult a selected group of Turkish officials based on Germany's secret intelligence experience during the First World War. These instructional seminars were conducted both in Turkey and Germany. However, due to a payment dispute between Walter Nicolai and the MAH, his consultant position was severed in January 1927 and MAH was left alone to develop its capabilities. We will see in Chapter 2, however, that during the Second World War the MAH found the British to be suitable partners to help build its capabilities.

On the basis of the 1926 memorandum, signed by the Turkish Chief of Staff, Fevzi Çakmak, the organization acted as a small unit mostly operating within the country's army structure. By the end of the year the organization had evolved into a more complex structure that consisted of four directorates. The first directorate, known as 'A Branch', was responsible for espionage activities. 'B Branch' was responsible for counter-espionage, 'C Branch' for propaganda and 'D' for technical assistance. Moreover, the agency initially set up three offices abroad, namely in Vienna, Cairo and Tehran, as well as a wide array of branches within the country. The agency was directly bound to the prime minister himself. Through this organizational structure, special emphasis was placed upon domestic counter-espionage activities. Moreover, the MAH was designated as the *primary* organization to undertake these duties, taking responsibilities from the Directorate of General Security, the national police force. However, the cadres of the MAH were still either appointed on the payroll of the police forces or through the military gendarmerie. The Ministry of the Interior thereby emerged as the body responsible for the activities of the MAH, although the Turkish General Staff remained involved as well, since a secret decree ordered the MAH to work closely with the military to cover their intelligence needs.

Concurrently with MAH, the Turkish General Staff also started increasing its intelligence capabilities but ordering specialized intelligence officers to conduct military intelligence, and counter intelligence when necessary. However, due to the lack of necessary framework, there were frequently disputes between the Turkish law courts and the General Staff since Turkish prosecutors were indicting Turkish intelligence operatives who were trying to cross the country's borders illegally to spy on foreign military targets.[46] This case demonstrates the hybrid character of the regime in Turkey, in which the intelligence apparatus does not have impunity in law, only receiving it when the political leadership wants to grant it.

The first spymaster of the agency was Şükrü Ali Öğel, who was an MP from the ruling Republican People's Party (CHP), who remained head of the agency until June 1941. He later said that, during the initial years of the agency, it mostly focused on counter-espionage activities without subjugating the agency to the private interests of political leaders. Moreover, among the initial successes of the agency, he notes that it triumphed in nationalizing the country's railways, telecommunication lines and other strategic infrastructure inherited from the Ottoman era. However, he resigned from his post due to the fact that the newly appointed prime minister, although from the CHP, tried to run the agency for his own domestic political gain. This is claimed to have led to a politicization of the agency in later years, as well as increasing its involvement on the domestic scene.[47]

It is important to note that the existence of the MAH remained secret until 9 March 1954, when the existence of this ultra-secretive agency was revealed, in a mundane way, in a decree which appeared in the official gazette regarding the appointment of agency personnel. However, until a major reformation of the agency in 1965, the MAH remained as an uncoordinated, low-budget agency. It operated through loosely organized networks, mostly using HUMINT, without any central mechanism for all-source intelligence evaluation mechanisms to produce a comprehensive national intelligence estimate. Moreover, even the name of the agency was ambiguous when it appeared in official documents. Although the officially designated name of the agency was properly MEH, from the early 1930s the acronym MAH appeared in official communications as well.[48] The reason for using the acronym MAH instead of MEH, as stated in the official history of the agency, was because MAH sounded more phonetically acceptable when pronounced in Turkish!

This ambiguity, which spread even to the official acronym of the agency, was also visible in the relative responsibilities of the military and ministry-level intelligence departments. Over time, the military intelligence branch became predominant over foreign intelligence gathering, SIGINT activities and the drafting of national intelligence estimates for policy makers. In explaining this development, it is particularly important to note the roles and powers of three intelligence agencies other than the MAH, namely military intelligence, the police intelligence unit and intelligence collection abroad made by the foreign ministry. When the CIA was under scrutiny regarding their enhanced interrogation techniques, an insider defended their policy by saying: 'We are an intelligence service, an espionage service. Not jailors, not policemen, not interrogators. We debrief people, don't interrogate them.'[49] This was not the case with Turkish intelligence. Since the domestic suppression of political dissidents was an important aim for the country's political leadership, the country's various intelligence services competed with each other to monitor dissidents in order to secure a more prominent position in the bureaucracy. Therefore, the work of police, the espionage service and others overlapped. Moreover, the prime directive of secret intelligence – 'laws to be obeyed at home and broken abroad'[50] – was not observed and hampered both the country's policing and intelligence agencies. Thus it is vital to take a glance at Turkey's political police in order to see the overlapping traits between secret intelligence and police work in Turkey.

According to the organizational law on national police forces, the political police was responsible for all activities surrounding the national security of the state.[51] These tasks ranged from subversive actions and propaganda to counter-espionage activities. However, although the political police was responsible for these tasks, 'they were not fully equipped to operate under full secrecy and even to counter against secret propaganda, espionage from foreign agents, and the subversive activities although the political police was going through an intense secret intelligence training'.[52] The content and limits of duties and responsibilities were only vaguely defined when it came to putting these duties into practice. The Turkish political police sought to broaden its powers, to include the ability to exercise its powers against political dissidents as part of its responsibility for counter-espionage. It defined its duties thus:

> Defending information against espionage, protection of infrastructure and facilities against sabotage, and protecting government personnel from subversive activities. Also, as a part of our law, the prevention and neutralization of harmful activities by dissident groups or individuals that could be harmful to national security.[53]

This broad definition of the counter-espionage duties of the political police led to two unintended consequences in terms of their activities. Initially, the political police developed a quite unique relationship with politicians from the ruling party; particularly by the 1950s it acted as a mechanism of oppression against political dissidents in the country. Under the CHP's single-party rule, the political police conducted surveillance missions on Turkey's intelligentsia on the grounds that they were opposed to the government and party politics, and that hence they were engaging in communist propaganda against the ruling party.[54] Thus, university students and scholars, who were not necessarily members of an underground communist network, were targeted, as being a dissident provided sufficient grounds for the political police to frame them as such and conduct extensive investigations into them. Several loosely connected networks also emerged from among the political police to act directly as a 'personal intelligence unit' overseeing politicians. Secondly, the political police, whose budget and personnel exceeded that of the MAH, also liaised with foreign intelligence agencies or even engaged in foreign policy issues as well. For instance, the Director of General Security, Cemal Göktan, who controlled the political police, did not hesitate to comment directly to the British Ambassador, Bernard Burrows, on Soviet propaganda directed towards Turkey's Kurdish minority, and Turkey's policy line on this issue.[55]

This ambiguity in the power and responsibilities of the political police led it to overlap its practices with diplomatic affairs and with national security policy more generally – a field that is normally outside the realm of authority of police forces. Moreover, as we will see in Chapter 6, the Turkish police force was even running its own network of agents in Syria to feed foreign intelligence to decision makers. Although this was not its legally authorized duty or responsibility, the politicization of Turkey's bureaucratic institutions enabled the police to overreach, and, more importantly, to undermine the progress of the primary intelligence agency – the MAH – in developing its capabilities further.

In the Turkish case both the MAH and especially Police Intelligence were highly politicized in the early period of the Cold War. This politically infused relationship between policy makers and intelligence personnel led some intelligence officers to gain further access to decision-making mechanisms and additional financial resources from politicians. As a result, on several occasions, intelligence officers appear to have told decision makers what the civilian politicians wanted to hear instead of accurate details on real threats. This problematic relationship between politicians and the intelligence community hampered the effectiveness of the intelligence agency on several occasions and made the country vulnerable to *unexpected* developments, such as the Kurdish independence movement and the fiasco in Syrian policy during the late 1940s and 1950s. The nature of politicization in the Turkish case is different from its American and British counterparts. As Joshua Rovner explains, in Western states, too, there might be a tendency to manipulate intelligence estimates to reflect policy preferences, in order to secure influence over policy makers. Political leaders appointing like-minded spymasters often reflect this process.[56] In the Turkish case, however, the intelligence apparatus was turned into a toy of domestic power politics.

The foreign ministry also participated in this competition, particularly in the collection of foreign secret intelligence. The main reason behind the utilization of foreign ministry personnel in secret intelligence collection derived from the lack of means and budget of the MAH, which lagged behind in this domestic rivalry, as a specialized intelligence agency. However, since diplomatic personnel were not specifically trained for secret intelligence collection, and since they were under strict surveillance when they did operate in the Soviet or Soviet satellite territories, the utilization of diplomats in intelligence collection was not an effective tool for intelligence gathering. When Turkish diplomats abroad observed a military parade or came across a new weapon technology, they were simply not equipped with enough background on military affairs to provide the necessary information. Thus, Turkish diplomats dealt mostly either with local photographers in exchange for their services (for an excessive price) in photographing the facilities, infrastructure or weapons, or they simply enlisted help through personnel connections with their colleagues from other countries who were indeed trained in secret intelligence matters.[57]

Also, dispatching 'political intelligence' regarding their host countries became a measure of competition between Turkish diplomats. However, since they did not have effective means to gather actual secret intelligence, numerous Turkish diplomats would frequently merely encrypt and classify local newspaper articles as if they were their own 'political intelligence estimates', and then dispatch them to Ankara. They thought that the increased quantity of dispatches in 'political intelligence' would gain them career promotion before their superiors. When the then General Secretary of the Ministry of Foreign Affairs, Fuat Carım, found that reports were not genuinely political intelligence estimates but just newspaper articles, he made diplomats pay for the cost of telegram dispatches![58]

Although secret intelligence collection and counter-espionage was partially conducted by civilian intelligence agencies and units (such as the MAH, political police and diplomats), the military still maintained control over the security policy of the country. Thus, army units were also heavily involved in secret intelligence activities that fell under the responsibilities of other institutions. For instance, the military police, the gendarmerie, also conducted counter-subversion, propaganda and counter-espionage, particularly in rural areas of the country. Between 1920 and 1960, only one third of the country was urbanized, thus, the scope of responsibility of the gendarmerie intelligence units exceeded the coverage area of the political police. In an internal publication of the Gendarmerie in 1936, it was claimed that 'foreign spies' could be in the country at any time and could try to stir up disturbances by subverting public opinion. The same internal publication urged gendarmerie officers not to be friends with any foreign nationals (even for the sake of language learning) and be vigilant of foreign nationals wandering around the country![59]

Regarding the Gendarmerie, it is also important to keep in mind that they conducted intelligence operations, either intelligence gathering or operations of a covert nature in their struggle against ethnic bandit groups in the country. After the official formation of the modern Turkish republic in 1923, bandits, and also some armed tribes in certain parts of the country, continued to loot properties and attack government targets. As a legacy of the multi-ethnic Ottoman Empire, bandit groups were organized according to their ethnicity, such as Georgian, Armenian, Kurdish, Abkhazian and Circassian. As these groups took advantage of the mountainous terrain and used guerrilla tactics, it was rather difficult for gendarmerie units to pursue them. Thus, an internal gendarmerie report from 1936 urges local commanders to recruit a wide network of informants in their areas.[60] It should be noted that having a wide network of human sources and intelligence is essential for conducting any counter-insurgency campaign. General the Lord Bourne, who was the General Commanding Officer in the Malaya campaign between 1954 and 1956, pointed out that intelligence is 'the key to success in dealing with bandits or with a full-scale rebellion'.[61]

The intelligence required for fighting against bandit groups and insurgencies differs from secret intelligence. As David Kilcullen argues, it is 'rather a cultural and demographic jungle of population groups to be navigated, "basic intelligence" – detailed knowledge of physical, human, cultural and informational terrain, based on a combination of open-source research and denied area ethnography'.[62] Therefore, the Turkish gendarmerie units in remote rural parts of the country were creating a vast network of spies and penetrating deep into the rural, and ethnically divided, segments of society.[63] However, the Turkish Gendarmerie's experience in counter-insurgency was different to Britain's post-war decolonization.[64] For the British, intelligence used in counter-insurgency operations was a tool for protecting influence on the decaying empire's overseas territories. For the Turks, however, it was a tool for constructing a new regime based on a secular Turkish nationalist character, upon the ashes of the multi-ethnic and multi-religious Ottoman Empire. Therefore, the gendarmerie's network of spies also acted as the new regime's agents of influence in remote parts of the country, reiterating the hybrid role of the Turkish intelligence apparatus.

The military's strong influence on intelligence was not only limited to the gendarmerie. Military attachés in Turkish diplomatic posts abroad were also involved in intelligence collection, and indeed their role in the intelligence collected was often praised by the embassy.[65] To add to this, the SIGINT activities and posts developed by the Americans and British in several coastal and highland areas acted in cooperation with the Turkish Military's Communications Command.

As early as 1946, just at the beginning of the Cold War, military intelligence officers were trained not only for the collection of military and tactical intelligence but also to comprehend multiple source intelligence activities, ranging even from biographical intelligence activities to economic intelligence.[66] Thus, the first branch of the Turkish General Staff's intelligence unit emerged as the multi-source intelligence unit that produced the national intelligence estimates. Particularly after Turkey's admission to NATO, Ankara asked NATO to establish joint intelligence training schools in Turkey to enhance Turkish officers' capacity in intelligence affairs and their role in NATO special projects.[67] NATO preferred more civilian officers' participation in projects, but the Turkish government preferred military officers to be involved, since these special projects were held in regions that bordered the USSR and where the Alliance's SIGINT bases operated. Such behaviour reflects the way that civilian authorities yielded increasing responsibilities to the Turkish military in national security affairs. Indeed, the increasing role of the military in national security decision making paved the way for the 1960 coup which ousted the elected civilian government of the country.[68]

## From intelligence to policy making

While secret intelligence is essential for policy making, it is not an apparatus for forming policy. Rather, secret intelligence acts as a mechanism to inform responsible policy makers. However, the institutional link between the policy makers and intelligence communities in the United Kingdom, the United States and Turkey sheds light on two important aspects of secret intelligence. Firstly, the institutional link reveals the influence of the civilian and military officers in the intelligence community on the formation of policy. Secondly, the same link sheds light on the function of the intelligence as well. Thus, it is important to discuss the role of the National Security Council in the United States, the Joint Intelligence Committee in the United Kingdom and the High Commission on National Security in Turkey.

The origins of an interdepartmental national security body in Turkey can be traced back to the establishment of the War Council in 1922, during the later stages of the Turkish Liberation war.[69] The War Council was not a constitutional advisory body but rather an executive body that could order parliament to take action. This wartime establishment was led by the Chief Commander, Mustafa Kemal himself, accompanied by the deputy chairman of parliament, minister of economics, minister of national security, joint chief of staff and heads of the national security and economic commissions. The War Council acted as a war cabinet by drawing up policies based upon the collecting of all relevant intelligence from pertinent departments. Changing threat perceptions during the interwar years, particularly Italian, Soviet and German belligerency, required changes in the Turkish national security apparatus. Thus, on 24 April 1933 the council of ministers issued a decree to form the High Defence Council.[70] This was again created by Atatürk. It was designed to convene at least once a month, with cabinet ministers in addition to the chief of staff. The importance of the High Defence Council was highlighted by decree no. 14819 in August 1933, which stated that it was commissioned to deal with issues of utmost importance to national security and take necessary precautions which could not be undertaken by other departments due to economic, legal and administrative restrictions.[71] The Council operated from 1933 until 1949 and acted as an executive body led by the prime minister. Its decisions were binding on all government departments. An appointed secretary of the council monitored both the flow of information into the Council and the implementation of its decisions.

In the post-war years, a more comprehensive national security council was needed to deal with the challenges of the Cold War, ranging from foreign policy to anti-subversion activities at home, as well as to strike a balance between civilian and military inputs. Thus, on 30 May 1949 the National Security High Commission (MSYK) was formed in accordance with the National Security High Commission Law no. 5399. This commission was inspired by the American National Security Council, founded in 1947.[72] The MSYK operated until 1961 and was led by the president, accompanied by the prime minister and chief of staff, as well as ministers of the interior, foreign affairs, economics, transportation, commerce, construction, agriculture and administration. The powers and responsibilities of the MSYK reflected both the Turkish fear of a hot war triggered by the Soviet Union, and the threat of Soviet subversive activities on the domestic scene. Aside from forming war plans and national security policy, the Commission even advised the cabinet to ban several labour strikes, censor the press and even deny passports to certain citizens on the basis that their travel abroad could jeopardise Turkish national security.[73]

The MSYK not only acted as an advisory board to the government, but also acted as an instrument to coordinate broader national security policies ranging from foreign policy to anti-propaganda measures. It is again important to note that, at first, the MSYK seems to be a mostly civilian body with a limited military presence. However, the chief of staff, through G-2 (military intelligence), was also responsible for national security estimates and used the MSYK as a means to implement and coordinate national security measures. Such a role of the Turkish General Staff in national security policy was also reflected in parliamentary debates, where even the minister of national security or the governors could not decide to open a coastal area to tourists – instead, such a decision was the responsibility of the Turkish General Staff.[74]

In contrast to the Turkish case, the British Joint Intelligence Committee (JIC) was created in 1936 and developed during the war and post-war years. However, it is crucial to note that the JIC did not form policies; it simply informed the responsible cabinet committees on possible action. Therefore, the Turkish Committee possessed both the JIC responsibilities and that of the cabinet committees. In the British system, however, such an attitude helped create a beneficial gap between the realms of politics and secret intelligence, helping prevent the politicization of the intelligence community, in contrast to the Turkish case. During the 1930s, however, the JIC was mostly associated with the military understanding of secret intelligence.[75] The origins of centralized intelligence machinery in Britain also paralleled developments in Turkey. Concerning the origins of the JIC, Goodman states that 'a centralized system of intelligence was not initiated before 1936 had nothing to do with the changing nature of British intelligence, but rather more with the appreciation of the international situation. [T]he JIC's origin lay in an external threat awakening consideration of the internal means of dealing with it'.[76] In the British case, this external threat was German belligerency in Europe, whereas for the Turks, Soviet designs on Turkish territory played a more important role.

Concurrent with post-war developments and a new necessity for a centralized intelligence apparatus, the JIC also went through reforms to encourage interdepartmental cooperation within the UK in 1948[77]; the Turks followed that trend a year later in 1949. In both countries, this centralized machinery of intelligence and national security policy making was re-devised for the Cold War international environment so that it could act as a bridge between intelligence and policy making.[78] Aldrich, Cormac and Goodman argue that the JIC was traditionally in the 'activist' camp of the intelligence community.[79] As the JIC was responsible for setting requirements and priorities for the collection agencies, and for dissemination of the finalized intelligence to its consumers, it thus monitored the collection agencies of MI5, GCHQ and MI6.[80] The JIC fine-tuned the intelligence agencies in line with political concerns, since 'in practice, the intelligence assessments are ripe with ambiguity and uncertainty. Political concerns permeate every aspect of intelligence work, from requirement setting all the way through to assessment and dissemination'.[81]

Nonetheless, the role of the JIC's brokerage between policy makers and the intelligence community is quite different from the Turkish context. In the JIC, only representatives of the civilian ministries, military intelligence and related advisors accompanied the heads of intelligence agencies, whereas in the Turkish context the ministers, president, prime minister and chief of staff all accompanied representatives of the intelligence agencies. Thus, the Turkish context reveals a closer and even blurred line between the intelligence community and policy makers, meaning it is easier to politicize the assessment and estimation process itself.

Compared with the role of the MSYK in Ankara, and the role of the JIC in London, the American National Security Council stands in a unique position, even if the Turks claimed to have copied the American example. The necessity for a peacetime coordinating council in the United States also emerged due to the necessities of the post-war era. As much as the changing world structure itself, the increasingly interventionist American role in global affairs required the president to be constantly advised on current foreign and national security issues and to take action accordingly. Thus, the National Security Act of 1947 founded the NSC as a body that would advise the president on all available intelligence, determine the targets and requirements for the intelligence bodies, and even draft the covert action plans that they would submit to the president. After reforms, the NSC assumed its final shape as a body that consisted of the vice president, secretary of defence, director of Central Intelligence and the chairman of the Joint Chiefs of Staff. In the initial phases, the NSC undertook two kinds of activities. The first, and more formal one, was to provide the policy papers drafted by the NSC's various departments and agencies to be discussed by the Council and later to be submitted for the president's approval or rejection. The second track provided spontaneous policy advice for the president to take action.[82] According to Truman:

> The council was to be a channel for collective advice and information regarding just one discrete part of the President's total range of responsibilities with complete freedom to accept, reject and amend the Council's advice and to consult with other members of his official policy and enforce it. The sole exception would be general direction and coordination of intelligence operations, for which the NSC was legally responsible under the National Security Act of 1947.[83]

This object made the NSC a very different entity from its Turkish and British counterparts. In the British context, the JIC's role was to submit the finalized intelligence as the American NIE system, while at the same time, taking a politically active position to craft the necessary political discussions between the Cabinet and the intelligence community. In the Turkish context, the MSYK held the ultimate decision-making power in national security matters. Truman wanted to avoid such a situation and only attended eleven of the sixty meetings held before the Korean War. Furthermore, he deputized either the secretary of state, and after the 1949 National Security Reform, the vice-president, to chair the meetings. The president used this 'arm's length' approach to ensure that no one would think he was captive to the NSC's decisions; the Council would discuss and advise him and the president would hold the last word on whether to approve their recommendations or not.[84]

## Conclusion

These comparisons between the machinery of Turkish, British and American secret intelligence apparatuses help us to frame the analysis of Turkish intelligence cooperation with the West in the early Cold War. Factors such as organization, capacity, responsibilities, politicization and a role in the decision-making mechanism crucially shaped the characteristics of intelligence diplomacy between the Turks and the West. Thus, it comes as no surprise that Turkish intelligence diplomacy with the West focused more on domestic concerns and political priorities rather than aiming to establish an effective channel for intelligence cooperation. As a result, reciprocal distrust between Turkey and its partners was a prevailing theme in their relations, even though there had been parallels and similarities between the evolution of the Turkish intelligence community and that of its Western friends. Turkish intelligence diplomacy during the interwar years and in the Second World War was the initial period when Ankara began actively to utilize intelligence diplomacy in its relations with the West. A survey of that period is therefore essential as the next step in this analysis.

## Notes

1   Bock, 'Anglo-Soviet Intelligence Cooperation, 1941–45', 890–912. In a recent study Jonathan N. Brown and Alex Farrington argue that regime type hardly matters, it is rather the perception of mutual threat that drives the depth of intelligence cooperation. Cf. J. N. Brown and A. Farrington,

'Democracy and the Depth of Intelligence Sharing: Why Regime Type Hardly Matters', *Intelligence and National Security*, 32:1 (2017), 68–84.
2   G. P. Hastedt, 'Towards the Comparative Study of Intelligence', *Journal of Conflict Studies*, 11:3 (1991), 57.
3   Ibid.
4   It is important to note Davies and Gustafson's attempt at comparative analysis. Their edited volume demonstrates the potential for comparative analysis in intelligence studies. However, it is an initial step lacking deeper understanding. For instance, one of the chapters in the book is titled 'Origins of an Arab and Islamic Intelligence Culture' which is self-explanatory as regards reflecting the limitations of the study. Cf. P. Davies and K. C. Gustafson, eds., *Intelligence Elsewhere: Spies and Espionage outside the Anglosphere* (Washington, DC, 2013).
5   D. Van Puyvelde and S. Curtis. '"Standing on the Shoulders of Giants": Diversity and Scholarship in Intelligence Studies', *Intelligence and National Security*, 31:7 (2016), 1040–1054.
6   Ibid.
7   R. Aldrich and J. Kasuku, 'Escaping from American Intelligence: Culture, Ethnocentrism and the Anglosphere', *International Affairs*, 88:5 (2012), 1027.
8   P. Davies, 'Intelligence Culture and Intelligence Failure in Britain and the United States', *Cambridge Review of International Affairs*, 17:3 (2004), 495–520.
9   T. Kılıç, 'Subayların İstihbarat Bilgileri', *Topçu Mecmuası* (1 İkincikanun 1944), 65.
10  Author's Collection: MAH, *Stratejik Istihbarat* (Ankara, 1945).
11  Author's Collection: MAH, *Komünist Faaliyetleri*, c. 1947.
12  A. B. Darling, *The Central Intelligence Agency: An Instrument of Government to 1950* (Pennsylvania, 1990), 48.
13  Ibid., 40.
14  Ibid., 42.
15  D. Alvarez, 'American Clandestine Intelligence in Early Postwar Europe', *Journal of Intelligence History*, 4:1 (2004), 12–15.
16  Darling, *The Central Intelligence Agency*, 48.
17  M. Warner, 'Salvage and Liquidation: The Creation of the Central Intelligence Group', *Studies in Intelligence*, 39:5 (1996), 117.

18  Darling, *The Central Intelligence Agency*, 58.
19  Ibid., 106.
20  Ibid.
21  S. Grey, *The New Spymasters: Inside Espionage from the Cold War to Global Terror* (London, 2015), 54.
22  Ibid., 50.
23  A. Tully, *The Central Intelligence Agency: The Inside Story* (London, 1962), 16.
24  J. Richelson, *The US Intelligence Community* (New York, 1989), 18; J. Ranelagh, *The Agency: The Rise and Fall of the CIA* (New York, 1986), 20.
25  Ranelagh, *The Agency: The Rise and Fall of the CIA*, 20.
26  For the origins of the London Metropolitan Police Special Branch as a political police organ, and the transition from a mid-Victorian liberal environment to an era of anxiety and tension due to the German threat and domestic terrorism please, see: B. Porter, *The Origins of the Vigilant State: The London Metropolitan Police Special Branch before the First World War* (Woodbridge, 1987).
27  K. Jeffrey, *MI6: History of the Secret Intelligence* (London, 2010), 3.
28  Ibid., 621.
29  Ibid., 621.
30  Ibid., 620.
31  R. Cormac, 'The Pinprick Approach: Whitehall's Top-Secret Anti-Communist Committee and the Evolution of British Covert Action Strategy', *Journal of Cold War Studies*, 16:3 (2014), 8.
32  Grey, *New Spymasters*, 36.
33  Cormac, 'The Pinprick Approach', 5–28.
34  Ibid., 12–13.
35  R. Cormac, 'Disruption and Deniable Interventionism: Explaining the Appeal of Covert Action and Special Forces in Contemporary British Policy', *International Relations* (2016): 0047117816659532.
36  See C. Hashimoto, 'Fighting the Cold War or Post-Colonialism? Britain in the Middle East from 1945 to 1958: Looking through the Records of the British Security Service', *The International History Review*, 36:1 (2014): 19–44; R. Arditti, 'Security Intelligence in the Middle East (SIME): Joint Security Intelligence Operations in the Middle East, c. 1939–58', *Intelligence and National Security*, 31:3 (2016), 369–396.

37  Jeffrey, *MI6: History of the Secret Intelligence*, 623.
38  P. Davies, 'From Special Operations to Special Political Action: The "Rump SOE" and SIS Post-War Covert Action Capability 1945–1977', *Intelligence and National Security*, 15:3 (2000), 55–76.
39  C. Andrew, *Defend the Realm: The Authorized History of MI5* (London, 2009), 3.
40  Ibid., 128.
41  Ibid., 324.
42  Ibid., 325.
43  Ibid.
44  N. Tamkin, 'Diplomatic SIGINT and the British Official Mind during the Second World War: Soviet Claims on Turkey, 1940–45', *Intelligence and National Security*, 23:6 (2008), 749–766.
45  Aldrich, *GCHQ: The Uncensored Story of Britain's Most Secret Intelligence Agency*, 1.
46  MKB (Milli Kütüphane Başkanlığı): Mahrem: Genelkurmay Başkanlığı XI.Şube no.60581: Espiyonaj, 20 June 1940 (Turkish National Library records based in Ankara, Turkey. Hereafter it will be referred as MKB).
47  Ögel, 'Millî Emniyet Hizmeti Nasıl Kuruldu?', 605–607.
48  İlter, *Milli İstihbarat Teşkilatı tarihçesi*.
49  Grey, *New Spymasters*, 12.
50  Glossary of Spying in Grey, *New Spymasters*, 2015.
51  M. Şenel and T. Şenel, *Siyasi Polisin El Kitabı: Temel Güvenlik Konularımız İstihbarat, Karşı İstihbarat ve Propaganda* (Ankara, 1972), 10.
52  Ibid., 2.
53  Ibid., 49.
54  BCA: 490.1.0.0.1191.176.2: 7. Büro: 'Üniversite talebeleri hakkında yapılan tahkikat ve Komünist Partisine dahil olanlar', 14 February 1947 (Turkish State Archives' Republic Era Collection, based in Ankara, Turkey. Hereafter will be referred as BCA).
55  TNA: FO 371/136521: 1822/53: Telegram from Bernard Burrows, Ankara to FO dated 17 December 1958.
56  J. Rovner, 'Is Politicization Ever a Good Thing?' *Intelligence and National Security*, 28:1 (2013), 55–58.
57  A. Yakın, *İstihbarat, Casusluk ve Casuslukla Mücadele* (Ankara, 1969), 5.
58  Ibid., 50.

59 MKB: Ş. Olcay, 'Gizli Kuvvet – Casusluk ve Jandarma', *Jandarma Mecmuası*, 2:46 (1936).
60 MKB: E. Baykal, 'İstihbarat – Haber Alma', *Jandarma Mecmuası*, 2:46 (1936).
61 K. Jeffery, 'Intelligence and Counter-Insurgency Operations: Some Reflections on the British Experience', *Intelligence and National Security*, 2:1 (1987), 118.
62 D. Kilcullen, 'Counter-Insurgency Redux', *Survival*, 48:4 (2006), 126.
63 See MKB: M. Rahmi, 'Çapulcu, Tahkik, Takip ve Müsademe', *Jandarma Mecmuası*, 10:38 (1934); B. Tümay, 'Çete Harbi', *Ordu Dergisi*, 67:146 (1948).
64 For the British counter-insurgency in the colonies, see R. Cormac, *Confronting the Colonies: British Intelligence and Counterinsurgency* (Oxford, 2014); J. Newsinger, *British Counterinsurgency* (London, 2016); T. R. Mockaitis, *British Counterinsurgency in the Post-Imperial Era* (Manchester, 1995).
65 Ibid., 5. For earlier interwar years examples for reports from Turkish military attachés, see MKB: Büyük Erkân-ı Harbiye XII. İstihbarat Şubesi, *Tahran ataşe militerliği raporu* (Ankara: Büyük Erkân-ı Harbiye 13. İstihbarat Şubesi, 1928).
66 MKB: C. Akyol, 'Subay İstihbarat Eğitimi', *Silahlı Kuvvetler Dergisi*, 80:202 (1962).
67 NATO: AC/19-D/198: 'Training of Communications-Electronics Personnel in Turkey', 24 September 1959 (NATO Archives based in Brussels, Belgium).
68 Please see Chapter 6 for more details.
69 H. Özdemir, 'Milli Güvenlik Kurulu', in *Cumhuriyet Dönemi Türkiye Ansiklopedisi*, Cilt II (Ankara, 1983).
70 Kararname 14443
71 S. Sezen, 'Millî Güvenlik Kurulu Üzerine', *Amme İdaresi Dergisi*, 33 (2000), 69.
72 R. Aybay, 'Milli Güvenlik Kavramı ve Milli Güvenlik Kurulu', *Ankara Üniversitesi SBF Dergisi*, 33:01 (1978), 73.
73 Ibid.
74 TBMM Tutanakları: 10. Dönem, 5. Cilt, 40. Birleşim.

75 R. Aldrich, R. Cormac, and M. S. Goodman, *Spying on the World: The Declassified Documents of the Joint Intelligence Committee, 1936–2013* (Edinburgh, 2014), 10.
76 M. S. Goodman, 'Learning to Walk: The Origins of the UK's Joint Intelligence Committee', *International Journal of Intelligence and Counterintelligence*, 21:1 (2007), 41.
77 R. Aldrich, R. Cormac, and M. S. Goodman. *Spying on the World: The Declassified Documents of the Joint Intelligence Committee, 1936–2013* (Edinburgh, 2014), 62.
78 Ibid., 1.
79 Ibid., 6.
80 Ibid., 2.
81 Ibid., 5.
82 J. Prados, *Keepers of the Keys: A History of the National Security Council from Truman to Bush* (New York, 1991), 27.
83 Ibid., 30.
84 D. Rothkopf, *Running the World: The Inside Story of the National Security Council and the Architects of American Power* (New York, 2006), 57.

# 2

# Historical Background, 1923–45

The Turkish government used every means at its disposal during the Second World War to protect its sovereignty and avoid becoming ensnared in the devastation of the war. One of the prominent mechanisms the Turks employed was 'intelligence diplomacy'. The experience of the Second World War shows us that Ankara exploited intelligence diplomacy, particularly in its relations with the British, to avoid being dragged into the war, and to deflect threats from the Germans and Soviets. Also, during the war, Ankara did not hesitate to serve the intelligence needs of France and the United States on occasions when Turkey derived material and strategic gains from them.

Turkish intelligence diplomacy during the war involved negotiations and the use of joint action with Britain, synchronized by diplomats and intelligence officers. While such efforts often resulted in an overlap between diplomatic and intelligence efforts, there is no clear indication that either the Turkish or British intelligence services acted at variance with their foreign ministries. In this relationship, the Turks, as the weaker state in the partnership, sought ways to influence their more powerful partner, through holding over them the possibility of granting or not granting the establishment of SIGINT posts on Turkish soil, or by refusing to accept the intelligence estimates provided by their partner. Thus, the intelligence diplomacy conducted by the Turks showed how, even during a war, a smaller power could seek ways to avoid becoming a mere 'stooge', and instead pursue its own strategic imperatives in the region. Aside from not becoming a 'stooge' of their powerful partner, the Turks avoided becoming ensnared in the conflict and increased their own technical capabilities in exchange for their partial support for British military and intelligence activities in the region. There were thus powerful, arguably compelling, reasons for pursuing such intelligence diplomacy.

Shedding light on secret intelligence diplomacy during the war era contributes to the debate surrounding Turkish diplomatic history. The official line of Turkish diplomatic history states that (although they signed an alliance treaty with the UK and France in May 1939) the reason the Turks did not enter the war was because the British failed to deliver on their promises of arms and material aid to them.[1] In contrast, the revisionist approach argues that Turkey was determined to maintain neutrality from the beginning, but that Ankara manoeuvred between the rival powers during the war, and adopted an opportunistic attitude to gain from whichever side emerged as the more suitable source for financial aid.[2] An analysis of intelligence diplomacy, both before and during the war, demonstrates that the materialist and opportunist features of Turkish diplomacy during the war extended to the dimension of intelligence as well.

This chapter initially focuses on the development of Turkish secret intelligence activities as an integral part of the country's foreign and security policies after the foundation of the Republic in 1923.[3] It highlights the fact that, while the newly established republic tried to portray itself as being committed to international law and friendly relations with other countries to solve problems, Ankara did not hesitate to utilize its intelligence apparatus for covert action and espionage to manipulate a situation for its advantage. Next comes an outline of Turkish intelligence diplomacy during the war years. It is noted that, while Turkey initially did not wish to abandon its responsibilities under the Anglo-Turkish Treaty, Ankara was mistrustful and cautious about British intentions, as well as about Soviet demands on Turkey, and thus crafted its strategy and policy in the first place to secure its political and territorial integrity. The discussion then elaborates on the conditions and characteristics of Turkish intelligence diplomacy in relation to pressure from its Western allies, as well as from Germany and the

Soviet Union. After exposing Ankara's pragmatist frame of mind, the chapter analyses cooperation on clandestine operations and staff talks to highlight the major strands of the Turkish approach.[4]

## Early steps

For centuries the Ottoman Empire had controlled vast swathes of territory in Asia, Europe and Africa. It entered the twentieth century as the 'sick man of Europe', facing almost inevitable dissolution and collapse due to economic, social and political corruption, as well as the rise of nationalist movements in every corner of the empire. The corruption was in every segment of society in every possible dimension. For instance, Servet Sürenkök, an intelligence officer who later became a governor in the 1950s, recalled that it was partly due to large-scale opium addiction among Ottoman army officers that the Ottoman military faced a fiasco by losing large portions of its European territory during the Balkan Wars of 1912–13.[5]

The Committee of Union and Progress (CUP) government in the Sublime Porte pushed the dissolution progress further by joining in the Great War in November 1914, in alliance with Germany. Defeated in the war, the empire practically ceased to exist after the Armistice of Mudros, signed on 18 October 1918 between the Ottomans and victorious allies. The Treaty of Sevres, signed on 10 August 1920, demanded the disarmament of the Ottoman army and the carving-up of Ottoman territory between the allies (with Britain the mandatory power in Iraq, Transjordan and Palestine; France in Syria and Lebanon; and the Greeks occupying areas of western Anatolia), alongside some newly planned states, including a Kurdish and an Armenian state in the eastern provinces of the empire. Meanwhile, as the Ottoman state approached its demise, a Turkish nationalist uprising, mostly comprising former Ottoman military officers, politicians and intellectuals, led by Mustafa Kemal, later known as Atatürk, emerged in Anatolia. While the Kemalist government in Ankara endeavoured to resist allied partition of the country, it began to utilize intelligence work and diplomacy alongside military force. This utilization emerged in support of two crucial aims in particular. The first was to obtain arms and material support from the Soviets for the Turkish resistance. The second was to conduct espionage and sabotage missions against the allied forces and other threats.

This intelligence work was initiated principally by former officers of the Ottoman Empire's intelligence agency Teşkilat-ı Mahsusa, who organized small cells such as Karakol, Zabitan, MM and Askeri Polis to conduct these operations.[6] Karakol and Zabitan pursued a political rivalry with Mustafa Kemal, and so these two groups were not credited with their successes and soon disappeared. The MM, however, was in the same political lineage as Kemal, and distanced itself from the political rivalry between Kemal and the CUP. Thus, the MM became the more useful secret agency working for the politico-military goals of the nationalist resistance. The experience of these organizations during the Great War and the ensuing War of Independence created the nucleus of modern Turkey's intelligence apparatus.

One of the most remarkable successes of the new organization was its seizure of a secret report by the commander of the allied occupation forces, General Sir Charles Harrington, based in Istanbul. The report outlined the weaknesses and strengths of the Greek and British forces occupying the country. Moreover, the report revealed disputes between the British and the Greeks. After seizing the report, Ankara was able to direct its military operations accordingly, as well as developing a policy to exploit the disputes between the two allies.[7] The MM was also involved in transferring arms from the Soviets to Turkish resistance fighters around the country. The Turkish resistance was not in any way a socialist movement, but the Soviets were keen to strengthen anti-imperialist movements in neighbouring regions, including Turkey, China and Afghanistan, as a part of their struggle against capitalist forces.[8] Thus the Turks and Soviets shared similar foreign policy concerns. As Stone explains, 'Turkey shows how domestic anti-communism was irrelevant for Soviet arms exports so long as a state's foreign policy remained pro-Soviet, or rather anti-imperialist. The Soviet goal was preventing Turkish dependence on Europe's capitalist powers while promoting good relations more generally.[9] During this period, it is difficult to define centralized and organized intelligence agencies on either the Turkish or Soviet sides. These joint operations were based instead on a rather loosely connected network of former military officers and their civilian auxiliaries. Such liaison with the Soviets contributed to the intelligence diplomacy culture of the MAH, helping define secret intelligence's role in diplomacy and security affairs in general. Particularly, having a multi-layered approach in their fighting against the allied occupation of Anatolia, the MAH not only received material help from the Soviets, but certain ranks within the military and intelligence were coming to believe that the 'Western' mode of government was not the only solution for Turkey's economic, social and political problems. Moreover, distrust and scepticism directed towards the West, partially reiterated by this early stage Soviet influence, later surfaced during the Cold War.[10]

However, during the course of Soviet support for Turkey, Mustafa Kemal became troubled by their growing influence. He was especially irked by the fact that while the Soviets helped the Turkish resistance against the British and the Greeks, they simultaneously endeavoured to infiltrate the resistance movement, evidently hoping to replace Kemal's regime with a communist government. This was a partnership based on distrust and it soon fell apart. From September 1920, Ankara grew increasingly concerned. The Bolsheviks were believed to be infiltrating the ranks of the Turkish army, as well as preparing a communist uprising in the eastern provinces. The MM, under orders from Mustafa Kemal, thus started to put military and civil officers with any possible connection to the Bolsheviks under surveillance.[11] They did so with some care. As revealed in an MAH report evaluating communist movements in Turkey during the War of Independence, the intelligence services did not want to put those movements under too much pressure in order not to sour relations with the Soviets while their cooperation remained valuable. The MAH further concluded that the MM was well informed about subversive communist movements within the country, and that it monitored the key Soviet agents, Sarafim and Gessenberg.[12]

However, when the Kemalist government consolidated its power after its victory over the Greek forces (which were driven out of Anatolia in 1922–3), it launched a mass investigation into communist groups within the country. That investigation resulted in numerous arrests and convictions. Once the new regime had consolidated power at home, Ankara was ready to use intelligence diplomacy to solve the 'remaining problems' in its foreign policy during the interwar years. However, due to a lack of material capability, Turkish leaders had to handle foreign policy delicately, mostly synchronized with secret intelligence, in order to prevent undesirable and unaffordable confrontation with Western countries.

## The interwar years

After Turkish liberation was concluded with the signing of the Treaty of Lausanne, on 24 July 1923, Ankara continued to exploit intelligence and covert action as essential tools to support its policies in Mosul (in Iraq), Hatay (in Syria) without directly confronting Britain and France. As Morgan Pelts explains, Ankara's foreign policy included a strong desire for influence over and protection of the so-called 'external Turks' (Dış Türkler), living in former Ottoman territories that were now outside its borders, most importantly in Mosul and Hatay.[13] Turkey was well aware of its own military, economic and political weaknesses. Thus, the government wanted to settle these disputes without military confrontation, while also creating military and political pressure on Britain and France, so that they would come to terms with the Turkish government. Moreover, Turkey was too weak to act overtly. This led Ankara to depend on covert links to achieve policy goals. (The desire to wield influence over the 'external Turks' endured and this point will be significant in Chapter 6, which investigates covert action.)

A senior intelligence officer, Özdemir Bey, organized an uprising against the British occupation of Mosul as early as 1920. He initially made contacts with Kurdish and Turkish tribes, who subsequently made significant advances in the area. In response, the Royal Air Force (RAF), under the command of John Salmon, organized a month-long counter attack against the rebellion. But Özdemir did not receive the necessary support for his campaign and fell out with military headquarters in Ankara, the chief of staff (COS) dismissing him as a maverick. Ankara did not want a direct military conflict with British forces.[14] By the time the Mosul dispute was settled by the League of Nations in 1926 in favour of the British, yielding the oil-rich region of Mosul to Iraq, Ankara was keen to develop good relations with the British in order to counter Soviet influence.

During the War of Liberation in 1921 Ankara signed a ceasefire with the French (who then left Britain and Greece to bear the brunt of the conflict with the Kemalists). As part of the ceasefire agreement, the Ankara government ceded the mostly Turkish-speaking province of Alexandretta (Hatay) to the French, a step subsequently confirmed by the Treaty of Lausanne. The treaty provided that Paris would set up an autonomous administration for Hatay in their Syrian mandate. However, when France and Syria signed an agreement on 9 September 1936 to end the French mandate and recognize Syrian independence, France also yielded her control over Hatay to the newly formed Syrian government. As a strategically crucial and Turkish-speaking province in the eastern Mediterranean, the Turks could not readily accept such a step and Ankara launched a bilateral campaign to achieve their aims in Hatay. First, through diplomatic channels, they applied to the League of Nations on 26 September 1936 to guarantee that Sancak (Hatay) should not be integrated into the new Syrian state. On 9 October 1936, Turkey also issued a *Note Signée* to France, demanding that it grant autonomy to Hatay. Second, Atatürk commissioned the MAH to launch a covert operation in Hatay to create disturbances in the province to Turkey's advantage.

As a result of this two-pronged policy, while diplomatic relations were progressing at the multilateral level in the League of Nations and at the bilateral level between the Turks and French, a violent conflict emerged on the ground between Turks in the province and the French Gendarmerie.¹⁵ As part of Turkey's covert operation in Hatay, which included propaganda and arming the population, the MAH infiltrated French political circles in the region, as well as in Paris. For instance, during Turco-French negotiations on Hatay, the MAH acquired a secret telegram from Paris directed to the French delegation in Ankara. In the telegram Paris instructed their delegation that if Turkish claims were to be limited to Hatay to the north of the Lazkiye-Aleppo line, Paris would compromise, otherwise an armed confrontation between Turkey and France would be inevitable.¹⁶ This secret intelligence helped Ankara to gear its covert operations and diplomacy accordingly. Moreover, Ankara appointed Celal Tevfik Karasapan of the MAH to be the Turkish Consul in Hatay.¹⁷ As a result of the intense Turkish intelligence activities in the province, the MAH's chief spymaster, Şükrü Ali Öğel, reported in January 1937 to the chief of staff in Ankara that 'the French were not prepared for a military action against the Turks and that the French were aligning more towards the Turkish proposal. Even Christians in Aleppo were alarmed that Turkey would invade the city.'¹⁸ Ankara's covert operation threatened a high political and military cost for the French administration in Syria if they did not agree to Turkey's demands. Indeed, following bilateral diplomacy in the League of Nations on 26 January 1937, the French delegation agreed to grant more autonomy to the Hatay region. Anthony Eden, the British Foreign Secretary, was also influential in settling the dispute, so that the Turkish Foreign Minister, Tevfik Rüştü Aras, issued a press release showing gratitude for British support.¹⁹ An independent Hatay (Sancak) state was formed in September 1938 and, on 29 June 1939, the Hatay parliament ratified a fait accompli to join Turkey. These events demonstrate that the Ankara government often employed two-dimensional relations with Western countries. Ankara utilized its secret intelligence service to manipulate conditions in its favour, making a diplomatic solution on Turkey's terms much easier to achieve. This complex foreign policy attitude, especially concerning critical issues in Turkey's adjacent regions, was inherited by Turkish governments in the Cold War era.

Similar in principle to its policies over Mosul and Hatay, the Turkish government was keen to assert its traditional domination over the Straits and was concerned over a clause in the Treaty of Lausanne that demanded their internationalization and disarmament.[20] Indeed, İsmet İnönü, Turkey's chief negotiator at the Lausanne conference, initially sought Soviet support for the Turkish position on the Straits, before deciding that the Soviets were acting like Tsarist Russia in trying to gain influence over the Straits for themselves, so as to access the Mediterranean. Eventually, Ankara decided that agreeing with the British over the Straits was more in line with Turkish strategic interests. It was largely as a result of working with the British that the Turks were able to gain full control over the Straits in the Montreux Convention of 1936. MAH's first spymaster Öğel hints that Turkish Intelligence was active during these negotiations to learn of frictions between the allies, and the allies' concerns regarding the Soviets gaining an advantageous position on the control of the Turkish Straits.[21] Thus, Turkish diplomats were able to exploit this information to gain full control of the Straits.

After Ankara settled its disputes with the UK and France regarding Mosul, Hatay and the question of the Straits, there were no remaining major outstanding disputes obstructing Turkey's development of good relations with these countries. Ankara was able to focus on strengthening its position in the face of rising tensions in the region. However, attempts to work with the Western powers did not go smoothly. As part of Turkey's eagerness to align itself with the UK, Ankara gave administrative rights over a major steel and iron plant in the city of Karabük to the British Brassert company, removing the German Krupp company's rights in 1937.[22] The same year Ankara asked Britain to sign a mutual defence treaty, but incoming prime minister Neville Chamberlain, as a believer in 'appeasement', rejected the proposal on the grounds that this would challenge the Soviet position.[23] Chamberlain's initial refusal of a mutual defence treaty only deepened Turkish concern over British aims and their fear of isolation in the face of a possible war.

## Turkey and the powers, 1939–41

In the late 1930s, both Benito Mussolini's Italy and the Soviet Union posed potential threats to Turkish territorial integrity. Italy's invasion of Albania in April 1939 especially alarmed Ankara, since it might foreshadow fascism's wider belligerency in the Balkans and the eastern Mediterranean. Moreover, when the Turkish foreign minister, Şükrü Saraçoğlu, visited Moscow in the same year, seeking to confirm the Soviet Union's policy of non-aggression towards Turkey, he did not find a friendly reception. Rather, the Soviet foreign minister, Vyacheslav Molotov, demanded the establishment of Soviet military bases on the Straits and the ceding of Turkey's eastern provinces, Kars and Ardahan, to the Soviet Union.[24] After this, while Ankara increased its military build-up on its Balkan borders, it also sought a mutual defence agreement with the UK and France.[25] With London and Paris also concerned over events in Albania, as well as by Germany's invasion of Czechoslovakia, an Anglo-French-Turkish treaty was signed in Ankara in May 1939.

The British were aware that Turkey would only actually join the war if directly attacked, or to serve her own interests. One of the primary interests of the Turks, as discussed during Staff Talks in May 1939, was to recapture the Dodecanese islands, in the Aegean Sea, occupied by Italy since their 1911 defeat of Turkey.[26] Therefore, during the Staff Talks the British promised to hand over control of the Dodecanese islands to Turkey as war spoils. At the same time, British promised the Dodecanese islands to the Greeks as well (Greece eventually took control of the islands after the war). However, it is likely that the Italians were aware of these discussions between the Turks and the British, as the Italian army's intelligence unit had been able to decode encrypted Turkish communications since 1938.[27] Thus, Italian diplomatic, military and intelligence efforts were directed towards a possible Anglo-Turkish deal on the islands. However, it was not only the Italians who were eavesdropping on Turkish communications: The Germans, Americans and British were all able to decipher high-level Turkish communications, a damning comment on the state of Turkish security at this point. It took time before Ankara was able to develop a secure communication system to protect its secrets.[28] At that point, it hampered Turkish intelligence diplomacy as regards taking action on the islands since it could not prevent its deceitful tactics being leaked.

The 1939 treaty stated that the UK and France were obliged to aid Turkey if an aggressor from the West attacked it, a measure designed to operate against Germany or Italy. However, the Turkish delegation insisted that the treaty's obligations would not be valid if they risked Turkey being drawn into a conflict against the Soviet Union. There were compelling reasons for the Turks' insistence on avoiding a direct conflict with the Soviets: Turkish defensive and offensive lines were directed towards the Thrace region, against possible confrontation with Italy, Germany or Bulgaria and there were insufficient resources to prepare defences against the Soviet Union in the East. In any case, British and French resources were also limited and it is apparent from Staff Talks, in May 1940, between Turkey and an Anglo-French delegation that on the Caucasus line, the Turks would be left to look after themselves in the event of armed confrontation with the Soviets.[29]

By taking this position, Ankara tried to secure its place if the coming war spread into the Balkans and if Italy launched a military campaign against Turkey through the Dodecanese islands. At the same time, Ankara did not wish to alienate its powerful neighbour, the Soviet Union, with which it was keen to prevent confrontation. Short of actual war, the Soviet Union had various subversion capabilities and Turkish intelligence was well aware of this situation. The first pillar of Soviet subversion was through communist infiltration within the country via illicit cells organized by the outlawed Turkish Communist Party.[30] The NKVD's spymaster, Lavrenti Beria, was also interested in exploiting the grievances of minorities in Turkey, for example by using the

Kurds as 'a dagger ready to be pointed at Turkey' and planning for the Armenian Soviet Republic to reorganize areas 'liberated' from Turkey.[31] A confidential report on the Kurdish population in Turkey, submitted to President İnönü in early 1946, articulates the administration's awareness of the Soviet Union's wartime subversion plans among the Kurds within the country.[32]

While Turkey was concerned about Soviet intentions, the UK was well aware of the importance of Turkish support for British war plans and tried to convince the Turks to join the war. In 1939, the British chiefs of staff were looking for ways to cut Italy's oil and coal supply, both essential for its war effort. If Italy was unable to receive its required energy supply, it would render the country a liability for Germany rather than an aid to Axis war efforts. The British chiefs of staff produced a report in 1939 stating that gaining Turkish support was a 'must' in order to cut the oil supply for Italian and German war machinery.[33] The major oil supply for their war efforts came from Romania, transported through the Straits to Italian ports and from there to Germany.[34] Turkey could therefore cut the transportation of oil through the Straits if she joined the war on the side of the Allies. Moreover, Turkey could also grant permission for British warships to enter the Black Sea.[35] Another factor highlighting Turkey's importance to the Allied war efforts was that Turkey blocked a possible Axis land bridge to the heart of the British Empire, India, via Syria, Iraq and Iran.[36]

Simultaneously, Germany was increasing its pressure on Turkey. Adolf Hitler appointed one of his top diplomats, the former chancellor, Franz von Papen, to Ankara. Von Papen essentially had two objectives. First, he sought a rapprochement between Turkey and Italy. Second, he aimed to drag Turkey over to the Axis side, since German policy makers considered Turkey to be vital to their interests in the long run, providing access to the Near East by possibly cutting Allied lines of communication.[37] German policy was to sow distrust in Ankara about the Soviets, and compel Turkey to seek protection from Germany should the Soviets then launch an attack on Turkey. To this end, in March 1941, Hitler summoned the Turkish ambassador and revealed

Soviet demands on Turkey.[38] However, Turkey in turn informed the British about these meetings.[39]

In reality, the Turks did not need to inform the British about their meetings with the Germans since, as noted above, London had broken Turkey's diplomatic codes. The strong anti-Soviet tone reflected in the intercepted Turkish communications was evaluated by the British as the 'Turks [being] simply idiotic'; the 'insane Russian complex' was attributed to Russophobia, which the British considered a traditional Turkish weakness.[40] But the fact that, after June 1941, Germany was at war with Russia – which could not then contemplate war with Turkey – suited Turkish interests and made it less likely they would enter the conflict. As the Italian ambassador in Turkey noted, 'the Turkish ideal is that the last German soldier should fall upon the last Russian corpse.'[41] Wartime communications between the Turkish and the British were coloured by the Turkish aim of weakening the Soviets rather than encouraging a rapid German defeat.

## Wartime clandestine cooperation

As a neutral country in the midst of a major conflict, around seventeen different foreign intelligence agencies operated in Turkey, from which they directed their operations in South Eastern Europe and the Middle East.[42] The MAH, however, had a 'special relationship' with the British intelligence service. In November 1940, the Anglo-Turkish Security Bureau was established and, in December 1940, a British Security Officer was appointed to it. This Bureau was unique in its scope and operations, since Turkey was the only non-British occupied country to employ such an officer.[43] It was funded by the British, but was largely operated by their Turkish counterpart. A former Turkish intelligence officer, Neşet Güriş, who joined the MAH in 1932, states that they cooperated with the British in a joint counter-espionage effort against German *Abwehr* agents operating in the country. A counter-espionage effort was mounted against the operations of Axis agents.[44] At one point, when the MAH was tailing a White Russian resident because of his suspicious activities in Istanbul, they found out that the Russian was actually working for the British and entering the British consulate's Passport Branch via its backdoor in the Galata district of Istanbul after dark. Güriş's superior then ordered him to stop the surveillance mission on the White Russian.[45]

The MAH connection proved a valuable asset for British intelligence, helping to gather information on Axis activities. However, such a 'special relationship' did not stop the MAH from spying on the British Ambassador. Between 1941 and 1944, someone inside the Ambassador's residence was opening his safe frequently and passing information to the Turks.[46] The British were not aware of this major leak until late 1944, due to the fact that the MAH was able to deceive the British about its aims, intentions and capabilities. For their part, the British always remained sceptical about the willingness of the Turks to collaborate against the Axis. Julian Amery, a Special Operations Executive officer in Turkey during the war, told his colleagues in Egypt in 1942 that 'this town [Istanbul] has now become such a rabbit-warren of agents that there are no honest men left; but surely you could find some Swiss, Swede, Frenchman, Portuguese or other neutral in Egypt?'.[47] It was easy for the MAH to exploit this situation to deceive the British.

Besides the MAH, the British were also involved in the development of Turkey's SIGINT activities, which were the responsibility of the Turkish General Staff (TGS), under the authority of the Cabinet. President İnönü signed a decree on 6 May 1941 to approve the reconnaissance of Turkey's coast by a British group, led by Captain S.N. Smith, with a view to establishing SIGINT facilities. Areas subject to reconnaissance included Çorlu, the eastern and western Black Sea, the environs of the coal-rich region of Zonguldak, and the Western coastal line of the Aegean Sea, Gelibolu and Foça.[48] The search for suitable sites in Turkish coastal areas to place radar and communication bases did not proceed very efficiently over the course of the war. Both the Turks and British tried to gain maximum benefit for their own side. For the Turks, this meant acquiring technical capabilities that they did not yet have. For the British, it meant dragging Turkey onto the Allied side and deploying more British personnel on Turkish territory against a possible Axis invasion of the country. A compromise between these aims was not achieved during the war and the issue of the SIGINT bases remained a major topic in the intelligence diplomacy that followed. However, these wartime discussions built the foundations of the Cold War liaison between the Turks and the British, including the establishment of GCHQ bases, which began operations against the Soviets soon after the war, in areas surveyed during the Second World War.

For its part, Turkish intelligence had an almost obsessive degree of focus on subversive activities within the country. Barry Rubin notes that the MAH 'kept detailed files on foreign residents, tourists in Istanbul, gathering information from numerous hotel, restaurant, embassy and transport workers, as well as others on its payroll.'[49] Significantly, the MAH's network of informants served to inform the Allied countries of Axis activities, while the Turks utilized their networks within Soviet diplomatic circles to gather information on Moscow's intentions. Ambiguous Soviet behaviour towards Turkey caused grave concern to the Turkish political leadership. Moreover, Moscow took all possible measures to break down the Turkish-German agreement of non-aggression and push Turkey to join the war in accordance with Soviet interests. A prominent example of this type of Soviet activity occurred by using German planes. In the spring and summer of 1942, the TGS reported that German airplanes were violating the country's airspace. However, when the Turkish minister of Foreign Affairs, Şükrü Saraçoğlu, contacted the German embassy to inquire about this, the embassy and the German chief of staff stated categorically that they respected Turkish airspace and had not been sending any scheduled flights near it. As a result of further investigations, the Turks found that the Soviets were repairing captured Messerschmitt 109 and 110, and Junkers 87-type airplanes and flying them into Turkish airspace, still with their German markings, to try to break the non-aggression agreement between Turkey and Germany.⁵⁰ This only caused more anger in Ankara about Soviet behaviour.

A remarkable example of these tensions is the case of Ismail Akhmedov, a Soviet intelligence officer based in the consulate in Istanbul. He was gathering inside information on the Soviets and passing it on to the MAH while working undercover as a Soviet 'press attaché' in Istanbul in 1941–2. Among other things, he repeated what the Soviet ambassador told him: 'Turkey is our enemy and one day she is going to pay for it. Remember!'⁵¹ Significantly, the Turks did not share with the British most of the intelligence they gathered on the Soviets. Once again, Turkish decision makers did not trust the British, fearing in the early years of the war that the Allies could make a secret deal with the Soviets (as the Germans did in the Ribbentrop-Molotov Pact), to win the Soviets over to their side at the expense of Turkey. Turkey sometimes manipulated the Allies to gain information on the Soviet Union for itself. Thus, early in the war, Ankara secretly allowed French reconnaissance missions so they could photograph the Soviet oil fields in Baku, on the grounds that these fields were fuelling the German war machine.⁵² The Turks were trying to show to the French that the Soviets were a real threat to the Allies, due to the Turkish claim that they were collaborating with the Nazis. Later in the summer of 1940, the Germans released documents regarding this mission, and plans for an Anglo-French-Turkish joint mission to bomb Soviet airfields. The Nazis hoped thereby to feed Soviet suspicion of Turkey and the Western allies.⁵³

After March 1941, Turkey felt further pressure from the UK for expanded cooperation. Upon the invasion of Yugoslavia by Hitler's armies, Churchill pushed Turkey to open a new front in the Balkans, so that Germany would be forced to divert units to that front. In turn, Churchill promised Ankara 4 to 6 army brigades, 20 to 30 squadrons of aircraft and the construction of the necessary airfields.⁵⁴ Ankara declined Churchill's offer, arguing that UK aid was not strong enough to resist the German army in the Balkans. Moreover, Ankara was concerned that if Turkey were invaded by the Germans, any 'liberation' armies who later came to it would not leave the country. It is important to note that Turkish military circles had little confidence in British military effectiveness. According to the Turks, the RAF was good but, except for Field Marshall Archibald Wavell, the British did not have effective generals. Some high-ranking Turkish officials knew Wavell from the Palestine campaign of the First World War. Though they were on the opposite side to Wavell, in the course of that campaign they developed an admiration of him.[55] In contrast to Churchill, the United States, which joined the war in December 1941, did not consider Turkey to be a strategic asset. Moreover, the rumours that Turkey was holding high-level meetings with the Germans and was continuing to export strategically crucial chrome to Germany in return for arms and ammunition caused the United States to avoid providing direct aid to Turkey. Instead, the United States provided aid to the United Kingdom, and in turn the United Kingdom delivered some of this to Turkey.[56]

One of the most remarkable examples of the competition between the Soviets, Germans and the British was the failed assassination attempt, of 24 February 1942, on the German ambassador, von Papen, who survived the attack with only minor injuries. The MAH traced the assassin, whose body was blown into pieces due to the early ignition of his bomb, to the Soviet Consulate in Istanbul. He was a communist of Yugoslav descent who had been ordered by the 'press attaché' in the Soviet Consulate to kill von Papen in order to provoke Germany to attack Turkey, thereby diverting military units from Germany's Russian campaign. Since the MAH revealed that the assassination attempt was not from a Turkish source but was a Soviet covert action, the consequences of the attempt did not work out as Moscow intended. As a result, Ankara aligned itself more towards the UK, to protect itself from both German and Soviet pressure.[57]

In early 1943 Turkey emerged as a crucial player for both overt military planning and covert action by the Western Allies. Especially after the Casablanca conference between British Prime Minister Winston Churchill and US President Franklin Roosevelt, on 30 January 1943, the allies were convinced that Turkey must be brought into the war on their side; as a result, Churchill met President İnönü on a train carriage in the Turkish city of Adana.⁵⁸ Here, İnönü agreed to join the war if Britain agreed to provide the necessary military support to the Turks in their efforts in the Balkans. However, İnönü cautiously warned Churchill that Turkey's main concern now was not Nazi Germany, but rather the possible victory of the Soviet Union. He told Churchill of his fear that if the Soviet Union entered into the Balkans first, Moscow would establish communist governments there as a part of its imperial project.⁵⁹ Before this meeting, in fact, Churchill knew from the British interception of Turkish diplomatic communications in early 1943 that Turkey was trying to establish an anti-Soviet bloc in the Balkans, including making contact with Hitler's allies, Romania and Hungary.⁶⁰

Soon after this bilateral meeting, joint Turkish-British preparations in the military, intelligence and political fields commenced. For instance, SOE was prepared to organize a local sabotage and resistance movement in case Turkey was invaded by the enemy. To create a 'stay-behind' network the British ambassador, Sir Hughe Knatchbull-Hugessen, approved SOE plans to develop small clandestine cells formed by Turks, equipped with wireless transmission devices, and to store explosive caches in Istanbul, Adana and Izmir.⁶¹ The ambassador was not always so cooperative on intelligence matters; nor was the relationship between Turkish intelligence and the SOE always good. During the war, in contrast to other areas of Europe and the Middle East, the SOE lacked a well-established organization in Turkey and this was mainly due to Knatchbull-Hugesson's negative attitude towards the organization, as well as to the MAH's vigilance against foreign espionage. Knatchbull-Hugesson feared that a visibly increased level of SOE operations in Turkey would push the neutral country towards the Axis. For him, it was preferable to form a consensus with the Turks rather than trying to coerce them through covert action. So, he frequently hampered SOE attempts to use Jewish agents in Turkey to assassinate German and Italian agents as well as Indian and Arab nationalists who had fled to Turkey. Without having its activities vetted by the British embassy, SOE could do no more than bribe certain railway officials in Turkey to delay German armament shipments to Iraq and Iran through the ports of Trabzon and Samsun. Acting on advice from the embassy, the Foreign Office imposed a strict ban on SOE activities in Turkey in December 1941, and extended this ban to its propaganda activities in April 1942.[62] Even when it came to the 'stay-behind' units, the SOE was only authorized to plan post-occupation organizations in Turkey and the Turks involved were personally vetted by the ambassador himself.

Gardyne de Chastelain, the head of the SOE in Turkey, did not share the Foreign Office's belief in Turkey's friendship towards Britain. In particular, since Turkey did not give up its profitable trade in exporting chrome to Germany, the SOE contemplated ways to sabotage this. By February 1944, SOE had a plan to destroy bridges near the Arda River, to sever the rail communication between Turkey and Germany. The British embassy in Ankara successfully advised against such action, because it would bring Britain into direct confrontation with Turkey, given half of both the bridges were in Turkish territory.[63] However, the American wartime intelligence organization, the Office of Strategic Services (OSS), considered launching a sabotage attack on the bridges as well. At that time Turkey did not have the leverage on the United States to prevent an OSS operation – an operation that might possibly harm Turkish interests (in this case disrupting chrome exports to Nazi Germany). Ankara attempted to do so, however, by exploiting the MAH's cooperation with the British, by asking their embassy in Ankara to halt the OSS sabotage missions. This showed how the Turks could conduct intelligence diplomacy, using British tactical dependence on Ankara to protect Turkish national interests, by hampering American strategic objectives during the war. But the British embassy had its own reasons for cooperating with Ankara: it feared that the OSS sabotage mission on Turkish territory could compromise SOE missions by upsetting the Turks. Thus, the embassy urged the Foreign Office to prevent the OSS from carrying out their sabotage mission.[64] This again shows that the asymmetrical character of intelligence diplomacy can give leverage to the weaker partner to pursue policy goals beyond its usual capabilities.

## An element of distrust

In 1943, military preparations were made by Turkey and Britain for the Turks to launch an attack through the southern Balkans towards Yugoslavia.[65] During the meetings, however, Turkey's military officers remained hesitant about giving accurate and clear answers to their British colleagues' questions regarding the Turkish military communication infrastructure, or on the positions and status of their military units.[66] This again reflects the fact that the Turks, even in desperate times, did not trust their allies. Leaving aside official Turkish policy, there was wide antipathy and prejudice against Britain in high-level diplomatic and military circles in Turkey.[67] The main source of this antipathy stemmed from the old enmities between the British and Turkey during the Great War and the Turkish War of Liberation. Losing battles against the British on almost all fronts (Gallipoli and the Siege of Kut being exceptions) and the British occupation of Istanbul were still vivid in the memories of the Turkish diplomatic and military elites. Many diplomats and military officers, discontented with Turkey's policy of developing close relations with the British, even passed crucial secret information to their First World War ally, Germany, via Abwehr agents, with whom they had developed contacts in the previous war. Ismail Okday and Said Erim were among those who had special responsibility for handling Abwehr informant circles within the Turkish Foreign Ministry and army, and who passed information to Paul Karl Gluech, an Abwehr agent in Turkey during the war.[68]

From early 1943, too, Washington changed its policies towards Turkey and started to consider it as a major asset to drive Hitler's forces out of Europe. The OSS founded its own branch in Istanbul, designed to coordinate all its activities in the Middle East and Balkans, on 4 May 1943. Rubin explains OSS-Istanbul's importance to the war campaign in the following way: 'Turkey offers a base of penetration into the entire enemy-occupied Southeastern Europe. From Istanbul, run only land routes into that territories, and from İzmir small boats can be operated into the Dodecanese and Aegean Islands and to the

Greek mainland.'[69] Apart from developing joint intelligence activities in the Balkans, which were mostly dominated by the Turkish military, the Americans also developed a need for communication sites on Turkey's Mediterranean coast. By the beginning of 1944, the OSS had established a communication and SIGINT site in Adana, at the summer residence of the American ambassador. The Americans wanted to establish this site without Ankara's knowledge, and instructed the responsible officer in the Adana station to be discreet. Since Turkey was a neutral country until the very end of the war, the American embassy in Turkey wanted to keep its operations clandestine in order not to annoy the Turks. The MAH was nevertheless able to detect the existence of the Adana station, although higher Turkish officials deliberately turned a blind eye to it.[70] The reason for this was that the Turks hoped to attract Washington more towards their own position. It can be argued that the Turkish approach was successful in this regard. The result was that the Adana station formed the nucleus of the Incirlik base, an extensive American military and intelligence base that began operating in the early Cold War, continues to operate today, and indeed acts as a major symbol of the American military and intelligence presence in Turkey.

The question of the deployment of British military personnel into Turkish ranks, as part of the development of Turkey's technical infrastructure regarding signals intelligence, also played a major role in improving relations with the Western allies towards the end of the war. It is important to note that the Turkish approach to this issue reflected the nature of their threat perception and their ongoing distrust of British aims. Ankara wanted to employ British officers as 'foreign specialists' instead of hosting them as officers who were infiltrated directly into Turkish ranks. This was a case of learning from earlier experience: during the First World War, infiltrated German officers played a major role in dragging Turkey into the war and Ankara did not want to repeat the same mistake.[71]

The minutes of the meetings between the British Colonel Lister and his counterpart, Major Remzi Soyoğuz, the representative of the TGS, on 24 August 1944, are a good reflection of this Anglo-Turkish distrust. Lister was assigned to install radar and reconnaissance posts in coastal areas as part of British technical aid to Turkey.[72] However, when he required further information on the technicalities and radar infrastructure of Turkey, Soyoğuz only provided him with a very limited range of information: he went through the approximate number of Turkish Air Force planes, but refused to provide information on Turkish radar systems. When Lister asked Soyoğuz how the Turkish radar system worked and whether it would support British endeavours to establish an early-warning system for air attacks, the Turk stated that the radar infrastructure was under the responsibility of the General Command for Air Defence and that he was not at liberty to discuss it with the British. Moreover, in terms of the intelligence cooperation with the British, Soyoğuz raised these obstacles, which needed to be tackled: (1) coordination problems between the radar and airbases; (2) the difference in radio frequencies between the radars and reconnaissance airplanes; (3) the training of personnel and the requirement for coordinated maps; (4) a lack of translators on the ground.

Interestingly enough, Lister agreed with Soyoğuz that Britain should help the Turks overcome these problems, except for the sharing of the radio frequency codes.[73] Although Soyoğuz insisted on acquiring the codes, the British were suspicious that the Turks would share the codes with the Germans, since there were a considerable number of pro-German officers within the Turkish army ranks. The intelligence relationship, even in the midst of war, suffered from a deep-rooted distrust on both sides, further encouraging the Turkish multi-layered approach to exploit all channels to increase its own influence.

After being briefed about the meeting with Lister, discussed above, the First Commander General of the Turkish Army ordered Major Soyoğuz to demand technical aid and geographical intelligence from the British at subsequent meetings. Initially, the TGS demanded the establishment of ground radio communication stations as well. Secondly, the TGS stressed that it was of the utmost importance for the Turkish military to acquire maps from the British for the use of the air force, as well as for Turkish ground artillery units. When it came to an upcoming Turkish reconnaissance mission in the Caspian Sea area, however, the TGS ordered Major Soyoğuz to share details on only a part of the mission with the British.[74]

These episodes reflect the fact that the British, with whom relations were friendliest in the war, were not trusted by the Turks when it came to intelligence sharing, even though Turkish soil was now being used for British radar installations. This lack of confidence was evident elsewhere. By 1944, a joint committee of intelligence was established by the British, Americans and Turks in Ankara. This was chaired by a Turkish Brigadier General; it compared and analysed Turkish and Allied intelligence reports.[75] However, through this committee the Turks tried to deceive the Americans and British both on Turkish capabilities and on possible threats from the Soviets and the Axis powers. The practice of Turkish intelligence diplomacy, by deceiving the British and Americans with regard to Axis capabilities in the Balkans and Caucasus, and by overestimating the Soviet threat to Turkey, helped Ankara in its endeavour to stay out of the war while getting the greatest possible military aid and capabilities from the British. In a negative sense, however, Turkish intelligence diplomacy in turn led to distrust on the British side regarding Turkey's intentions and capabilities.

Yet another problem emerged regarding the use of British personnel to operate SIGINT facilities on Turkish soil.[76] In a letter from N.S. Allison, a RAF Air Officer serving at the British radio-location service in Ankara, to the chief of the TGS, Kazım Orbay, the former stressed that by August 1944 there were 1,251 British SIGINT officers operating in Turkish radio and radar posts but that that number was still insufficient to pursue an effective intelligence operation.[77] Allison required an additional 960 personnel to be deployed and he tried to convince the Turkish COS by writing that 'the number of extra personnel which I require for the Control Staff in Ankara may seem rather large to you, but I examined this most carefully and am convinced that they are necessary'.[78] Yet the TGS fiercely opposed the idea of such a large number of British SIGINT personnel being deployed in the country. Two reasons lay behind this decision. First, the

TGS feared that, when the British acquired certain positions on Turkish soil, particularly over the strategically important SIGINT posts, they would not leave after the war was over. An excessive number of British personnel could also attract German action against Turkey.[79] But the Turks' biggest fear was of the British and Russians agreeing upon jointly exercising power over Turkey when the war was over, thus jeopardizing national independence. The British knew of this fear and called it the 'Turkish Complex'. After one meeting with the Turkish foreign minister, Numan Menemencioğlu, Knatchbull-Hugessen reported that the Turks suspected a secret British pact with Russia. The foreign minister argued that, in effect, there was an unholy pact between the Russians and the British to force Turkey into the war regardless of Turkish interests.[80] The British suspicion of a Turkish complex was not, therefore, without any basis.

Another problem leading to hesitation over working with British officers on SIGINT was made clear by COS Kazım Orbay, in a memorandum to the TGS's head of operation. According to Orbay, before agreeing on the chain of command and the role of the staff, initial cabinet approval would be necessary concerning the division of respective roles. The deployment of British personnel would also affect the chain of command in both operational and SIGINT activities, and the TGS would not yield command to British officers.[81] According to Orbay, if the Turks did cede the chain of command at some points to the British, the quantity of the British staff at specific sites should exceed the Turkish forces only under the strict condition that the defence of the country should be under Turkish command. Concern emerged within the TGS that the British were asking to deploy the maximum possible number of personnel; certain officers within the TGS's bases even suggested that at least half of the British personnel should be cut.[82] Air Marshall Francis John Linnel, the Deputy Commander-in-Chief in RAF Mediterranean and Middle East, told the Middle East headquarters that even Britain's Turkey embassy was getting worried about the increasing number of personnel sent to Turkey. He stated that the usual number of staff in the embassy was forty-five, yet by January 1944 it was over five hundred, some of them concealed from the Turkish authorities. If the Turks were to discover this excessive number, it might jeopardize future talks.[83] In fact, Turkey had already issued a note to the British regarding the personnel issue; moreover, Menemencioğlu sent a letter to Knatchbull-Hugessen stating that Ankara feared the British objective was to drag Turkey into the war and that 'infiltration' (as he termed the personnel deployment) was a trick to bring this about.[84] Indeed, Menemencioğlu's hesitation had some basis in fact: the liaison staff were tasked with the formation of the nucleus of a British headquarters operating in Turkey, as if it was inevitable that Turkey would enter the war on the British side.[85]

While the Turks were considering their conditions for intelligence sharing with London, and mulling over the chain of command for the SIGINT posts, the British were aware that the Turkish military was in great need of these listening and radar posts. Furthermore, they readily used the threat of withdrawing the radar equipment and UK personnel from Turkey as a bargaining chip. On the other hand, even if the provision of arms supplies and training to Turkey were to cease, the British did not want to terminate the operations of the SIGINT posts, since these were of great value to the British war effort. The complexity of the relationship was again exposed when the embassy suggested that military aid to Turkey should be cut back, since Ankara seemed hesitant about supporting the British war effort. The Middle East HQ then argued:

> Nothing is more likely to give impression to the Turks that we intend to leave them high and dry than withdrawal of RADAR personnel and especially of RADAR equipment. Such a move would stifle the story which Turks otherwise start that we are ceasing to arm Turkey but continuing those preparations of particular interest to ourselves, thereby indicating that we intend to seize bases and force Turkey's hand.[86]

Another remarkable episode deserves a mention here. When, in February 1944, Knatchbull-Hugessen met with Menemencioğlu and the Greek ambassador, to try to convince the Turks to join in the war on the

Balkan front, the foreign minister resisted the idea on the grounds that the British were not aware of the capability of German forces in the region or the risk that they posed to Turkish forces. He insisted that there were twenty-four German brigades there, beside the Bulgarian forces allied to them, that Tito's Yugoslav resistance forces would soon be wiped out and that the Germans would then advance towards the Turkish Straits.[87] Menemencioğlu was certain about his intelligence on the German troops in the region, as well as Tito's resistance capabilities, and considered Turkey's participation in the war to be suicidal. The Turks refused to believe in the alternative estimates presented by the British.[88] The Middle East HQ then asked the RAF Special Signal Office, probably upon a request by the Turks, whether they could personally parachute a Turkish intelligence officer into Yugoslavia, to see Tito. They also hoped to send Turkish officers to visit the Middle East HQ to see the British intelligence estimations on the spot.[89] But the Middle East HQ refused these suggestions for the following reasons:[90]

- [The officer sent to Tito] would have to be dropped by parachute and there would be considerable difficulties on getting him out again quickly. Moreover, it would take considerable time for him to form any impression as he would have to travel largely on foot and even so it would be impossible to cover the whole area.
- We fear that a totally different impression might be obtained from that desired.
- On security grounds it is certain that any information gained would reach the Germans.

The refusal to accept a Turkish visit to observe British wartime intelligence gathering and estimate-making probably reflected the fact that the British did not want to share their methods and sources of intelligence. The Turks just tried their luck, hoping perhaps to reveal British sources and methods. But distrust triumphed over their 'special' bilateral relationship and Turkey only joined the war on the Allied side in February 1945, after the Germans had been driven from the Balkans.

In the event, Turkish soldiers did not fire a bullet during the war. Turkey nevertheless received an invitation to participate in the San Francisco Conference – which launched the United Nations Organization – as an allied country.

## Conclusion

Turkey, as a relatively weak power during the Second World War, tried to use intelligence diplomacy in order both to increase its wartime military and intelligence capabilities, and to convince the British, its major partner, about Turkey's concerns in the war, especially the danger posed by the Soviet Union. This intelligence diplomacy was conducted not only through diplomats, but also via specialized intelligence agencies and military officers. However, the Turkish leadership demonstrated repeated doubts and hesitancy about British aims, even fearing an Anglo-Soviet agreement which would jeopardize the country's political and territorial integrity. As the host country of various radar and SIGINT facilities, the Turks tried to do more than just take their share from the intelligence. They endeavoured to direct intelligence liaison in their favour, which was not necessarily in the British interest. In this intelligence diplomacy, Turkey's attitude was shaped by a desire to share necessary information with the British, especially to convince them about Turkish estimations, while at the same time taking precautions to avoid becoming a British 'stooge' and finding themselves dragged into the war without securing significant national gains.

While the Turks sought to ease British distrust and convince London of the emerging Soviet threat, they were also aware that, on the technical plane, Ankara was in need of British aid to develop its SIGINT capabilities. Therefore, the Turkish clandestine service MAH worked closely with their British counterparts to conduct counter-espionage missions against Abwehr agents in Turkey to demonstrate that the Turks supported British efforts and so deserved to receive technical aid. However, the differing interests of the Turks and British were further reflected in the fact that, at the same time, the Turkish ministry of foreign affairs conducted negotiations with two of Hitler's allies, Romania and Hungary, to form an anti-Soviet bloc in the Balkans.[91]

After the war, when the Soviet threat openly emerged and the Americans began more actively to counter Soviet expansionism in the Eastern Mediterranean, the Turks again emerged as a partner for the secret intelligence activities of the Americans and British in the region. However, the Turks learned important lessons from their practice during the Second World War, when they had largely achieved their aims. With the advent of the Cold War, as we will see in the next chapter, Ankara conducted more elaborate intelligence diplomacy to play the British and the Americans against each other, and gradually but steadily increased the price of Turkish cooperation with Western intelligence activities on such issues as permitting British or American SIGINT bases to operate on Turkish soil.

## Notes

1. B. Millman, 'Turkish Foreign and Strategic Policy 1934–42', *Middle Eastern Studies*, 31:3 (1995), 483–508; A. Türkkaya, *Turkish foreign policy, 1939–1945* (Ankara, 1965).
2. E. Weisband, *Turkish Foreign Policy 1943–1945: Small State Diplomacy and Great Power Politics* (Princeton, NJ, 1973); S. Deringil, *Turkish Foreign Policy during the Second World War: An 'Active' Neutrality* (Cambridge, 2004); M. Tamkoç, *The Warrior Diplomats: Guardians of the National Security and Modernization of Turkey* (Salt Lake, UT, 1976); F. G. Weber, *The Evasive Neutral: Germany, Britain, and the Quest for a Turkish Alliance in the Second World War* (Columbia, MI, 1979); N. Tamkin, *Britain, Turkey and the Soviet Union, 1940–45: Strategy, Diplomacy and Intelligence in the Eastern Mediterranean* (London, 2009).
3. Excerpt from this chapter is published in E. Bezci, 'Turkey's Intelligence Diplomacy during the Second World War', *Journal of Intelligence History*, 15:2 (2016), 80–95.

4　The Staff Talks are the meetings between assigned military and intelligence officers (as well as diplomats) from Turkey and Britain to negotiate the conditions of Turkey joining the Second World War. The Staff Talks took place between 1939 and 1944.
5　MKB: Servet Sürenkök, 'Emniyet', *Ordu Dergisi*, 67:145 (1948).
6　On Teşkilat-ı Mahsusa see, Y. Yiğit, 'The Teşkilat-ı Mahsusa and World War I', *Middle East Critique*, 23:2 (2014), 157–174; P. Stoddard, *The Ottoman Government and the Arabs, 1911 to 1918: A Preliminary Study of the Teşkilât-i Mahsusa* (Princeton, NJ, 1963).
7　N. Ekinci, 'Kurtuluş Savaşında İstanbul ve Anadolu'daki Türk ve Düşman Gizli Faaliyetleri', *Ankara Üniversitesi Türk İnkılap Tarihi Enstitüsü Atatürk Yolu Dergisi*, 14 (1994), 174.
8　D. R. Stone, 'Soviet Arms Exports in the 1920s', *Journal of Contemporary History*, 48:1 (2013), 58.
9　Ibid., 60.
10　For instance, Lieutenant General Cemal Madanoğlu, one of the leading architects of the 27 May 1960 coup, on 9 March 1971 supported a left-wing coup called '*Milli Demokratik Devrim* – National Democratic Revolution'. However, the attempt did not involve the Turkish Military's chain of command, and was suppressed. Although the literature does not refer to the wartime origins of distrust of the West, there are studies to reflect the growing anti-Western attitude of certain portions of the army during the Cold War. See H. Sahin, 'Reading the Memoirs: Some Notes on Turkish Soldiers' Political Thoughts', *Mediterranean Quarterly*, 27:2 (2016), 28–46; P. B. Koelle, 'The Inevitability of the 1971 Turkish Military Intervention', *Journal of South Asian and Middle Eastern Studies*, 24:1 (2000), 38–56.
11　E. Akal, *Moskova-Ankara-Londra Üçgeninde İştirakiyuncular, Komünistler ve Paşa Hazretleri* (İstanbul, 2013), 191–196.
12　Author's Collection: MAH, *Komünist Faaliyetler*, c. 1947.
13　M. Pelt, *Military Intervention and a Crisis Democracy in Turkey: The Menderes Era and Its Demise* (London, 2014), 39–97.
14　Z. Türkmen, 'Özdemir Bey' in Musul Harekâtı ve İngilizlerin Karşı Tedbirleri (1921–1923)', *Atatürk Araştırma Merkezi Dergis*, i 17 (2001), 49–80.

15 M. Gönlübol, et al., *Olaylarla Türk Dış Politikası, 9th edition* (Ankara, 1996), 129. Hereafter will be referred as OTDP.
16 Öğel, 'Milli Emniyet Hizmeti Nasil Kuruldu', 607.
17 BCA: 030.10/224.511.6, printed in E. Karakoç, 'Atatürk'ün Hatay Davası', *Bilig*, 50 (2009), 109.
18 ATASE archives: No: 7–037-1, 'Information by MAH's Şükrü Ali Öğel', Classified: TOP SECRET, Date: 16 January 1937. (ATASE: Turkish Military Archives based in the TGS in Ankara, Turkey).
19 Gönlübol, et al., *OTDP*, 130.
20 Gönlübol, et al., *OTDP*, 51.
21 Ş. Â. Ögel, 'Millî Emniyet Hizmeti Nasıl Kuruldu?', *Türk Kültürü*, 128 (1973), 607.
22 Gönlübol, et al., *OTDP*, 115.
23 Ibid., 119.
24 W. Hale, *Turkish Foreign Policy since 1774* (London, 2012), 85.
25 Deringil argues that the major threat was initially Italy and the dislike of Italy goes back to the 1911–12 Tripolitanian War between the Ottomans and Italians. See Deringil, *Turkish Foreign Policy during the Second World War: An 'Active' Neutrality*, 36.
26 TNA: WO 201/1185: 'MOST SECRET: Comments on the instructions to the British Delegation at the Staff Talks, 23 January 1944'.
27 M. Williams, 'Mussolini's Secret War in the Mediterranean and the Middle East: Italian Intelligence and the British Response', *Intelligence and National Security*, 2:6 (2007), 887.
28 D. Alvarez, 'No immunity: Signals Intelligence and the European Neutrals, 1939–45', *Intelligence and National Security*, 12:2 (1997), 22–43.
29 Churchill Archives Centre, Cambridge (CAC): The Papers of Air Marshal Sir Thomas Elmhirst (ELMT): ELMT 2/3: Beirut Conference: Allied C's-in-C and Marshal Çakmak, 20–21 May 1940.
30 Author's Collection: report by Erkanıharbiyei Umumiye Riyaseti İstihbarat Başkanlığı (Classified SECRET), Ankara, Untitled, c. 1947.
31 E. Beytullayev, *Soviet Policy towards Turkey, 1944–1946*, unpublished thesis (University of Cambridge, 2005), 117–120 quoted in Tamkin, 'Diplomatic Sigint and the British Official Mind during the Second World War: Soviet Claims on Turkey, 1940–45', 758. Same point also echoed by J. Hasanli, *Stalin and the Turkish Crisis of the Cold War, 1945–1953* (Lanham, MD, 2011), 126.

32  Toplumsal Tarih Vakfı BBM: Necmetttin Sahir Sılan Papers, report by Kadri Kemal Kop, Ankara, to İsmet İnönü, 'Türkiye ve Kürtler yahut Doğu Anadolu'ya "politik bir bakış"', 6 March 1946. (Private Papers of Turkish President İsmet İnönü's COS Necmetttin Sahir Sılan, based in the archives of the Toplumsal Tarih Vakfı in İstanbul, Turkey).
33  L. Curtright, 'Great Britain, the Balkans, and Turkey in the Autumn of 1939', *The International History Review*, 10:3 (1988), 435.
34  Ibid., 438.
35  Ibid., 444.
36  F. Marzari, 'Western-Soviet Rivalry in Turkey, 1939 – I', *Middle Eastern Studies*, 7:1 (1971), 75.
37  Ibid., 76.
38  Hale, *Turkish Foreign Policy, 1774–2000*, 86.
39  Ibid., 89.
40  Tamkin, 'Diplomatic Sigint and the British Official Mind during the Second World War: Soviet Claims on Turkey, 1940–45', 756.
41  Hale, *Turkish Foreign Policy, 1774–2000*, 90.
42  B. M. Rubin, *Istanbul Intrigues* (New York, 1992), 5.
43  H. O. Dovey, 'The Intelligence War in Turkey', *Intelligence and National Security*, 9:1 (1994), 60.
44  CREST: 25-Year Program Archive: CIA-RDP80R01731R001200050065-7, 26 August 1943: Indeed, the director of Turkish Intelligence informed the American Naval attaché during the summer of 1943 how he was enjoying upsetting the German intelligence operations in the broader region by exploiting the lack of coordination between the German intelligence organizations' operations in the region.
45  T. Özkan, *Bir gizli servisin tarihi: MİT* (Istanbul, 1996), 112.
46  C. Baxter, 'Forgeries and Spies: The Foreign Office and the "Cicero" Case', *Intelligence and National Security*, 23:6 (2008), 810.
47  Churchill Archives Centre, Cambridge (CAC) Julian Amery Papers (AMEJ): AMEJ 1/1/28: Letter from D/H8 to A/HA, 29 January 1942.
48  BCA: 30.18.1.2.94.36.19: 241–198: 2//15704: Council of Ministers: 'Permission for British Officer S.N. Smith to enter forbidden zones to survey locations for setting up SIGINT posts, 6 May 1941'.
49  Rubin, *Istanbul Intrigues*, 25.
50  BCA: 30.10.0.0.232.562.11: 420/255, 'From Turkish MFA to COS and PM regarding Soviet Planes disguised as Germans, 11 June 1942'.

51  Rubin, *Istanbul Intrigues*, 13.
52  Ibid., 39.
53  Tamkin, 'Diplomatic Sigint and the British Official Mind during the Second World War: Soviet Claims on Turkey, 1940–45', 754.
54  Gönlübol, et al., *OTDP*, 153–159.
55  A. S. G. Lee, *Special Duties: Reminiscences of a Royal Air Force Staff Officer in the Balkans, Turkey and the Middle East* (London, 1946), 31.
56  Ibid., 160.
57  M. S. Bilgin and S. Morewood, 'Turkey's Reliance on Britain: British Political and Diplomatic Support for Turkey against Soviet Demands, 1943–47', *Middle Eastern Studies*, 40:2 (2004), 24–57.
58  Gönlübol, et al., *OTDP*, 165.
59  Ibid., 166.
60  Tamkin, 'Diplomatic Sigint and the British Official Mind during the Second World War: Soviet Claims on Turkey, 1940–45', 757.
61  S. Kelly, 'A Succession of Crises: SOE in the Middle East, 1940–45', *Intelligence and National Security*, 20:1 (2005), 132.
62  Kelly, 'A Succession of Crises: SOE in the Middle East, 1940–45', 131.
63  TNA: WO 201/1185: MOST SECRET AND PERSONAL: 'Telegram from Ankara Embassy to FO, 6 February 1944'.
64  TNA: WO 201/1192B: 'MOST SECRET: Telegram from Ankara to FO, 22 November 1943'.
65  H. Özlü, 'Arşiv Belgelerine Göre, İkinci Dünya Savaşı'nda İzmir ve Trakya'nın Savunmasına Yönelik Türk- İngiliz Heyetlerinin Görüşmeleri ve Alınan Önlemler', *Çağdaş Türkiye Tarihi Araştırmaları Dergisi*, 10:23 (2011), 240; also see for the British plans in regard to the Soviet Union: B. Millman, 'Toward War with Russia: British Naval and Air Planning for Conflict in the Near East, 1939–40', *Journal of Contemporary History*, 29:2 (1994): 261–283; P. R. Osborn, *Operation Pike: Britain versus the Soviet Union, 1939–1941* (Portsmouth, 2000).
66  ATASE archives: File no: 6–111-1, 'Minutes of the war plan meeting between General Arnold and Colonel Kayabalı', c. August 1943; also see Churchill Archives Centre, Cambridge (CAC), The Papers of Air Marshal Sir Thomas Elmhirst (ELMT): ELMT 2/3: Middle East Joint Planning Staff Paper no. 36: Memorandum for British Liaison Staff to Turkey, 4 January 1941.
67  Lee, *Special Duties*, 8.

68 CIA Declassified Files: No: 519cd81e993294098d5166ac: 'U.S. Army. European Command. Intelligence Division Wartime Activities of the German Diplomatic and Military Services during World War II', 18 November 1949.
69 Rubin, *Istanbul Intrigues*, 116.
70 R. Cossaboom and G. Leiser, 'Adana Station 1943–45: Prelude to the Post-War American Military Presence in Turkey', *Middle Eastern Studies*, 34:1 (1998), 73–78.
71 Lee, *Special Duties*, 13.
72 ATASE archives: File no: 1–077-2, 'Minutes of the meeting between Radar Specialist Colonel Lister in the General Staff, in 24 August 1944'.
73 Ibid.
74 ATASE archives: File no: 1–077-4, 'First Commander General's orders to Major Soyoguz', 25 August 1944.
75 Cossaboom and Leiser, 'Adana station 1943–45', 74.
76 CREST: 25-Year Program Archive: CIA-RDP80R01731R001200050065-7, 26 August 1943: It is important to note that the Turkish concern regarding increasing foreign intelligence was not only confined to the British. During a meeting, the Turkish director of intelligence also conveyed a similar message of concern to the Americans, stating that 'he was responsible for security and counter-espionage throughout Turkey, but he did not employ as many people or spend as much money as the Office of War Information does in Istanbul'.
77 ATASE: File no: 1–111-1, 'TOP SECRET: Letter by Allison to COS Kazım Orbay, in 25 August 1944'.
78 Ibid.
79 TNA: WO 201/1185: 'MOST SECRET AND PERSONAL: Anglo-Turkish Staff Talks, 23–30 January 1944'.
80 TNA: WO 201/1185: 'SECRET: Telegram from Ankara to FO, 17 January 1944'; also please see for changing role of Turkey during the war for the British policies in regarding to Anglo-Russian relations: Tamkin, *Britain, Turkey, and the Soviet Union, 1940–45: Strategy, Diplomacy, and Intelligence in the Eastern Mediterranean*, chapters 5–7.
81 ATASE archives: File no: 2–054-1, 'Memorandum by COS Kazım Orbay'.
82 ATASE archives: File no: 5–028-10, 'Calculation for the British infiltration of personnel'.

83. TNA: WO 201/1185: 'Secret Cyper Message from Ankara to Middle East HQ, 28 January 1944'.
84. TNA: WO 201/1185: 'SECRET: Telegram from Ankara to FO, 20 January 1944'.
85. Churchill Archives Centre, Cambridge (CAC), The Papers of Air Marshal Sir Thomas Elmhirst (ELMT): ELMT 2/3: Note on the Function of British Liaison Staff, 7 March 1941.
86. TNA: WO 201/1185: 'MOST SECRET: Telegram from MIDDLE EAST to FREEDOM, 5 February 1944'.
87. TNA: WO 201/1185: 'MOST SECRET: Telegram from Ankara to FO, 28 January 1944'.
88. Indeed the Turkish concern was not without basis especially after the British failure in the Aegean and Balkan campaign between October and November 1943. See Robin Denniston, *Churchill's Secret War: Diplomatic Decrypts, the Foreign Office and Turkey, 1942-44* (London, 1997), 105-128.
89. TNA: WO 201/1185: 'MOST SECRET: Telegram from Middle East HQ to Air Force Special Signal Office, 18 January 1944'.
90. TNA: WO 201/1185: 'MOST SECRET: Telegram from Air Force Special Signal Office to Middle East HQ, 19 January 1944'.
91. Tamkin, 'Diplomatic Sigint and the British Official Mind during the Second World War: Soviet Claims on Turkey, 1940-45', 757.

# 3

# (Dis)Trusting Your Allies: NATO and CENTO

Both the North Atlantic Treaty Organization (NATO), formed in 1949, and the Central Treaty Organization (CENTO), known in its early years as the Baghdad Pact, formed in 1955, emerged as crucial regional mutual defence organizations during the Cold War. While NATO acted as a security mechanism which cemented the transatlantic partnership, the Baghdad Pact played a more local role, creating a Western-oriented defence apparatus operating in and around the soft underbelly of the Soviet Union. Although CENTO ultimately proved ineffective, for Turkish secret intelligence it played a major role. Intelligence liaisons in both NATO and CENTO shared many things in common. These commonalities can be identified in two major ways: military intelligence and the security of intelligence. Both of these mechanisms were directed against Soviet military and subversive activities in the countries covered by these organizations. For Ankara, intelligence cooperation in these organizations also acted as a means to implement policies that were not only aimed against the Soviets. Ankara used intelligence diplomacy in CENTO and NATO mostly to attract further economic and military commitments from its Western partners. Ankara also constantly sought further cooperation in these multilateral organizations against what it defined as the subversive activities of minorities and leftist political opponents.[1] Again, intelligence diplomacy was a useful tool for Ankara to exploit in this way.

It is important to note that during the early post-war era Ankara tried to overlap its interests with Western security concerns in the region. Cohen describes this overlapping of security concerns by stating that 'Soviet behaviour prompted fears that one of the current, "local" crises might escalate out of control, even if by mistake, into a wider conflict'.[2] Stalin's increasingly belligerent rhetoric against Turkey, especially at the Yalta conference, at the same time as the increased subversion and espionage activities that the Soviet bloc directed inside Turkey, made the country a theatre of conflict between the Soviets and the West, and one where a minor clash could have led to a major confrontation. Thus, by March 1946 the US Joint Chiefs of Staff started drafting a strategic series called the *Pincher* series. The first of this series was code-named *Griddle* and focused on Soviet pressure on Turkey, and on the consequences of that pressure. The Griddle report warned that Soviet belligerency against Turkey could lead to a Third World War by undermining the British position in the Eastern Mediterranean and in the Middle East. The report further warned that the British might resist the Soviets militarily, and concluded that the Americans could not stand neutral in the conflict and would have to join the conflict on the British side.[3]

The Truman Doctrine and Marshall Aid Programme alleviated Turkey's vulnerable position against the Soviets to some extent. Yet these measures did not provide a full guarantee concerning the defence of Turkey. Ankara was convinced that British interests in the region were permanent due to its commitments to the Commonwealth. At the same time, however, Turkish decision makers were not convinced that post-war Britain was able to provide the security assistance and guarantee that they needed. The Americans, on the other hand, were capable of providing the security that the Turks needed – but Ankara perceived American interests in the region as short term and temporary. They worried that the Americans might see Turkey as disposable, and leave the country exposed to Soviet interference or even invasion.

American assistance to Turkey prioritized military hardware, in terms of modernizing the Turkish armed forces and improving transportation networks.[4] However, prior to Turkish admission to

NATO, Washington was more concerned about whether a military build-up of Turkey would trigger a *casus belli* for Moscow to embark on a general war. Thus, the CIA concluded:

> The Soviet reaction to tangible security arrangements (i.e. a specific military build up) including Greece and Turkey, whether or not NATO were also involved, would depend on the scope and implication of the arrangements. So long as Moscow did not regard them as of sufficient magnitude to pose a serious threat to Soviet security, we believe that these arrangements alone would not cause the USSR to resort to preventive war.[5]

The American decision to grant further economic and military support to Turkey was restricted by that consideration. As the Turkish government was aware of this, and as it also felt certain that a third global conflict was imminent, the Turks sought other security alliances to better secure their position. Even admission to NATO in 1952 did not calm Ankara's search for security in the Balkans and Middle East, and such worries led it to take active roles in regional pacts such as CENTO. Turkey's policy on the Balkans and Middle East thus aimed at synchronizing Western and Turkish interests in the region through an active foreign policy, and perceived NATO and CENTO as possible platforms to do so.[6] Even before admission to NATO, Foreign Minister Fuat Köprülü told George McGhee, the US Ambassador to Ankara, that the United States and Turkey should view their world problems together.[7] Turkish intelligence diplomacy at a multilateral level aimed to convince the Americans that their problems in the region were essentially the same. In both of the multilateral organizations, the Turks therefore overemphasized the Soviet threat around the Black Sea and the Middle East in order to gain a long-term American commitment to their security interests.

Although NATO and CENTO acted as important mechanisms for intelligence cooperation, establishing confidence between the Turks and the West proved problematic. This is not surprising: confidence between the various parties is a crucial factor in all secret intelligence cooperation.⁸ For the Turks to feel confident about this cooperation, American assurances of Turkish independence and resistance against the Soviets had to be expressed through a formal commitment, ratified by the US Senate, binding the United. States to go to war if Turkey were to be attacked.⁹ The Turks preferred bilateral commitments rather than multilateral commitments through NATO.¹⁰

Building up confidence in a multilateral organization was more difficult for Ankara than in its bilateral relations. Ankara's concerns about NATO were shaped by two distinct elements. As explained by Feridun Erkin, its ambassador in Washington, 'the Turkish government considered that it might weaken the Turkish position to be placed in the position of receiving a unilateral assurance of support from such countries as Luxembourg and Holland'.¹¹ The Turkish contribution to a Western security arrangement could only be achieved either through bilateral relations as equal partners or through Turkish admittance to the multilateral organization. Ankara did not accept any assurances from other countries which Ankara perceived as equal or inferior to Turkey. Thus, even in NATO, the Turkish government needed a formal assurance from Washington concerning Turkey's security. To them, the other smaller members of NATO were not a match for Turkey's extensive knowledge on the Soviets or for the Turkish defence budget. As Foreign Minister Köprülü told American Ambassador McGhee, Turkey would provide an example for these smaller European countries in NATO rather than receiving security commitments from them.¹² Therefore, the Turks utilized intelligence diplomacy by highlighting their knowledge of the Soviet Union in their quest to be equal partners with the United States and the United Kingdom.

However, there was a problem when it came to confidence building regarding Turkish involvement in a Western security organization, and that problem stemmed from US military assistance. The Turks were always reluctant to give detailed information of their military capacity to other parties. As a part of the *7th Quarterly Report on Aid to Greece and Turkey* in July 1949, Dean Acheson commented on American military assistance:

It occurs to me that this is of considerable Intelligence value to a certain foreign power, which will be able, simply by looking at this report, to find out what modern training methods, equipment and techniques are available to the Turkish armed forces. That power could probably find out these facts eventually, but why hand them out on a silver platter?[13]

According to Acheson, the Soviets could easily access these evaluation reports. The Turks saw the acquiring of this intelligence by any other third party, not only by the Soviets, as a national security threat. These concerns soon created an obstacle to the building-up of confidence in multilateral alliances.

Another obstacle was created by the fact that intelligence security in NATO and CENTO was supervised by MI5. The supervision and training given to the Turkish authorities by MI5, designed to establish a culture of secrecy and control over secret intelligence, also influenced the Turkish security culture even as it developed Ankara's capabilities in that respect. While doing so, Ankara had to keep its own existing military and intelligence capabilities hidden, so that it could use multilateral intelligence channels to deceive the Americans and British about Turkish capabilities and keep them in line with Turkish intelligence estimations.

## Intelligence Security and Confidence Building

Multilateral intelligence cooperation during peacetime was a new feature of the Cold War. The necessity of building a permanent defence organization to counter possible Soviet offensives in all realms, including subversive activities and military preparedness, triggered the necessity for multilateral intelligence sharing within NATO and CENTO. However, even when under an umbrella defence organization, countries usually prefer to conduct intelligence cooperation within bilateral relationships rather than multilaterally.[14] The motivation of each country to hide their methods, sources and capacities is a major characteristic of multilateral intelligence cooperation. Moreover, intra-alliance relations (such as between Turkey and Greece), differences on the perception of the common threat and lack of compatibility in intelligence cooperation structures created weakness in multilateral intelligence sharing, creating opportunities for the Soviets to exploit.

Particularly given the large scope of the intelligence activities of NATO and CENTO, including anti-subversion, military intelligence and covert action, building trust among member countries and ensuring the security of information emerged as a prerequisite during peacetime intelligence cooperation under NATO and CENTO. This prerequisite for intelligence cooperation emerged due to the need for security of information, and for common ground among members who each had their own distinct culture of secrecy. Moreover, NATO intelligence cooperation by its very nature not only covered cooperation on assessed intelligence reports, but also covered discussions on NATO's Special Committee, Military Committee and Committee on Civil Organization in Time of War, dealing with intelligence priorities and sharing, military and covert action policy planning, as well as detailed information on the deficiencies and weaknesses of each member country in case of a war with the Soviet Union.

Being aware of these conditions, Soviet military and civilian intelligence agencies, especially the Soviet Main Intelligence Directorate (GRU) and Ministry of State Security – MGB (later renamed KGB in 1954) – took every possible opportunity to gain information on NATO activities, and to mostly do it through the weak link in the chain, Turkey. Their efforts preceded Turkey's NATO admission in 1952, and dated back to the initial staff talks between Turkey and NATO that included Ankara as an associate in some phases of NATO's military planning.

At the same time that the Turkish government began its association with NATO military planning for the defence of the Mediterranean, the MGB sent one of its Turkish agents to Ankara as an illegal resident. That agent had been previously supervised by another illegal resident in France, named Aleksander Korotkov, an assassin sent to liquidate Trotskyites and other defectors from the Soviet Union.[15] Available records illustrate that there was an ongoing KGB espionage mission codenamed SAMANTA to spy on the Turkish intelligence and security apparatus, and its connection to the US and UK intelligence services.[16] Thus, it is safe to suggest that MGB activities through this illegal resident were successful, and one record even suggests that during that period the Turkish intelligence agency, MAH, discovered a communist network within the army.[17] Moreover, by the late 1950s, when Turkey increased its activities in both NATO and CENTO, the Soviets increased their offensive espionage activities to infiltrate the Turkish army.

## Reds in the Ranks

Oleg Penkovsky was a GRU agent in Turkey between January 1955 and November 1956. He was working under the official cover of the assistant military attaché in the Soviet embassy. His memoir sheds light on Soviet espionage in Turkey during that era. Penkovsky states that there was a rivalry between the KGB and GRU in Turkey.[18] Although the KGB was more extensive and efficient in its espionage activities, the GRU focused on the Turkish army, using more crude tactics. Penkovsky describes their 'crude' tactics by stating that they would meet people on the streets of Ankara, invite them for dinner at a restaurant and ask them to bring a military manual in exchange for monetary gain.[19] They focused on the creation of additional GRU-directed illegal residents in Turkey. They mainly used Bulgarian-born Turks as well as Bulgarians who had settled in Turkey some time before.[20] Increased GRU attempts to infiltrate the Turkish army did not escape the attention of the Turkish intelligence agency, MAH. One of the assistants in the military attaché's bureau in the Soviet Embassy, named Ionchenko, was apprehended by MAH in September 1956 while he was meeting one of his agents. Thanks to his diplomatic cover, Ionchenko was bailed out by Penkovsky, and sent back to Moscow. While both the KGB and GRU increased their activities in Turkey, the MAH also had some success in penetrating the Soviet espionage network in Turkey.

An initial lead came from the confessions of an Armenian-born reserve officer in the Turkish military. When he was apprehended by the MAH in early 1957, he confessed that he had previously trained at a 'special NKVD espionage course' in Austria in order to obtain information on NATO defence plans and the cryptographic system used in NATO communications. This intelligence was shared through subcommittee meetings of CENTO to raise awareness of Soviet intelligence activities.[21] After a series of counter-espionage operations against the Soviet agents in Turkey, the MAH successfully caught two KGB officers red handed in 1957, Alexander Mikhalovich Marlagin and Mikhail Lishcin.[22] The two KGB officers, who had operated under the diplomatic cover of the Soviet embassy in Ankara, were subsequently deported from Turkey in 1957. The counter-espionage operation involved a Turkish agent, who was disguised as a disgruntled and communist-inclined Turkish army officer of Bulgarian descent, approaching the Soviets. After he had gained their trust, the MAH apprehended them at a subsequent meeting where he was supposed to hand over NATO military positions along the Turkish Straits. Such operations proved that the Soviets were indeed seeking to obtain NATO plans in the regional theatre, and information on the Turkish military's role in the event of a war against the Soviets. The MAH, at least being aware of the Soviet operations, increased its efforts to discover these plots and immediately shared them with their Western partners, particularly the Americans. These Soviet espionage efforts, although raising scepticism regarding the safety of Turkish information security, helped Turkey to attract the necessary capacity-building assistance from MI5 and the CIA for information security.

## NATO

NATO's security arrangements for counter-espionage measures were led by the British Security Service, MI5.[23] MI5's crucial role in NATO's security arrangements mostly emerged due to the fact that the British already had wide experience in counter-espionage and boasted a solid record of efficiency dating back to the First World War. The NATO Standing Group, which was the main NATO organ on military affairs, commissioned the MI5 to find common ground between the member countries, in order to implement the necessary regulations as the first step in intelligence cooperation. In this respect, John Alexander Sinclair, head of the British Secret Intelligence Service between 1953 and 1956, advised MI5 to consult documentation from the Second World War and accumulated knowledge on the subject, in order to draft an efficient organization of counter-espionage within NATO.[24]

The common ground between the member and associate countries for the security of information, the NATO Security Coordinating Committee, was formed including American, French and British representatives.[25] Another body, titled the Joint Security Council, was also formed and was made up of a representative from each member country to liaise with the Security Coordinating Committee for the implementation of the NATO security measures and the COSMIC system.[26] NATO's COSMIC security system, an ultra-secret measure to prevent the leaking of sensitive alliance documentation, was introduced by all member countries by 10 July 1950. Thus, on 3 July 1950, NATO's Standing Group sent a top-secret message to all members and agencies of the organization stating that:

> Members and agencies are reminded that all personnel, both civilian and military, having access to COSMIC and other classified NATO material must be fully aware of the great responsibility which devolves upon them. Any breach of security will affect not only their own country but all countries of the North Atlantic Treaty Organization.[27]

However, establishing such a potent security system as COSMIC did not protect NATO from the leakage of information. Numerous accounts of leakage occurred. Most of these were not due to Soviet espionage activities, but to the press, and took place as a result of differences in the understanding of secrecy and security among the politicians and officials of the various member countries. For instance, before and during the NATO ministers meeting in May 1953, a considerable amount of classified NATO information was leaked to the press. The North Atlantic Council immediately took action on this matter and launched a survey to standardize legal prosecution of the leakage of NATO information.[28] Moreover, The Security Committee reminded the member nations:

> that the Secretary General circularises Heads of Delegations asking them to bring home to their staff and advisers the dangers of careless talk and indicating that instances of unauthorised disclosure of classified information will in future require to be fully investigated.[29]

As an associate of NATO military planning as early as 1950, Turkey was not exempt from these arrangements. The North Atlantic Council, NATO's main decision-making body, decided in 1950 to include the Greek and Turkish governments for the defence of the Mediterranean region. In the light of Turkey's association with NATO's military planning, particularly in the eastern Mediterranean region, liaison between NATO's Standing Committee and with the regional military commands was an initial step to take. The Turkish Representative, General Egeli, attended the Standing Group's 37th meeting in November 1950. At the meeting General Egeli and the Standing Group mutually agreed on Turkey's strategic importance, and on the need to deny Turkish territories to enemy forces, deny the passage of enemy naval units through the Bosphorus and Dardanelles, to use Turkish naval and air bases and maritime forces, and to facilitate the protection of maritime lines of communication in the Eastern Mediterranean. However, NATO left the protection of Turkish territory to the national authority. There were compelling reasons to do so. While the Turks and NATO agreed that the country was able to repel possible Soviet bloc incursions, the CIA came to a different conclusion. The CIA concluded that:

> It is estimated that the Turks will put up a very stubborn resistance with the means at their disposal but they are only capable of withstanding attacks by relatively minor forces. Against an all-out attack mounted by Soviet Forces, they are not believed to be capable of prolonged

resistance but only of delaying action. As the Soviet forces advance, there should be excellent opportunities offered for guerrilla warfare along the lines of communication.[30]

At this stage, Ankara's attempts to convince NATO that Turkey was an asset rather than a liability did not work well. In the case of a Soviet Bloc invasion, Turkey was left to itself but help would be granted in forming stay-behind networks to delay the Soviet advance. If the Turks were attacked only by a minor force, such as Bulgaria, they would be able to thwart their attacks by themselves.[31] Therefore, the Turkish military attaché in Washington was appointed to liaise with NATO's standing group. Since military planning and monitoring Soviet naval activities along the Turkish straits, including establishing air-warning systems, required an intense level of intelligence cooperation, the Standing Group firstly aimed to establish the necessary security system in Turkey, and bring the Turkish security system in line with NATO requirements. Without the establishment of an efficient security system in Turkey, the Standing Group stated that they could not hold further meetings with the Turks.[32]

In accordance with the Standing Group's decision, the British Security Service conducted a security survey of Turkey. This preliminary security survey was conducted without the notification and knowledge of the Turkish government. Moreover, the planned official survey was conducted by the Security Team and scheduled to be held between 19 and 23 January 1951. The official security survey was conducted within the framework that MI5 had provided in its memorandum.[33]

In accordance with the preliminary survey, the NATO security team conducted the scheduled survey of Turkish premises, but it was limited to a security survey of the military sections of the Turkish government. The head of the G2 (Intelligence Unit) of the Turkish Chief of Staff, Admiral Aziz Ulusan, guaranteed to the NATO team that all NATO files would be kept in the Turkish General Staff registries. For communications with NATO an X-2 type cypher machine would be used, and the Turkish government would use American State Department couriers to transfer the documents. Most importantly, the

Security Team insisted that even the President and Prime Minister were not allowed to take NATO documents and highly sensitive military plans to their offices. If they had to consult certain documents, they needed to visit the Turkish General Staff building. The Security Team made two observations for the security of information in the Turkish government. First, the Turks were asked to develop similar protective measures in other civilian departments such as the Foreign or Finance departments which could handle NATO documents. Second, the Security Committee was concerned about the influx of Bulgarian refugees to Turkey in the late 1940s, a quarter of a million in total. The committee noted:

> It is obvious that a number of these persons may be Communist agents and a few have indeed already been detected. Although the Communist party has no legal existence it cannot be assumed that there are no Communists in the country, though it seems probable that the organisation is not sufficiently effective to permit direct and consistent penetration of Government organisations.[34]

The committee observed the limited threat of communist infiltration of the Turkish government, yet the committee did not completely trust Admiral Ulusan's guarantees concerning the security of Turkish intelligence. The committee agreed to make the Turkish government appoint a security officer from the army, of the rank of colonel, or higher, to an executive role in order to supervise the security of NATO-related information. This newly appointed officer would be trained by the NATO Security Committee according to NATO regulations and procedures.

Following Turkey's admission to NATO in February 1952, the NATO Security Committee conducted a thorough survey of the COSMIC system in Turkey. In order to maintain the efficiency of the system, the NATO Security Committee conducted regular surveys in Turkey and the last survey conducted between 22 and 28 May 1952 is particularly important as a measure of NATO influence in Turkey's security apparatus.

The committee observed that after Turkey's association with NATO had begun in 1950, the security system had been developed to a high standard. The increased level of the security of information within the Turkish government was well developed by NATO standards. The established security system of the Turkish government was directed by the Central COSMIC Bureau, headed by a senior figure from the ministry of Foreign Affairs and assisted by a high level military officer. This bureau was under the control of the bi-weekly central national security committee, which consisted of the General Secretary of the Ministry of Foreign Affairs, the Deputy Chief of the General Staff, the Chiefs of Staff of each of the military services and the Undersecretaries of the Ministries of Defence, Finance and Communications.[35] The establishment of a NATO-compatible security committee within the Turkish government fostered Turkey's increased multilateral intelligence sharing within NATO. Moreover, regular security surveys of the Turkish government also helped the process of building confidence for greater intelligence sharing. However, the security of information within CENTO caused much greater problems when it came to multilateral intelligence cooperation.

## Baghdad Pact

In 1958, the Baghdad Pact Security Organization, like its European counterpart NATO, started to run security inspections of registry systems in its member countries, namely the UK, Turkey, Iraq, Iran and Pakistan. The Security Committee was mainly composed of military officers from member countries, Turkey and the UK being the exception, sending civilian intelligence officers to the committee. The inspection of UK registries was led by Major Ghani on behalf of the Pact. He held a meeting with the British Security Policy and Methods Committee and concluded that the British departments handling the classified documents of the Baghdad Pact were satisfactory.[36] However, the main outcome of the Pact's security inspection was to learn about the practices of the British Security Service and NATO procedures regarding the security of information. Thus, Kemal Menderes, the chief Security Advisor of the Baghdad Pact who was originally an officer from Turkish intelligence, requested information from his British counterparts on the means by which NATO and MI5 tackled that problem.[37] Even US President Eisenhower praised the superiority of the British Security Service in this regard at the time.[38]

The British decided that their own Joint Intelligence Committee (JIC) could recommend actions for member countries to take in order to preserve the security of their intelligence. Thus, MI5 took action under the direction of the JIC to create the necessary training material, including short clips of how to handle secret materials. Accompanied by MI5, the Baghdad Pact Security inspection team surveyed the Turkish Chief of Staff and Security Service registries. As Turkey had previously acquired the necessary training and procedures due to NATO membership, MI5 found the security implementation in Turkey in good standing.[39] However, the MI5 and Baghdad Pact security

**Figure 1** Baghdad Pact Military Council Meeting, Lancaster House, London, UK, July 1958. Turkish Chief of Staff Fevzi Mengüç chairing the first meeting after the 14 July revolution in Iraq. Source: Papers of Air Marshal Sir William Dickson, Churchill Archive Center.

inspection in Iran was not satisfactory since five top secret Baghdad pact documents were found to be missing in the registries.[40] This point was also raised by the Turkish chairman of the National Security Authority, who argued that security inspections were designed to build confidence between the different security partners while guaranteeing that member countries protected each other's confidential information. He added that without guaranteeing the implementation of the agreed security procedures in every detail, confidence building among the member countries could not proceed.[41]

While the Turks were concerned about the security of information in other regional countries, during the initial phases of the Baghdad Pact military planning committee in 1956, the British ambassador in Baghdad, Sir Michael Wright, informed the Foreign Office about the Turkish Security Advisor's complacent attitude in the military planning committee. His concerns led the British Security Service to take additional measures to prevent any breach of intelligence.[42] They decided to prevent any dissemination of documents to member countries before the necessary security arrangements were in place, in order to prevent leakage. General Jazi, the Iranian deputy on the committee, personally informed Wright that Iran had no security service other than the police forces to undertake responsibility for the security of information. The Ambassador commissioned Mr. Clayton of MI5 to personally provide information to General Jazi to develop a competent security service in Iran, and to supervise the Turks and other members to prevent them from taking a complacent approach to intelligence security.[43] Ambassador Wright was satisfied with Clayton's conduct of this, telling the Foreign Office, that 'Mr. Clayton is a first-class man and I am sure he will do much to dispel the Turks' complacency. I am glad he is watching over security arrangements for the present planning cycle'.[44]

The Baghdad Pact member countries sought to eliminate any leakage of intelligence to so-called 'undesired parties', meaning either Soviet agents or other subversive elements such as communists or Nasserists. However, unlike in NATO countries, coups, assassinations, and political intrigues were common trends in the Middle East. The July 1958 coup d'état carried out by Arab nationalist officers of the Iraqi army demonstrated the validity of these concerns. The new Iraqi government, led by Iraqi Brigadier Abd-ul Karim Qasim, immediately withdrew from the Baghdad Pact and took the country away from its previous Western orientation. It meant that the previous Baghdad Pact documents held by the Iraqis, such as those relating to counter-intelligence and counter-subversion methods and policies as well as documents of the military planning committee, were also likely to be compromised by undesired parties. Since the Baghdad Pact headquarters were in the Iraqi capital, and the previous security arrangements at the premises there were not at a desirable level, there were not sufficient security safeguards to prevent the exposure of Pact documents to the coup government.

Following the coup d'état, MI5 immediately issued new security procedures for the remaining member countries, at the same time moving the Baghdad Pact headquarters to Turkey, seen as the most stable country. Also, as will be discussed in Chapter 6, the British position in the Pact became more passive as it had lost the country that was seen as the most pro-British regime among the members. The Pact was renamed the Central Treaty Organization (CENTO). The new security procedures stated that all CENTO and Military Planning Staff documents that had been circulated to the Iraqi government before July 1958 were presumed to be compromised.[45] In order to minimize such incidents in the future, CENTO representatives held a meeting with the British Security Methods and Policy Committee on 25 September 1959 to limit the bilateral circulation of confidential CENTO documents and imposed higher restrictions on the personnel involved in information security.[46] The new procedures involved more duplication and a stricter imposition of NATO-inspired regulations, such as a clearance process and restricted access to documents. However, in CENTO the problem with security of information was not the major cause of ineffective intelligence cooperation. The major cause was the ambiguity regarding issues on which to cooperate. Therefore, as is demonstrated in the following sections, intra-alliance behaviour and norms are as important (and sometimes more) a prerequisite of intelligence cooperation. Certainly, CENTO was lacking in that regard.

Although the security of information and confidence building was an important aspect of the multilateral intelligence cooperation under NATO and CENTO, military intelligence played a significant role as well. Spying on the Soviet Union and Soviet clients, as well as determining the military vulnerabilities of alliances, posed two important tasks for military intelligence. The first task involved gaining accurate intelligence on the enemy, and the second task was not to provide intelligence about the alliances' military vulnerabilities to the enemy. Yet the partners in the alliances, such as Turkey, had other priorities according to their own national imperatives. They did not hesitate to employ intelligence diplomacy in military affairs to deceive their partners.

## Military Intelligence

### NATO

The military intelligence aspect of NATO covered the majority of the topics of intelligence cooperation. NATO was founded as a multilateral defence organization against the Soviet Union. The defence and war planning of NATO member countries, as well as determining the weakness and strength of NATO armies in relation to the Communist Bloc, was based on intelligence gathered concerning Soviet military, political and economic trends. Moreover, based on this intelligence, the command structures of NATO militaries, and priority areas of force improvement, were discussed as well. NATO intelligence analysts assumed that 175 Soviet military divisions would be available in the European theatre in case of war. The USSR's comparative supremacy over NATO countries was the main factor determining Western threat perceptions.[47] NATO intelligence assessments on the Soviets were also mostly synchronized with American assessments.[48]

Since military intelligence analysis in NATO was dominated by American perspectives, disagreement between the members on Soviet military capabilities was also an inevitable consequence. Such disagreement about NATO intelligence estimates was more visible when it came to intelligence outcomes prepared by the alliance's working group on Trends and Implications of Soviet Policy during the 1950s, due more to the ideological biases of the analysts themselves than to tactical/military intelligence estimations which counted Soviets troops and warheads.[49] Yet the most pressing concern regarding multilateral intelligence, for military intelligence purposes, was to 'coordinate the NATO member's views and responses to the ascent of Soviet Power'.[50]

This problem manifested itself in two different ways, both in relation to countries' own concerns and capabilities. In other words, a major country like the United Kingdom desired to shape NATO intelligence estimations in such a way as to overestimate the British capabilities. The British aim was to ensure its leading role in the Eastern Mediterranean and its control over the Middle Eastern theatre. The ramification of this British endeavour was two-fold. First, London wanted to assure the Americans that Britain still had the capability to protect its own interests in the region and those of the alliance. Second, the British wanted to assure the smaller powers in the alliance, such as Turkey, that London could still provide them with the necessary security and so prevent them from moving closer to the Americans.

This double-pronged British strategy was visible in NATO discussions on the NATO Mediterranean Command between 1950 and 1953. After the association of Greece and Turkey to NATO in 1950 and their later admittance to NATO in 1952, NATO reorganized its command structure to integrate Turkish and Greek forces. The command reorganization was structured in a way to counter a possible Soviet military advance in the Near East. Military intelligence on the status of NATO forces in the Eastern Mediterranean theatre, and estimations on possible Soviet actions in the theatre, resulted in the American 6th Fleet, ultimately under the command of an American, Admiral Robert Carney, being deployed in the area. The Sixth Fleet was formed in 1948, and upon

NATO's formation in 1949, this same fleet took responsibility for the Eastern Mediterranean. Until the mid-1960s the fleet held a paramount position in the Mediterranean due to the lack of any significant rival force. As John Chipman states: 'the Sixth Fleet was therefore able to move within the Mediterranean, and show the flag with full confidence that its political weight would be felt by those it wished to influence'.[51] And it was true for Turkey as well. When it visited Istanbul as early as February 1951, the Chief of the Turkish Navy, Admiral Sadık Altıncan, and the Major of Istanbul, Fahreddin Kerim Gökay, told Admiral John Ballentine, the admiral of the 6th Fleet, how deeply touched they were by the American presence.[52]

American dominance over the Eastern Mediterranean caused the British to be warier of NATO military intelligence estimates, as these negatively affected British prestige and strategic aims. A British command in the Eastern Mediterranean would provide the country with a permanent presence in the region. The Americans, among others, were confident that Britain did not have the capacity to prevent regional or large scale conflict in the region. Thus, the military intelligence of NATO proposed the necessity of American command in the theatre, and Admiral Carney, commander-in-chief of NATO forces in Southern Europe, supported the view reflected in the intelligence analysis by stating that: 'the sensitiveness of British pride is understandable but the immutable fact is that the British Navy is not only smaller than the US Navy, but it also lacks the comprehensive inventory of weapons and techniques possessed by the US Navy'.[53]

These differing views on NATO intelligence between the Americans and the British created an opportunity for small powers in the alliance to shape the situation according to their own strategic imperatives. Turkey, as one such minor power, was able to accomplish this in a productive way. Although Turkish and British relations improved during the Second World War, in the early Cold War the Turks were uncertain about British aims in the region and were not confident that London could provide the necessary external support to resist Soviet aggression.[54] Turkish military cadres also distrusted Britain for historical reasons, and still saw it as a power which had fought against Turkish independence after the First World War. For these reasons, the Turks did not want to fall under a NATO Eastern Mediterranean sub-command led by the British.[55] Therefore, Ankara sought ways through intelligence diplomacy to attract American interest on a permanent basis.

This tension between the two major powers helped Ankara to influence certain NATO studies in its favour, as it did in the NATO Mediterranean command. Moreover, the Turks, like other minor powers in the alliance, did not have the capacity to produce detailed technical intelligence on the Soviets, including on the Soviet military. American-dominated NATO intelligence therefore proved immensely valuable for Ankara as a basis for its own policies.[56] The Turkish secret intelligence service also pursued its own course of action against the Soviet bloc. This arose due to the MAH's ability to infiltrate human agents through the Soviet Union's Caucasian border, and its ability to gather intelligence on Bulgaria and Syria as well.[57] In addition, the geographical importance of the Dardanelles made it easier to spy on Soviet naval activity. However, the intelligence produced by the Turks was crafted in a way to exaggerate Soviet activities and capabilities in the region when it was passed on to NATO. In order to conceal their exaggerations, Turkish intelligence officers claimed that they lacked personnel in other areas, thus dedicating all their resources to spying on Soviet activities in the Caucasus line.[58] Through these exaggerations, Ankara aimed to attract more American aid and attention to Turkey's security, by highlighting the importance of the country as an indispensable defence against common adversaries.

In order to trace Turkish secret intelligence activities in relation to military intelligence, it is useful to survey intelligence production before and after the country's admission as a NATO member. MAH, the Turkish Intelligence Agency, engaged in gathering military intelligence on the Soviet Bloc continuously through the post-war period. However, the technical capacities of the agency were limited, especially when compared to the British and American agencies. The United States was engaged in preparing aerial reconnaissance of the Soviet Union, starting from the early post-war years, through US Navy and Air Force missions carried out by Boeing RB-47 aircraft. The British also used Canberra aircraft for high altitude reconnaissance missions over the Soviet Union. These experiences of British and American air forces of high altitude reconnaissance missions led to the CIA's U-2 program in 1954. US bases in Turkey were crucial in the success of that programme.[59] It is also important to note that even after the Soviets shot down one of the CIA's U-2 flights in May 1960, the Turkish government offered no objection to the continuation of U-2 operations from bases in Turkey.[60] Although the Turkish government saw the continuation of the deployment of the U-2 planes as a sign of American commitment, Washington was worried that the incident would expose Turkey to the risk of Soviet retaliation.[61]

Furthermore, Ankara did not have the means to acquire the technological capacity to conduct aerial reconnaissance of the Soviet Bloc. Moreover, the Soviets were quite vigilant about possible foreign agents trying to infiltrate their country. Consequently, the Turks used their own diplomats or casual travellers to acquire military related intelligence, even in regions adjacent to Turkey.

For instance, until Turkey gained admission to NATO in 1952, the MAH produced military intelligence for the Turkish General Staff based upon verbal information provided by diplomats and 'casual travellers' behind the Iron Curtain. For instance, the hand-drawn map of the Soviet naval port in Batumi was drafted upon information given by the Turkish Consul General at Batumi, Georgia in July 1951. However, another top-secret intelligence report on the Soviet Bloc's natural resources in 1955 after the Turkish admission to NATO clearly demonstrates the influence of NATO-distributed intelligence to the Turkish General Staff, rather than in-house intelligence gathered by the MAH. The intelligence was also clearly produced in accordance with NATO intelligence guidelines, which laid special emphasis on the economic development of the Soviet Bloc. This is important to note since it shows that Turkish intelligence had to re-shape itself in

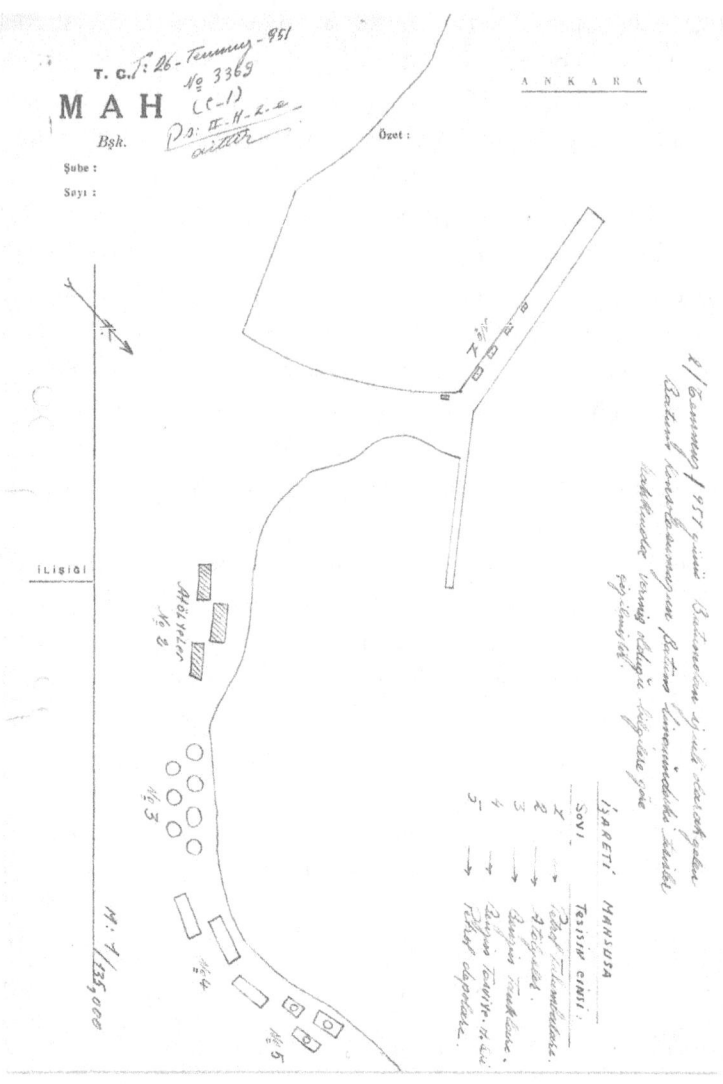

**Figure 2** Author's Collection: MAH drawing of Soviet Georgia's Batumi Port. 26 July 1951.

line with NATO procedures and requirements in order to conduct effective intelligence diplomacy. The transition of intelligence to meet NATO norms was not a swift one, since Turkish agencies lacked the necessary trained personnel and capabilities to analyse the economic, social and political trends of the Soviet Union. The intelligence reports of the 1950s indicate that the Turks remained heavily dependent on economic and political intelligence obtained from NATO channels, from the Turkish foreign ministry and from available open sources. This lack of capability meant that Turkish military planning depended on estimations produced by NATO.

After Turkey joined NATO, the Turkish army's need for military intelligence against the Soviet Bloc was mostly supplied by the alliance, and particularly by the Americans. For instance, in several Turkish military intelligence reports on developments in Soviet weapon systems, dating from around 1958, photos and blueprints of new Soviet weapons had 'SECRET' watermarks in English, which is an indication that the intelligence was passed to the Turks by the Americans or British within the NATO context.

Concurrently with Turkey's NATO accession, the MAH enhanced its pre-existing capabilities in HUMINT to conduct espionage activities on the Soviet Bloc. In particular, the MAH's ability to run agents in regions adjacent to Turkey, in order to acquire military intelligence on Soviet activities, put Turkey in a position where it could feed intelligence to the alliance. The NATO Standing Group Intelligence Committee held regular meetings with their Turkish counterparts to feed Turkish intelligence into NATO channels as effectively as possible.[62] NATO staff regularly visited the Turkish General Staff in Ankara for the meetings. In a meeting held in February 1953 in Ankara the MAH was not present, yet the intelligence division of the Turkish General Staff informed NATO about the country's intelligence capabilities and aims.[63] The MAH was not directly involved in intelligence cooperation with NATO, yet the intelligence acquired by the MAH was presented to NATO through Turkish military representatives. In the meeting, Colonel Gökçe, working in the G-2 (Military Intelligence), informed NATO about the organization and methods of operation of the intelligence service, stating that they were 120 officers and non-commissioned officers with no civilians assigned to the Intelligence Division. All were army personnel with the exception of one naval and one air force officer.[64] Colonel Gökçe did not inform the NATO staff about MAH and its activities. Since most of the foreign intelligence was conducted by the MAH, and not by military intelligence, Gökçe was hesitant when it came to informing NATO staff about the MAH's capabilities and activities. By keeping the MAH away from NATO eyes, Ankara had greater freedom to engage the MAH in solo and bilateral missions. Examples of MAH deception will be covered in Chapters 4, 5 and 6, which deal respectively with nuclear weapons, subversion and covert action.

NATO staff were concerned about the punctuality of the intelligence provided by Turkey. The Turks frequently delayed sending requested intelligence to NATO. The Chief of Staff, General Yamut, and his deputy, General Okan, explained that the intelligence division was short of staff, and especially short of the personnel that had the language capabilities to translate the intelligence into English and/or French. This shortage of staff meant that it would take a long time for Ankara to reply to requests.[65] Knowing the curriculum of officer corps training, it is safe to assume that the Turkish officers on duty during the 1950s were equipped with French.[66] The excuse for delaying the documents would almost certainly not depend on the lack of staff. The delay was presumably a part of Turkish intelligence diplomacy, designed to craft reports that would put Ankara's priorities first, rather than simply provide NATO with its requested intelligence. As veteran Canadian Intelligence officer Stephane Lefebvre argues, multilateral intelligence agreements are more political in their purpose, and limited in their effect, since they tend to reflect each national imperative, or agreed-upon intelligence policy objectives.[67] Moreover, in this politically characterized multilateral intelligence scene, minor partners who may have more access to human intelligence sources could use their comparative advantage to shape the intelligence cooperation according to their policy objectives.⁶⁸ This is what Turkish intelligence tried to accomplish in the context of NATO.

Thus the Turkish staff recommended that NATO should prioritize its requests and clearly indicate urgent requests so that Ankara could respond in a timely manner. Yamut added that their main concern was the variation in the intelligence estimates produced by different NATO National Staffs and laid stress upon the dangers of an underestimation of enemy forces.⁶⁹ He recommended that periodical meetings of the NATO National Staff should be used to overcome this divergence in estimates. Again, Turkish intelligence diplomacy aimed to keep NATO on alert by overestimating Soviet activities in the region, and then to obtain more aid and commitment to boost Turkey's defence as a country on the southern flank of the alliance. Yamut stressed the NATO National Staff's underestimation of enemy forces in the Black Sea region, and proposed two questions for study: first, the objectives of the relatively large Russian fleet in the Black Sea; second, the objectives of the Russian armed forces concentrated directly north of the Black Sea.⁷⁰ General Akçakoca, from G-2 (Military Intelligence) of the Turkish General Staff, later joined the meetings and stated that the Turkish Staff were best informed on Bulgaria, with Romania and the Caucasus next in line.

The Turkish emphasis on the Soviet Naval threat in the Black Sea, owing to constant alarming intelligence received by Ankara, affected NATO's Defence Planning in the following years. Nikita Khrushchev's Naval Seven Year Plan, introduced in 1959 to prepare the Soviet Navy 'to carry out a true internationalist mission in every major body of water over the globe', also underlined the importance of the Soviet Navy's possible penetration of the Mediterranean.⁷¹ The promotion of Admiral Sergey Gorshkov, from the commander of the Soviet Black Sea Fleet to the chief commander of the Soviet Navy in 1956, revealed the great ambition behind Soviet naval activities.⁷² Turkey strictly monitored the Soviet Bloc's naval activities along the Turkish straits, and denied access to Soviet warships that did not fall under the Montreux Convention of 1936. In order to circumvent the treaty's obligations and penetrate the Mediterranean, the Soviets also tried covert methods to disguise their ships. Turkish intelligence needed more comprehensive technical capabilities to see through these disguises.

In the Defence Planning Multilateral Meetings in February 1956, the issue of the Soviet Naval threat in the Black Sea and in the Straits was emphasized by Admiral J. Wright, the Supreme Allied Commander Atlantic, as reflected in the minutes of the meeting:

> He could not over-emphasise the importance which he attributed to operations aimed at making unprofitable any attempt of enemy submarines to issue from their existing concentrations. The main areas concerned were the Turkish and Baltic Straits, and also the Straits of Gibraltar, here access from the Mediterranean to the Atlantic could be denied.[73]

The safety of the Turkish Straits and Black Sea, which was one of the crucial passages connecting the Soviet Bloc to the Mediterranean and then to the Atlantic, also emphasized the Turkish role in monitoring Soviet surface and submarine activities. These concerns were then shared by the alliance. However, the Turks lacked major SIGINT capabilities to produce and disseminate comprehensive intelligence on the Soviet Bloc's naval activities along the Black Sea and Turkish Straits. The NATO Standing Group responded with new guidelines in June 1959, titled Systems on 'Reporting by Signal the Movements of Soviet Bloc Warships and Auxiliaries in Peacetime'.[74] The goals of this intelligence work were '(a) to gain intelligence; (b) to prevent the Soviets from using such vessels to gain intelligence on members of the alliance either as regards individual or collective activities; (c) to prevent the development of a surprise threat'.[75] These guidelines also made national authorities responsible for the production and dissemination of the necessary intelligence. However, regarding the Turkish Waters, the Mediterranean and the Black Sea, the British Admiralty, the US Sixth Fleet (COMSIXTHFLT) and the US Office of Navy Intelligence under the Chief of Naval Operations were also required to produce and disseminate intelligence in addition to that produced by the Turkish General Staff.⁷⁶ The responsibility of the British and Americans to collect intelligence in and around the region under the NATO scheme encouraged the Turks to look for other ways to highlight their intelligence contribution in the alliance. Especially from the late-1950s, the MAH developed stronger ties with its American and British counterparts and prioritized joint covert action, and the infiltration of human agents inside the Soviet Union. Although most of these attempts were futile, and the Soviets immediately captured most of the infiltrated agents, the MAH's constant efforts to support the American and British operations provided the necessary political grounds for Ankara to continue its intelligence diplomacy.

## Baghdad Pact

Particularly for HUMINT activities, MAH was keen to recruit 'causal travellers' for espionage missions in the Balkans and Caucasus. The intelligence produced by the Turks on the Soviet Bloc's military activities around the Black Sea made NATO pay special attention to the region. Just as in the NATO example, CENTO's military committee was a platform for military intelligence cooperation, yet in the broader Middle Eastern context, the bilateral regional grievances between countries made intelligence cooperation rather ineffective and untrustworthy. Thus, for Ankara, the CENTO's military committee became a channel for cooperation with the British concerning Middle Eastern politics and convincing the other regional members of the threat from the Soviet Bloc, and from subversive elements at home since the regional members could not create a consensus on what were the subversive elements, since one's subversive could be another's 'freedom fighter'. Yet finally, at a CENTO meeting in Lahore in 1962, the definition of subversive elements was broadened to include non-communist groups.⁷⁷ However, this did not necessarily foster more effective intelligence cooperation. For the British, the CENTO military committee was an indispensable way to influence regional countries' strategic thinking.

CENTO made its first serious steps towards regional military planning with the appointment of a Combined Military Staff in late 1957 to work permanently on the question of military planning. It should be noted that the United States also became a full member of the military committee in 1957. There was also pressure from the British to make the United States a full member of the organization. The British Ambassador in Washington, Sir Harold Caccia, urged that the United States should promptly join the Baghdad Pact as a full member,[78] but Secretary of State John Foster Dulles declined the idea by saying that they were 'hesitant about the merits of joining a pact which was not merely anti-communist but interpreted as being anti some of the anti-Communist Arab countries, notably Saudi Arabia'.[79] Dulles added that if the British were willing to settle the Buraimi dispute with Saudi Arabia in favour of the Saudi claims, then they were willing to change their stance and give full support to the Baghdad Pact.[80] This was not a price that the British were willing to pay. The Americans consequently offered only limited support to the Pact in military terms and left the British with most of the military burden in the region. Moreover, the American approach once more reiterated that the Baghdad Pact was not solely an anti-communist defence organization, but rather a platform that regional powers used to intrigue against each other and their western partners.

For instance, the Turkish government took the initiative to convince other regional members to issue an invitation to the United States to join the Pact's Military Committee in March 1957.[81] Iran appreciated this development, since it thought that the existence of such a powerful country within the organization would feed the needs of the Iranian military and intelligence services, particularly in terms of military aid.[82] Yet Iran also tried to exclude Turkey from any steps of the military planning of the Pact, although Turkey was a major member of the organization. Iranian intentions to exclude Turkey from the military planning sparked concerns in other member countries, particularly in Pakistan. When Pakistani President Iskender Mirza met British premier Harold Macmillan on 30 October 1957, he raised his concerns that the exclusion of Turkey from the military committee would mean the collapse of the organization, and he successfully sought British support against the Iranian proposal.[83] As a result, Macmillan called the Iranian proposal 'absurd'.[84]

However, the lack of trust between members and disagreements about the major threats facing the Pact remained major problems. Without agreement on the major threats facing the Pact countries, intelligence cooperation efforts proved rather futile. In the meetings, Pakistan, among other countries, wanted to draw attention to India and Afghanistan, and suggested that they draft war plans against these countries as well.[85] The Pakistani emphasis on drafting military plans covering India set an obstacle for intelligence cooperation and defence planning. If the military committee were to produce studies on India as well, member countries' effort to collect military intelligence would be focused on India. If word leaked out that Britain was drafting war plans against another commonwealth country, the results would likely be catastrophic.[86] In the end, the British were able to convince the Pakistani delegation that a war between two commonwealth nations was unthinkable, and that if such an incident occurred, Britain was likely to support the victim of aggression in the UN.[87] The Pakistani authorities still did not compromise on their position.

Every study drafted by the military committee was subject to approval by the British MoD and the JIC.[88] Besides the involvement of the MoD and JIC through official channels, service attachés stationed in British embassies also acted to influence the threat perception and strategic thinking of the regional members of CENTO, while engaging in bilateral discussions concerning the Pact's military planning. For instance, in April 1956, R.B. Stevens, the British Ambassador in Tehran, informed the Foreign Office that two of his service attachés had established close contacts with the Iranian Chief of Staff, General Hedayat, and other individual joint staff members over the discussions around military planning. These two service attachés thus had access to Iranian strategic thinking and military planning, and were able to send fully informed reports to the Foreign Office. According to Ambassador

Stevens' judgement, their close engagement with high level Iranian military figures enabled them to exert British influence over Iranian military planning. The Ambassador asked the Foreign Office to support their local mission by appointing these service attachés to special advisory positions within the Baghdad Pact since it is 'best, perhaps the only channel, for obtaining information about Iranian strategic thinking and for influencing the Iranian General Staff'.[89]

Military intelligence cooperation within the Baghdad Pact was dominated by local grievances and utmost distrust between the various parties, and this made military planning and intelligence cooperation rather difficult to obtain. For instance, the British Chiefs of Staff concluded that the slow tempo of military cooperation was to their advantage because the preparation of detailed operational plans would reveal true British strength in the area and what other capabilities they had. They were anxious to avoid the release of such information to Pact members.[90] Two implications followed from this British attitude. First, the British wanted to create ambiguity among members about their own capabilities, so as to prevent the members from drawing closer to the Americans. The second aim was to prevent the Pact members from falling under the rising Turkish influence in the region, influence that would be multiplied by an effective multilateral mechanism there.[91] In military planning, and in intelligence sharing, ambiguity and deception on all sides made effective coordination very difficult.

When the military committee agreed on study plans, the member countries did not even share the logistic routes or their naval and air capabilities with each other. The Pact countries did not even prepare a direct study on the Soviet Union, and focused instead on more local threats, namely the Kurds, Afghanistan and Chinese Sinkiang (Xinjiang), under the title of 'War Short of Global War'.[92] Even then, however, the members could not agree on study topics because initially Iran and Turkey were reluctant to include Afghanistan as a study topic. Pakistan also expressed their reservations, saying that any study that did not include India as a target would not be accepted by them. Such a compromise was not acceptable to the British. Therefore, the committee was not able to agree on the target study and military intelligence cooperation within the Pact remained weak and inefficient. The only exception to this concerned nuclear warfare, and the identifying of priority targets for RAF tactical nuclear weapons in the event of war.[93]

The unexpected level of cooperation in nuclear warfare planning proved an exception to the rather slow paced progress made by the military committee.

There were two main reasons for this relatively more efficient cooperation regarding nuclear weapons. First, the main security provider to the region, the UK, was not capable of providing the conventional land forces necessary for the protection of the Pact area in time of war. Second, the regional members of the Pact had little conception of the use and effect of air power in modern war, and therefore their military intelligence cooperation regarding nuclear weapons was to 'demonstrate the effectiveness of nuclear weapons and the over-riding advantages which their use would give to the defence of the Baghdad Pact area'.[94] Moreover, due to the lack of nuclear ballistic missiles in the region, in case of a global war with the Soviets in the Middle East theatre, the United States and the United Kingdom would provide nuclear weapons for the region through their Air Forces to inflict maximum damage on possible Soviet land communications. Therefore, the British and US liaison to the Baghdad Pact estimated that Iran would lose large parts of its northern territories in case of a Soviet advancement.[95] However, the British did not imply that Iran would lose the majority of its territory in the study regarding the use of nuclear weapons, in order not to anger Tehran. However, the study suggested that the United States and the United Kingdom would drop nuclear weapons in the member countries' territories to delay the Soviet advance until reinforcements arrived to defence the Pact area. This included targets around major transportation hub cities, such as the Trabzon-Batumi Road in Turkey and the Djulfa-Tabriz Road in Iran.[96]

Facing this concrete danger from the Soviet Union, the regional countries were even willing to allow strikes on their own territory. The deception by the United Kingdom and the United States of their partners, especially in their underestimation of possible causalities caused by these strikes, did not exactly help to speed up cooperation in military intelligence matters. As for the Turks, they were aware of the limited reach of British military capabilities, and estimated that the British would not divert their military to support the Pact area in case of war.[97] Therefore, Turkish intelligence diplomacy in the Pact's military matters focused on exploiting the decline of the British in the region (also rising anti-British sentiment following the Suez debacle) and, as we see in Chapter 6, on claiming its leadership over the regional members to support Turkish plans in Syria, and post-July revolution Iraq. For Turkey, the military intelligence cooperation in the Pact remained a political tool for pursuing Turkish intelligence diplomacy.

## Conclusion

In order to develop an effective mechanism of multilateral intelligence cooperation, the members of the alliances needed to ensure that their capabilities and sources would not be revealed to other parties and constitute a risk to their own national security. Under NATO's cooperation scheme, which included the COSMIC system and supervision by the British Security Service, confidence in each other quickly built up among the members. The Turkish conception of what constituted secrecy of information, and their own national mechanism for achieving that aim, was also shaped according to the NATO system. In NATO, moreover, and especially in terms of military intelligence, the level of cooperation between member states was rather efficient because the target of intelligence, the Soviet Bloc, was unanimously agreed upon. Therefore, even a minor country like Turkey had the opportunity to benefit from the technical assistance of NATO while at the same time gaining the opportunity to feed NATO with intelligence by utilizing its home capabilities. For this reason, Turkish intelligence diplomacy was quite effective, in spite of constant distrust between Turkey and some other members within the alliance.

In CENTO, however, local grievances and disputes hampered intelligence cooperation within the alliance. For Turkey in particular, CENTO's military intelligence focused mainly on regional problems, such as the Kurds and subversive activities, since its military commitments fell mainly under the NATO umbrella. From the British and American perspective, military intelligence cooperation under CENTO was less about the Soviet threat and more about influencing regional members' strategic thinking and trying to shape the future course of action in the region. Moreover, constant distrust and intrigue between the regional members made CENTO less likely to become an efficient defence mechanism against the Soviets. The next chapter, dealing with nuclear intelligence, further shows how Turkey conducted intelligence diplomacy to gain more Western aid and security commitments, even on the crucial issue of nuclear weapons.

## Notes

1 Please see Chapter 5 for further discussion on intelligence diplomacy in terms of counter-subversion matters.
2 M. Cohen, 'From "Cold" to "Hot" War: Allied Strategic and Military Interests in the Middle East after the Second World War', *Middle Eastern Studies*, 43:5 (2007), 725.
3 Ibid., 727.
4 American Diplomatic Training Service (ADTS) Oral History Interview with William M. Rountree (1945–46; special assistant to the director, Office of Near Eastern and African Affairs, Department of State, 1946–48; member of the American Economic Mission to Greece, 1947; diplomatic service in Greece, 1948–49, Turkey, 1952–53, and Iran, 1953–55; Deputy Director, 1949–50, and Director, 1952, Office of Greek, Turkish and Iranian Affairs, Department of State), interviewed by Arthur L. Lowrie, 22 December 1989.
5 CIA-RDP79S01011A000400010007-8: 'To Estimate Soviet and Satellite reaction to the inclusion of Greece and Turkey in NATO', *c.* 1950.

6   Ibid., the same point is also supported by N. B. Criss, 'Strategic Nuclear Missiler in Turkey: The Jupiter Affairs 1959–1963', *Journal of Strategic Studies*, 20:3 (1997), 98.
7   Truman Presidential Library and Archives: George McGhee Papers: Box 1: 'Memorandum of Conversation between Ambassador McGhee, and Foreign Minister', 15 January 1952.
8   Aldrich, 'Transatlantic Intelligence and Security Cooperation', 738.
9   Truman Presidential Library and Archives: Dean Acheson Papers: Box 65: Memorandum of Conversation with the British Ambassador and Others: 'Revised British Attitude on Proposed Statement on Greece, Turkey, and Iran', 15 March 1949.
10  However after being admitted to NATO, Turkey utilized NATO as the institutionalization of the Turkish-American Alliance. See Ş. Yılmaz, 'Turkey's Quest for NATO Membership: The Institutionalization of the Turkish–American Alliance', *Southeast European and Black Sea Studies*, 12:4 (2012), 481–495.
11  Truman Presidential Library and Archives: Dean Acheson Papers: Box 65: Memorandum of Conversation with the Turkish Ambassador: 'Turkish Interest in Proposed Declaration on Greece, Turkey, and Iran, and in Eventual Creation of Mediterranean Pact', 17 February 1949.
12  Truman Presidential Library and Archives: George McGhee Papers: Box 1: Memorandum of Conversation between Ambassador McGhee, Turkish Prime Minister and Foreign Minister, 8 February 1952.
13  Truman Presidential Library and Archives: Dean Acheson Papers: Box 65: 'Memorandum of Conversation with the President', 11 July 1949.
14  Adriana N. Seagle argues that intelligence sharing within NATO has not been one of trust and mutual cooperation even at the height of Cold War. Numerous tactical, political, and structural obstacles, she argues, have limited NATO intelligence sharing. See A. N. Seagle, 'Intelligence Sharing Practices within NATO: An English School Perspective', *International Journal of Intelligence and Counterintelligence*, 28:3 (2015), 557–577.
15  P. Sudoplatov, et al., *Special Tasks: The Memoirs of an Unwanted Witness, a Soviet Spymaster* (Boston, 1995), 244.
16  AIPN (Archiwum Instytutu Pamięci Narodowej): 02386/130: 'plan to gather information about SAMANTA'.
17  TBMM Tutanakları: 8. Dönem, 4. Cilt, 37. Birleşim, 29 January 1947.

18 O. Penkovsky, *The Penkovsky Papers: The Russian Who Spied for the West* (London, 1965), 62.
19 Ibid.
20 Ibid., 85.
21 TNA: FO 371/127861: VB1692/9: 'Report by the Turkish Delegation on Communist Activities in Turkey', 23 May 1957.
22 *Milliyet*, 14 September 1957.
23 R. Aldrich, *The Hidden Hand: Britain, America and Cold War Secret Intelligence* (London, 2001), 430.
24 TNA: KV 4/264: 'MI6 to JIC', 22 June 1954.
25 The NATO Security Coordinating Committee was responsible for regulating and implementing a common information security framework among the Allies.
26 NATO: C/4-D-4/7: North Atlantic Council Fourth Session: 'International Working Group Report on Implementation of the Security System for North Atlantic Treaty Organization', 15 May 1950.
27 NATO: SGM-0164-50: Standing Group, 'Implementation of COSMIC Security System', 3 July 1950.
28 NATO: AC/35-D/6: Security Committee: 'Leaks of Information (Questions Raised by Council in C-R(53)25 for Examination by Committee on Legal Position in Member Countries)', 15 May 1953.
29 NATO: C-M(53)101: North Atlantic Council: 'Leakages of NATO Information: Report by the Chairman of the NATO Security Committee', 10 July 1953.
30 CIA-RDP79R01012A000300020005-0: G-2 Contributions to NIE-9 – Turkey, c. 1950.
31 NARA: RG59: Box 4069: FW 782.5/8-1450: From Berry to Matthews: Capability of Turkey to deal effectively with an attack by Bulgaria in which the Soviets do not overtly participate, 14 August 1950 (US National Archives and Records Administration, hereafter will be referred NARA).
32 NATO: SG 080-2: Standing Group, 'Report by International Working Team to the Standing Group: Association of Turkey and Greece with NATO military planning', 20 November 1950.
33 Ibid.
34 NATO: SG 007-35: Standing Group: 'Final- Security Surveys in Greece and Turkey', 13 February 1951.

35 NATO: SG 007-52: Standing Group: 'Final – Examination of the COSMIC Security System in Greece and Turkey', 17 June 1952.
36 TNA: CAB 21/4049: 'Baghdad Pact Organization: The Report on the First Inspection of the British Embassy Sub-Registry at Washington', 10 December 1958.
37 TNA: CAB 21/4049: 'Security Policy and Methods Committee Meeting Minutes', 13 August 1958.
38 Eisenhower Presidential Library and Archives: Papers as President, Ann Whitman Files: DDE Diary Series: Box 27: Memorandum of Conversation between the President, Admiral Strauss and General Goodpaster, 30 October 1957.
39 TNA: CAB 21/4049: 'Security Service Comments on Report on Baghdad Pact Security Procedures in Turkey', 19 June 1958.
40 Ibid.
41 TNA: CAB 21/4049: 'Discussions with the Turkish National Security Authority on the Security Structure', 10 April 1958.
42 TNA: FO 371/121276: V1076/18: Wright from Baghdad to FO: 'Report of the Meeting between the Military Deputies at the Planning Committee', 30 January 1956.
43 Ibid.
44 Ibid.
45 TNA: CAB 21/4747: 'Compromise of Classified Documents Issued by the Central Treaty Organisation Before July 14, 1958', 21 December 1958.
46 TNA: CAB 21/4747: 'Minutes of the Meeting held in Room "C"', 25 September 1959.
47 P. A. Karber and J. A. Combs, 'The United States, NATO, and the Soviet Threat to Western Europe: Military Estimates and Policy Options, 1945–1963', *Diplomatic History* 22:3 (1998), 399–429.
48 E. Hatzivassilliou, 'Images of the Adversary: NATO Assessments of the Soviet Union, 1950–1964', *Journal of Cold War Studies*, 11:2 (2009), 113.
49 Ibid., 111.
50 Ibid., 94.
51 J. Chipman, 'NATO and the Security Problems of the Southern Region: From the Azores to Ardahan', in J. Chipman, ed., *NATO's Southern Allies: Internal and External Challenges* (London, 1988), 26.
52 Library of Congress: The Papers of John J. Ballentine: Box 8: Letter from Sadik Altincan, 24 February 1951; Letter from Gokay, 20 March 1951.

53 D. Chourchoulis, 'High Hopes, Bold Aims, Limited Results: Britain and the Establishment of the NATO Mediterranean Command, 1950–1953', *Diplomacy and Statecraft*, 20:3 (2009), 439.
54 Please see Chapter 2 for a detailed discussion.
55 Chourchoulis, 'High Hopes, Bold Aims, Limited Results: Britain and the Establishment of the NATO Mediterranean Command, 1950–1953', 445.
56 Hatzivassilliou, 'Images of the Adversary: NATO Assessments of the Soviet Union, 1950–1964', 114.
57 Please see Chapters 4 and 6 for a detailed discussion of these operations.
58 NATO: SGM-0341-53 – Report on the Visit of the Intelligence Committee to National Staffs in Ankara, Turkey, Athens, Greece and Rome, Italy, London, United Kingdom and the Supreme Headquarters Allied Powers Europe, 9 March 1953.
59 CIA: G. W. Pedlow and D. E. Welzenbach, *The CIA and the U-2 Program, 1954–1974* (Center for the Study of Intelligence, 1998), 11–15.
60 CIA-RDP62B00844R000200160038-5: 'Future of the Agency's U-2 Capability', 7 July 1960.
61 Ibid.
62 NATO: SGM-0341-53 – Report on the Visit of the Intelligence Committee to National Staffs in Ankara, Turkey, Athens, Greece and Rome, Italy, London, United Kingdom and the Supreme Headquarters Allied Powers Europe, 9 March 1953.
63 Ibid.
64 Ibid.
65 Ibid.
66 MKB: C. Akyol, 'Subay İstihbarat Eğitimi', *Silahlı Kuvvetler Dergisi*, 81:202 (1962), 25–37.
67 Lefebvre, 'The Difficulties and Dilemmas of International Intelligence Cooperation', 537.
68 Ibid., 534. Richard Aldrich also states that multilateral intelligence sharing is rare and difficult. cf. R. Aldrich, 'International intelligence cooperation in practice', in H. Born, I. Leigh, and A. Wills, ed., *International intelligence cooperation and accountability* (London, 2011), 18–41.
69 NATO: SGM-0341-53 – Report on the Visit of the Intelligence Committee to National Staffs in Ankara, Turkey, Athens, Greece and Rome, Italy, London, United Kingdom and the Supreme Headquarters Allied Powers Europe, 9 March 1953.

70  Ibid.
71  Chipman, 'NATO and the Security Problems of the Southern Region: From the Azores to Ardahan', 18.
72  E. Mawdsley, 'The Russian Navy in the Gorshkov Era', in P. P. O'Brien, ed., *Technology and Naval Combat in the Twentieth Century and Beyond* (London, 2001), 166.
73  NATO: AC-100-R-4: Record of Meeting: Summary Record of Discussions at the Palais de Chaillot after Defence Planning Presentations held on Friday, 20 February 1956 at 11 a.m.
74  NATO: MC-0090: 'The Dissemination of Intelligence: Reporting by Signal the Movements of Soviet Bloc Warships and Auxiliaries in Peacetime', 26 June 1959.
75  Ibid.
76  NATO: MC-0090: 'The Dissemination of Intelligence: Reporting by Signal the Movements of Soviet Bloc Warships and Auxiliaries in Peacetime', Appendix 'A', 26 June 1959.
77  C. Hashimoto and E. Bezci, 'Do the Kurds Have "No Friends but the Mountains"? Turkey's Secret War against Communists, Soviets and the Kurds', *Middle Eastern Studies*, 52:4 (2016), 648.
78  Eisenhower Library: John Foster Duller Papers: General Correspondence and Memorandum Series: Box 1: Memorandum of Conversation with Sir Harold Caccia, 24 December 1956.
79  Ibid.
80  Ibid.
81  PREM 11/1943: 'Telegram: UK Delegation Bermuda to FO', 22 March 1957.
82  PREM 11/1943: Baghdad to FO: 'Baghdad Pact Military Planning', 10 December 1957.
83  PREM 11/1943: FO to Baghdad: Telegram dated 5 November 1957.
84  Ibid.
85  FO 371/121276: Baghdad to MoD: Telegram dated 27 January 1956; FO 371/121277: Middle East Land Forces to MoD, Telegram dated 22 March 1956.
86  Ibid.
87  FO 371/121277: From Commonwealth Office to Islamabad: Telegram dated 20 March 1956.

88  FO 371/121277: MoD to G.H.Q. Middle East Land Forces, 3 April 1956.
89  FO 371/121277: Tehran to FO: Telegram dated 4 April 1956.
90  FO 371/121277: Chief of Staff Committee Joint Planning Staff: The Baghdad Pact – Military Committee in Tehran April 1956, 9 April 1956.
91  These points were also raised in M. Cohen, *Strategy and Politics in the Middle East, 1954–1960: Defending the Northern Tier* (London, 2004), 108–112 and also in B. K. Yesilbursa, *The Baghdad Pact: Anglo-American Defence Policies in the Middle East, 1950–59* (London, 2005), 113.
92  Ibid.
93  Ibid.
94  FO 371/121278:V1076/57: 'The Baghdad Pact Future Planning: The Impact of Nuclear Weapons on the Form of Global War in the Middle East', 6 July 1956.
95  Ibid.
96  FO 371/121278:V1076/57: 'The Baghdad Pact Future Planning: The Impact of Nuclear Weapons on the Form of Global War in the Middle East– Appendix B: Estimated Delay on Routes by Nuclear Weapons', 6 July 1956.
97  MKB: M.M.V. Erkanıharbiye Umumiye Riyaseti Karargahı İstihbarat Başkanlığı, İngiltere'de gelecekte takibedilecek milli müdafaa politikası (Ankara, 1958).

# 4

# Spies, Atoms and Signals

One of the most horrific threats during the early Cold War was the possibility of a nuclear war between the Soviet Union and the Western bloc. Thus, while Soviet intelligence was trying to acquire nuclear secrets from the United States and United Kingdom through espionage, London and Washington aimed to produce an accurate estimation of how and when the Soviets would acquire its first nuclear bomb. As early as 1940, a commission of Soviet scientists received rumours that a 'superweapon' was being built in the West, but they concluded that it was practically impossible to create an atomic bomb.[1] Yet the Soviets kept a vigilant eye on the American nuclear programme. The NKVD in particular operated networks of illegals and émigrés who managed to gather confidential information on the American and the British nuclear programme, including figures such as Julius and Ethel Rosenberg, and the physicists Alan Nunn May and Klaus Fuchs.[2] The vigilance of Soviet intelligence concerning atomic matters helped Moscow to gain at least a year's advantage in its quest to obtain a nuclear capability.[3] The head of the NKVD's Special Tasks Unit reported that 'by July 1943, [Soviet] agents in the United States had provided [Moscow] with 286 classified publications on scientific research in nuclear energy'.[4]

As a result, the Soviets successfully detonated their first atomic bomb on 29 August 1949. Moreover, the Soviet bomb was a copy of the American one. Klaus Fuchs confessed during his interrogation by MI5 that 'he had given the Russians, all the information in his possession about British and American research in connection with the atomic bomb'.[5] The Soviet leadership were assured that the Americans only became aware of the bomb after its detonation. Indeed, it was a 'rude shock' for both the Americans and the British when a US weather reconnaissance plane captured footage of the debris caused by the blast over the North Pacific on 3 September 1949.[6] Thus, it became an imperative for the West to accelerate its espionage efforts on the Soviet Union. These efforts required cooperation with the countries in regions adjacent to the Soviet Union. Hence, Turkey found itself in an advantageous position to contribute to the Western espionage missions on the Soviets, but in return Ankara did not hesitate to demand intelligence missions to the country as a means of leverage on the West.

This chapter argues that the intelligence cooperation between Turkey and the West in operations using human agents did not translate into the SIGINT field. The lack of in-depth cooperation required significant amendments to the Turkish-American relationship. SIGINT operations from Turkish soil, including spy-planes, were concealed behind thick layers of secrecy. In most cases the secret nature of the operations caused Ankara to underestimate the political and military risks these operations entailed. Ankara merely saw nuclear matters and the technical aspects of SIGINT operations as a way to obtain more US aid, and as a tool to pressure the American government.

After the first Soviet bomb test, efforts to acquire a more accurate picture of their adversary's capabilities became the priority for both Whitehall and Washington. These efforts required firm cooperation with their smaller allies who were in the proximity of the Soviet Union and could provide the logistical support required for SIGINT and human espionage operations. London was capable of using its Imperial-Commonwealth connections in adjacent regions for its own spy missions, such as using facilities in Cyprus. However, lacking those connections, Washington needed a reliable ally. Turkey was an ideal partner, especially for the Americans, since the Soviet missile and testing sites were believed to be located in the Caspian Sea region. Ankara was eager to obtain America's commitment to its security and to obtain as much economic aid for its ambitious domestic economic development during the 1950s. Thus, when US officials approached the Turkish leadership for help in spying on the Soviet nuclear programme and to install nuclear missiles to deter the Soviets, Ankara did not hesitate.

However, this transformation was not an easy one. One important point is that Turkish politicians and the military did not fully realize the significance of nuclear weapons. The lack of scientists in Turkey able to analyse the correlation between uranium production and nuclear weapons led to an inability of the Turks to create their own estimates in this field. Ankara therefore had to depend on intelligence passed on by the Americans. However, although the United States had been using NSA-supervised bases and CIA-orchestrated spy flights in Turkey to spy on the Soviets' military and nuclear programme, only a very small part of this intelligence was being passed to the Turks – and almost nothing was passed on about nuclear matters. This was due to security concerns, especially possible leaks from the Turkish side, and also the tendency of Ankara's political leaders to use foreign policy for domestic purposes. This was even apparent when the Turks so willingly hosted nuclear Jupiter missiles on its soil while other countries rejected the idea, so as not to be a target of a nuclear exchange during the war. Indeed, Turkish Foreign Minister Fatin Rüştü Zorlu told the secretary of state, John Foster Dulles, that 'IRBMs would be very useful in Turkey, it would be particularly helpful if there was some progress on the negotiations prior to the opening of the Turkish Parliament on July 15'.[7] We can see from Zorlu's conversation that the Turkish political leadership desired to use the deployment of nuclear missiles to gain domestic leverage. Even a crucial issue such as nuclear weapons was a bargaining issue for Ankara, notwithstanding the fact that it risked the exposure of the country to possible nuclear attacks. It might be noted that Washington, being aware of the dangers of exposing US personnel to Soviet nuclear retaliation, aimed to deploy intermediate-range ballistic missiles (IRBMs) away from the areas where there were already concentrations of US personnel.[8]

The lack of human agents behind the Iron Curtain able to provide the West with the necessary intelligence on Soviet military capabilities gave the USSR an advantage over the Americans, not least in judging the seriousness of the threat posed by the other side. Moscow presumed that the American and British stockpile could be sufficient to destroy the USSR by 1955.[9] Interestingly, American intelligence analysts made the same estimate about the Soviet Union, although the British disagreed.[10] In fact, even before the Soviets tested their first atomic bomb, the Western powers tended to overestimate their opponents. Stalin initiated the Berlin blockade in 1948 and it can be argued that, by taking advantage of the ambiguous perception in the West concerning Soviet war readiness, he helped to secure a communist victory in the Chinese civil war, in 1947–9.[11] For Stalin knew that Washington did not have sufficient capability to use nuclear weapons in both China and Berlin simultaneously, and Western overestimation of Soviet conventional warfare capabilities prevented the Americans using the nuclear threat to support Chinese nationalists.[12]

The former head of the CIA's Soviet Desk, Milton Bearden, states that the Soviet penetration of the US nuclear programme, paradoxically, did some good. Otherwise, in Bearden's words, 'Stalin would have been hysterical about the American burgeoning nuclear development if he had not penetrated the entire Manhattan Project with a whole array of people. Julius and Ethel Rosenberg kept Stalin from doing something goofy. That betrayal of the US probably saved us [West] a huge war.'[13] Yet, the lack of Western intelligence on the Soviet capabilities triggered US exaggeration of them. Clearly, American and British sources did not have a clear picture of Soviet nuclear developments at that time. This chapter will next discuss how Ankara used joint human operations to infiltrate agents behind the Iron Curtain to its advantage, in order to increase its capability and bargaining power with the West. Despite various obstacles, Ankara's willingness and ability to smuggle agents across the frontier to determine Soviet capabilities acted as an initial confidence-building mechanism for later Turkish operations.

## Human intelligence and smuggling of agents

After the Cold War began, Turkey's most populous city, Istanbul, became an invaluable base for human intelligence operations targeting the Soviet Union and communist governments in the Balkans and Central Europe. Large numbers of émigrés living in Istanbul provided an excellent pool from which to recruit human assets to penetrate the Soviet Union.[14] Kim Philby, MI6 chief in the city between 1946 and 1949 (and a KGB agent within the British ranks who passed a great deal of intelligence to the Russians), coordinated MI6 efforts with MAH to recruit potential agents from among the Armenian, Georgian, Bulgarian and Albanian communities, as well as from communist students who originated in the Balkans.[15] This pool of potential recruits, who still had links with their home countries and knew the region and its languages, emerged as suitable assets who could unearth Soviet military and nuclear activities in the surrounding region.

At the same time, MI6 was also spying on Turkey. Most of this concerned military-related matters, including a detailed survey of possible landing places around Iskenderun and Trabzon, and an analysis of Turkish war preparedness. The recently established Joint Intelligence Bureau (JIB) started a three-year project in 1948 that compiled a detailed intelligence handbook on Turkey.[16] Philby was responsible for the first twelve months of the project.[17] It is reported that he used local and professional photographers, as well as embarking on intelligence gathering missions himself, to produce an accurate survey of Turkey's military capabilities and positions. The British consulate in Istanbul acted as the main base for the securing, storage and development of the intelligence gathered in these operations. For security reasons, to prevent leaks to the Turks and to avoid diplomatic embarrassment, it was not permitted to collect intelligence in any other British consular posts in the country. The MI6 post in Turkey was attached to the British consulate in Istanbul at that time, thus, the embassy believed that all the intelligence-related work should be collected in Istanbul since it had implemented the necessary security measures there. Although, as at that time Kim Philby was leading the station in Istanbul, in retrospect the embassy's security warning is somewhat ironic. The intelligence gathered on Turkey and the emergence of the MI6 mission in Istanbul had two important implications. First, Whitehall became aware that Britain could not afford to grant more military assurance to the Turks in the event of a war, since the Turkish army would require a substantial amount of British economic and military commitment to defend itself against the Soviets. Second, the convenient position of the MI6 Istanbul station became crucially important for British attempts to understand developments behind the Iron Curtain, an understanding that both the British and Americans previously lacked.

In order to gain insights into Soviet military activity, the MI6 station in Istanbul had to coordinate its activities with MAH to a certain extent. However, this was a rather peculiar kind of cooperation. According to Philby, the MAH would ask for money and the agent who was to be smuggled into Soviet territory, and would then do the rest of the job itself. However, such cooperation was not always effective. The MAH lacked modern technology, such as advanced cameras and transmission devices, or the practical experience to carry out this kind of action. The success rate of the operations was therefore low. According to Philby, even the best agents in MAH sometimes botched their operations.[18] Yet, although he concluded that cooperation between Turkish and Western intelligence agencies did not uncover significant findings about Soviet military activity, the estimates prepared by British and Turkish intelligence in the early 1950s suggest that this cooperation *did* pay off to some extent. This reiterated the importance of the Turks as an intelligence partner.

In July 1951, for instance, the JIB prepared a survey of the Soviet military defences in the Caucasus and the Black Sea. It is true that some of the intelligence estimates, for example on the locations of Soviet defence establishments in South Crimea, Sevastopol and the Kerch Straits, lacked accuracy. The JIB noted the estimations on these areas were mostly derived from wartime information going back to 1941. However, in the areas where the SIS cooperated with its Turkish counterparts, such as Batumi, Transcaucasia and Baku, the information was up-to-date, accurate and more detailed.[19] This again shows that Turkish intelligence was justified in its claims that the strategic advantage of the country's location, and its experience in accessing local agents, made Turkey a suitable base for operations behind the Iron Curtain. But, although the MAH proved itself to be a reliable partner, as Ankara tried to gain more prominence in Western security arrangements, by the late 1950s there was a growing irritation in Washington regarding the Turks.

The Turkish military representative to SHAPE, in 1958, asked NATO to construct an additional radar early warning system in the city of Kars, near the Soviet border.[20] By making this request, Ankara aimed to complete defence projects with external assistance that Turkey was not capable of doing on its own. At this point, however, the United States became wary about providing military and economic aid to Turkey. It is important to note in this context that, by the late 1950s, the United States had begun to have doubts about Turkey's economic stability, and about the effectiveness of previous military aid to Turkey. By evaluating military and economic conditions in Turkey, in July 1957 the US National Security Council concluded that although Washington had sent 2 billion dollars to the country:

> On the military front there is no doubt that but that Turkish armed forces have gained greatly in their defensive capabilities, although the army is still far from being a fully equipped, well-trained fighting machine, and problems continue to exist in the Air Force and Navy. On the economic front, despite some noteworthy development projects which the United States has financed, the nation has not achieved economic stability nor is it a viable economic unit.[21]

As a solution to these problems, the NSC suggested that, instead of focusing on short-term projects – such as providing large amounts of complicated and expensive military equipment that had only limited effectiveness due to the lack of adequate, literate and technically trained personnel – military aid to Turkey should focus instead on increasing the Turks' basic economic strength.[22] According to Joint US Military Mission for Aid to Turkey (JUSMATT), it would take more than a decade to modernize the Turkish military. Given the nature and urgency of the current nuclear threat, JUSMATT recommended that 'in the view of the time required to build adequate Turkish military strength, that US units, with an atomic capability, be stationed in Turkey as quickly as possible'.[23] However, such a change in the US attitude posed a risk to the domestic and regional ambitions of the Menderes government, which wished to build up Turkey as a powerful actor.

In particular, as reported by the US ambassador to Turkey, Fletcher Warren, there was a strong element of 'negativism' in US policy to Turkey.[24] This negativism was mostly caused by the fear that Ankara's desire for rapid economic and military development could actually render Turkey instable. It is important to point out that this negativism was not unique to Turkey. The actions of Greece and Iran, key recipients of American aid at the same time, were also leading Washington to question the efficacy of the whole aid programme. However, the deputy secretary of state, Lampton Berry, wrote to Warren that the 'aspect of the Turkish problem that gives it a peculiar character has to do with the fact that the Turks have apparently been less successful than other countries in sensing the temper of Washington'.[25] Berry added that there was an increasing trend in Washington, as apparent in the 1958 budget hearings, to reconsider American aid and commitments abroad more generally – and, again, the Turks seemed unable to understand this trend as well.[26]

In response to Berry's letter, Warren explained his own perspective on this failure of understanding:

> I agree with you that the Turks do not sense the temper of Washington. We have done our best here to get this across, but as you point out, the Turkish Embassy in Washington has failed to report the situation back here objectively. In my opinion, this is because they are afraid to do so. It is true that Ürgüplü [the current Turkish Ambassador in Washington] speaks up and thinks independently, and that he may be an improvement over Görk [the previous Ambassador].

On the other hand, as we reported to the Department, the British government was not exactly enthralled with Ürgüplü. Among other things, they thought he spoke up too much and was just a little too independent.[27]

The over-politicization of Turkish institutions, including the Foreign Service, thus hampered an objective flow of information between Ankara and Washington.

It is important to note that, in this framework of intelligence diplomacy, the MAH and CIA established their own projects to conduct espionage missions across the Soviet border. These espionage missions were not necessarily independent of the broader security agreements between Ankara and Washington, being rather a complimentary dimension which the Turks used as leverage for broader diplomatic relations. Even as scepticism in Washington grew regarding the effectiveness of American aid to Turkey, the beginning of joint CIA–MAH espionage operations to spy on the Soviet nuclear programme came to the rescue of Turkish intelligence diplomacy. Justin O'Donnell, the CIA station chief in Ankara during the mid-1950s and one of the CIA's long-term career agents, provided the necessary equipment and infrastructure for the Turks to conduct these operations. Anthony D. Marshall, the CIA's Istanbul station chief in 1958–9, with the official title of vice consul, states that they mostly recruited third-country nationals to use in these operations. This cooperation was important, but it did not prevent the CIA from recruiting Turks to spy on Turkey as well. Marshall states that he 'recruited some Turks to do some works for them'.[28] Given that the agents used in the joint operations were vetted by both the MAH and CIA, Marshall recruited these Turks without the knowledge of MAH to spy on Turkey. The MAH's tolerant attitude enabled the CIA to target Turkey. However, the American dependence on the Turks' human agents did not last long. The changing character of the MAH–CIA operations, moving away from human agents to SIGINT, depending on the US listening posts on Turkish soil starting from 1954, encouraged the Turks to gradually acquire their own SIGINT capabilities as well.

Tighter Soviet patrols starting from the mid-1950s along the Turkish border spectacularly decreased the success rate of the joint operations.[29] The CIA–MAH operations then focused on other targets, such as Syria and Bulgaria, which were relatively easier to infiltrate. The high cost of the MAH–CIA spy infiltration operations also encouraged a shift to SIGINT operations, using spy planes and listening posts, to detect Soviet missile tests. Cooperation in the SIGINT field proved difficult, engendered distrust and on several occasions raised serious problems in the relationship between Ankara and Washington. Before we discuss SIGINT in more detail, however, it is important to note an episode that demonstrates how Ankara utilized its cooperation with her Western allies to pursue its own strategic imperatives, in this case sparking disturbances among the Turkish minority in Bulgaria. Considering the course of Turkish intelligence activities and the MAH's hesitancy in conducting joint psychological operations with the British aimed at the Turkish-speaking people in the Soviet Union, it is safe to assume that the MAH converted Ankara's own aim to increase its influence over the Turkish minority in Bulgaria into broader Western-backed operations.[30] How did the MAH do this?

## Running errands in Bulgaria

In the 1950s, Bulgaria, Turkey's northwest neighbour, was a prominent target for Turkish intelligence and an area of great interest to Turkey's Western friends. Animosity between Turkey and Bulgaria stretched back the better part of a century. After Bulgaria had shaken off Ottoman authority in the nineteenth century, it was viewed by the Sublime Porte and by later governments in Ankara as a serious military threat. After Bulgaria gained independence in 1878, its ethnic Turkish minority began to emigrate to Anatolia. This decrease in the Turkish population climaxed during the First and Second Balkan Wars in 1912 and 1913 when the Balkan League, led by Bulgaria and Serbia, waged war against the Ottomans to seize the remaining territory in the Balkans. As a result of these wars, hundreds of thousands more Turks migrated from Bulgaria to Anatolia. Ankara's problems with Bulgaria then continued after the country signed the Tripartite Pact in 1941 to join the Axis during the Second World War, a move that brought Nazi troops to Turkey's doorstep.

Bulgaria itself emerged as a major threat to Ankara when it aligned with the Soviet bloc and a communist regime took power in 1947. The poor treatment of its remaining Turkish minority and its military build-up made Bulgaria a major threat in Ankara's eyes during the early Cold War. However, since Turkey and Bulgaria stood on opposite sides during that period, an overt clash between the two countries was impossible.[31] The clash mostly occurred by covert means, in line with the general trend of the Cold War. Bulgaria tried to implement Soviet designs towards Turkey, in particular to export communist ideology there via emigres.[32] Meanwhile, the MAH had its own agenda to utilize the emigres as human intelligence assets against Bulgaria and the rest of the Eastern bloc.[33]

During 1950 and 1951, Bulgaria's communist government eased exit restrictions for its Turkish minority.[34] As a result, nearly a quarter of a million Turks from Bulgaria moved to Turkey to escape political repression and discrimination. During the same period, NATO decided to involve Turkey and Greece in military planning for the defence of the Mediterranean. Even though the two countries would not become NATO member states until the following year, both hosted significant United States and United Kingdom intelligence missions. NATO's Security Committee, the body responsible for protecting the alliance from subversion, was concerned that communist agents could blend in with Turkish migrants from Bulgaria:

> It is obvious that a number of these persons may be Communist agents and a few have indeed already been detected. Although the Communist party has no legal existence [in Turkey] it cannot be assumed that there are no Communists in the country, though it seems probable that the organisation is not sufficiently effective to permit direct and consistent penetration of Government organisations.[35]

However, as MI5 informed NATO, the threat of communist penetration from Bulgaria was well met by the MAH. MI5 noted that 'the degree of infiltration to Government offices by Communists or fellow travellers can be described as negligible or possibly even non-existent as this is one thing about which the Turks are eternally vigilant'.[36] Acting as both domestic security service and foreign secret intelligence service, the MAH not only prevented communist infiltration, but also successfully recruited human intelligence assets from among the immigrants.

After Turkey's admission to NATO in 1952 as a full member, the Turkish military intelligence, G-2, and the MAH synchronized their aims and policies to bring them into line with NATO requirements. In terms of SIGINT and other technical capabilities, Ankara had to depend on help provided by NATO, especially in terms of the interception of Soviet bloc communications and photographic reconnaissance. The Turkish Air Force only had two very outdated reconnaissance planes as late as the early 1960s.[37] Yet partial dependence on NATO intelligence did not mean an absence of effort from the Turks. Indeed, the Turkish intelligence service pursued its own operations against the Socialist bloc. As General Akçakoca from G-2 informed his NATO counterparts in 1953, the Turkish General Staff (TGS) were best informed on Bulgaria, with Romania and the Caucasus next in line.[38] The MAH utilized this advantage to conduct its own operations in Bulgaria, while covering its activities under the rubric of the Western Alliance.

Turkey, as a NATO member, also directed its intelligence activities at the Soviet bloc's nuclear agenda and uranium production. Until the mid-1950s, however, Ankara's attempts to collect intelligence on the Soviet nuclear programme proved rather futile. A 1955 G-2 report on Soviet uranium production even bluntly admitted that Ankara did not have 'any clue about the actual figures of the Soviet uranium production'.[39] However, after the mid-1950s, agents recruited among Turkish immigrants from Bulgaria played a crucial role in revealing some figures to the MAH, leading to very real improvements in Turkish intelligence efforts. For example, the MAH's intelligence activities targeted Bulgarian uranium production.[40] In this regard, it is important to note that although the McMahon Act of 1946 severed cooperation between the United States and United Kingdom in terms of nuclear energy, there was still efficient cooperation between MI6 and CIA when it came to spying on the Soviet nuclear programme.[41] Joint CIA–MI6 activities increased further after the formation of the Cooperation Regarding Atomic information for Mutual Defence Purposes on 15 June 1955 to locate Soviet tests, and to discover key sites for Soviet nuclear research and development.[42] One of the most important ways, for instance, to spy on the Soviet nuclear programme, was to monitor the level of uranium production in mines in Saxony. Thus, a joint CIA–MI6 mission penetrated these mines by 1950.[43] Ankara wanted to prove its usefulness to the Western allies by doing something similar. In particular, the MAH was able to penetrate the uranium mines in Bulgaria's Buhova region. The MAH was soon able to reveal the logistics of uranium production in these mines and its route of shipment to Soviet Russia for further enrichment. This information was passed to the CIA.

Another noteworthy example of the MAH's joint activities in Bulgaria came in 1960.[44] Turkey and its Western allies were, by then, eager to reveal the details of missile systems in the Ludogorie region of northeastern Bulgaria. NATO was aware of the existence of missile systems in the region, but the Bulgarians also built several fake missile ramps to divert attention from the real facilities. NATO asked Turkey for help in mapping out the properties and locations of the missile systems. The earliest Turkish efforts – the capture and interrogation of two Bulgarian agents – did not bear much fruit. After this failure, the MAH recruited a group of agents selected from the 250,000 Turkish immigrants from Bulgaria. These immigrants were good covert assets for missions in Bulgaria because they were fluent in Turkish and Bulgarian, knew the country and had a feasible excuse to be there under the cover of visiting their families. After the MAH smuggled these assets into Bulgaria, they were able to detect the exact location of the missile ramps. They returned to Turkey with their findings, and this intelligence was passed on to NATO's Intelligence Committee via Turkey's G-2.

The MAH's activities in Bulgaria proved useful for the broader efforts to spy on the Soviet nuclear programme. However, Turkish efforts in Bulgaria went beyond joint covert intelligence collection, including independent covert action.[45] Once Ankara increased its capabilities in Bulgaria, and gained the necessary infrastructure through its joint intelligence operations to spy on nuclear targets, it had the means to conduct operations within the country on its own. These were covert operations to increase Ankara's influence over the Turkish minority in Bulgaria and accorded with Turkey's own strategic goals. The British, at least, had no official knowledge of them. It is safe to suggest that the MAH wanted to use its own capabilities and experience this time to conduct an independent mission. However, this mission ran the risk of being perceived as an irredentist action by other regional partners of the United States and United Kingdom, such as Greece and Iran. Moreover, developments in Bulgaria – such as increasing oppression by the Bulgarian Communist Party against the Turkish minority by claiming there was a 'Turkish' threat inside the country, and accusing the Turkish minority of acting as agents of 'enemies of Bulgaria' – reduced relations between the two countries to a very low ebb. For instance, a Bulgarian note to Turkey dated 10 March 1951 'accused Turkey of instigating the Turkish minority to revolt'.[46]

And these Bulgarian accusations were not groundless: the MAH was indeed trying to organize a Turkish revolt within the country. Initially, the MAH formed opposition groups to encourage the repatriation of Turks in Bulgaria to Turkey. A secret telegram sent to London by the British mission in Sofia provided the details of Turkish covert action which caught British attention.[47] From the available archives it is not possible to argue that the British or Americans approved the Turkish action, but knowing the other examples of Turkish covert action in Syria, it is safe to suggest that the Western allies were wary of the possibility of Turkey dragging them into an unnecessary conflict. However, regardless of Western approval, the Turkish minority in Bulgaria remained the focus of Turkish intelligence for a long time. That is why this episode from the Cold War is particularly illustrative as regards showing Ankara's long-term interest in territories of the former Ottoman Empire. In 1956, MAH regional chief, Major Kamil Bey, based in the border city of Kırklareli, recruited a group of Bulgarian emigres to engage in subversive activities in Bulgaria, including sabotage against military and economic targets. These agents were provided with cash, encrypted transmission devices, arms and forged documents. Details of their targets and the outcome of their missions are not yet declassified. However, it is safe to suggest that in accordance with Turkey's relations with the Soviet bloc, and with the West as well, the MAH pursued its efforts even until the 1990s.

## Signals: Listening to the atoms

Apart from the joint HUMINT operations between MAH and its Western partners from the late 1940s onward, cooperation also grew in terms of SIGINT activities. These activities were designed to intercept Soviet bloc communications, and to spy on the Soviet nuclear programme. However, the character of cooperation in SIGINT activities was substantially different from that involving HUMINT, being spiced with distrust and an urge on both sides to conceal their capabilities from each other. This meant that Ankara had much less room for manoeuvre when it came to embedding Turkish interests more actively in SIGINT missions. In addition to this, the intelligence collected by Western SIGINT and ELINT missions based in Turkey was rarely passed to the Turks, and Turkish officers had limited access to SIGINT facilities. Why was this the case?

With the onset of the Cold War, and the development of nuclear weapons and ballistic missiles, governments were forced to restructure their intelligence capabilities to prevent a devastating surprise attack. Concurrent with these developments, according to Richard Aldrich, military leaders in the Western world 'demanded better intelligence and concluded that global SIGINT coverage was indispensable to the Western allies'.[48] However, both the Americans and British failed to predict the first Soviet atomic bomb in August 1949 or the outbreak of the Korean War in 1950.[49] Such failures pushed the Eisenhower administration to form the NSA, to prioritize intelligence collection from the Soviets through electronic means. However, the Americans faced a major problem. They had no bases sufficiently close to the Soviet Union, unlike the British who could count on bases in Cyprus and other Commonwealth countries.[50] Turkey proved indispensable for the Americans in this respect, due to its geographical proximity to the Soviet Union and to missile test sites such as Kapustin Yar, from where Sputnik I&II were launched.

Cooperation between the Americans and Turks was solely conducted by the Turkish military's signal intelligence branch since the MAH, as the civilian branch of Turkish intelligence, did not have a SIGINT organization at that time. The NSA decided that their cooperation with the Turks in SIGINT intelligence provided the United States with near-real-time intelligence on military air, naval, ground and paramilitary targets in the surrounding region.[51] This cooperation was greatly facilitated by Turkey's accession to NATO in 1952. Following the Turkish accession, Turkey ratified a Status of Forces Agreement (SOFA) with the United States on 23 June 1954. This allowed the Americans to maintain a military presence in Turkey as a part of the 'Implementing Status of Forces Agreement of June 19, 1951, between the Parties to the North Atlantic Treaty'.[52] By ratifying the SOFA treaty, Ankara accomplished her aims of attracting a long-term American commitment to Turkish security, gaining further material aid from the West, proving its usefulness to the Western Alliance and leading to a greater political influence for Turkey in NATO. For Washington, aiding this poor and volatile country, so willing to accept Western influence, would serve as the means to expand American influence in the region and avoid the necessity of depending on the British for the collection of intelligence on the Soviets.

Following the ratification of SOFA, a series of secret formal and informal agreements were also concluded between the Turks and the Americans, which envisioned the establishment of US military and intelligence sites in Turkey.[53] The important point to note is that, while the SOFA treaty was concluded with the approval of the Turkish Cabinet, future secret agreements allowing American intelligence sites to operate in Turkey were generally concluded directly by Turkish military officials or by the Ministry of National Defence. This point is illustrative regarding the conduct of intelligence diplomacy more generally. Diplomatic conduct regarding intelligence activities was left to the chief JUSMMAT officer and a liaison officer on the TGS, which bypassed both the American embassy in Ankara and the Turkish Foreign Ministry.[54] These two institutions would be involved in further discussion only in situations that required further political action. Indeed, the original suggestion that intelligence diplomacy should be conducted between specialized officers instead of diplomats came from the Americans, on the grounds that it would stimulate 'smooth operation and effective coordination'.[55]

There was, however, an unintended consequence of this for both the Turks and the Americans. The Turkish army soon increased its weight in national security matters, and even in Turkish foreign policy. As the military gained a larger diplomatic role (as discussed in more detail in Chapter 6), it gradually shifted civilian–military relations in its favour and eventually facilitated the coup of May 1960, which ousted the country's civilian leaders, followed by the execution of several of them. Moreover, after the coup the ruling military junta did not extend the same tolerance to American intelligence activities based in Turkey as the civilian governments had done. Instead, Turkish-American relations were greatly altered since the new government wanted to pursue a more independent foreign policy. Most importantly, the status of the American bases in Turkey was altered in Turkey's favour, and in a way that limited US operations from these bases.

According to the initial SOFA, the Turkish government devoted 32 million square metres of land to these bases, and was responsible for security as well as the storage and maintenance of the weapons deployed at the military sites. By 1958, the estimated annual cost of these sites to the Turkish budget was around $11 million.[56] Although this placed a considerable burden on the Turkish budget, it was an indispensable opportunity for Ankara to attract America's solid commitment to Turkish security and establish an efficient intelligence liaison with the Americans, while feeding the Turkish need for SIGINT coverage of Soviet targets. However, this investment did not mean that the Americans simply handed over the intelligence gathered from the bases to their hosts. Instead they conducted a bi-weekly intelligence exchange in Ankara, where they shared only the portion of intelligence that they believed the Turks needed to know. Ankara had to gather the rest itself by strengthening Turkish radar systems – albeit with American aid.[57] Again, this deal, including the terms and conditions surrounding the operation of the US bases, was not negotiated by diplomats. It was instead negotiated between the Turkish COS, General Hakkı Tunaboylu and the chief of JUSMMATT, General Lawrence Russel Dewey.[58]

It should be noted that this SIGINT cooperation between the Americans and the Turks faced major obstacles, even though Turkey played a crucial role regarding highly sensitive missions to spy on the Soviet Union. An example of the sensitive matters involved was the CIA spy-plane programme, including the U-2s operating from US Air Force TUSLOG Detachment 10-10 located in Adana (renamed as İncirlik Airbase in 1958) that commenced operations in mid-1954. In accordance with Operation OVERFLIGHT, approved by President Eisenhower for covert reconnaissance missions over the Soviet Union, TUSLOG Det 10-10 became one of the embarking locations for these missions. They had a vital objective. Soviet missiles posed an enormous threat, made worse by the lack of adequate alert systems and other intelligence. American planners also worried about the so-called 'missile gap' that could open in favour of the Soviets in the future, as evaluated by the US National Security Council's Technical Capabilities Panel in 1955, and the Net Evaluation Subcommittee in 1956. They concluded that it would be necessary to deploy the Strategic Air Force as a deterrent, while also developing a more comprehensive system of intelligence concerning Soviet missiles. Otherwise, in the event of a surprise nuclear attack, the Soviets could be the 'dominant world power in twenty-four hours'.[59]

Eisenhower's CIA director, Allen Dulles, stated in classified testimony to the US Congress that U-2 reconnaissance flights over the Soviet Union had five targets: bombers, missiles, atomic energy, submarines and air defence.[60] All these targets were interconnected, and could reveal Soviet capabilities in terms of producing and delivering tactical and strategic nuclear weapons at a variety of different ranges. However, when Eisenhower authorized the U-2 spy flights, confidential partners were needed for these highly secretive and risky missions – and these might not be forthcoming. For instance, the French President Charles de Gaulle replied, when approached, that he did not want to be any part of this mission. However, the Turkish prime minister, Adnan Menderes, agreed to the use of the Incirlik base (TUSLOG Det 10–10) in U-2 operations. Initially, Richard Mervin Bissel, Arthur C. Lundahl and Anthony D. Marshall from the CIA, who were responsible for the U-2 project, met Menderes and acquired his authorization to use Turkish territory. After this initial step, Marshall, the most junior of the initial team, visited Ankara and Adana several more times regarding the U-2 flights and became the CIA station chief in Istanbul in 1958.[61]

Before going into a detailed elaboration on the contribution of U-2 flights to gathering intelligence on Soviet nuclear and missile developments, it is essential to analyse the motivation behind Ankara's authorization for these flights to take place from Turkey. These missions again placed a high economic burden on an already-struggling Turkish economy. As NATO's International Staff pointed out in a Top Secret Annual Review of Turkey in 1958, during the mid- to late-1950s Turkey's two major economic problems were the control of inflation and the balance of payments situation caused by the Turkish development programme outstripping the ability of the national economy to pay for it.[62] Moreover, the same report indicated that the Turkish defence budget, which also covered items relating to the TUSLOG bases, was at its limits. The NATO report suggested that Ankara should delay domestic development programmes and allocate the necessary funds (which were around 25 per cent of the efforts) to NATO priority areas, which certainly included the maintenance of the American bases. The Menderes government complied with this suggestion at the cost of hampering its own economic development, despite the vital need to raise the very low standard of living in the country. Moreover, from the outset it was recognized that the political risks of U-2 operations were potentially high. President Eisenhower instructed his negotiators that they should explicitly warn their counterparts that, if these operations were exposed, the consequences could be catastrophic.[63] However, Menderes was more focused on the leverage he could have over Washington to maintain the flow of US economic aid to his economy. For Menderes, maintaining American economic aid meant that he could also maintain his rule in the country. There were already protests due to rising inflation and the badly managed economic structure. Thus, the cost of losing power was more important for Menderes to consider than exposing the country to a nuclear confrontation with the Soviets.

The political risks became visible when the Soviets shot down a U-2, piloted by Gary Powers, in May 1960. The military regime in Turkey, which overthrew the Menderes government on 27 May 1960, then used the U-2 incident as an excuse to reopen the issue of American bases in Turkey. The regime claimed that the Americans were violating the 1954 SOFA by not informing the Turkish government about its activities. However, as discussed in Chapter 3, Turkish claims were not accurate. Washington and Whitehall did not waste any time before instructing their ambassadors in Ankara to 'conduct business as usual' with the new Turkish government.[64] This initial change of attitude in Ankara following the coup d'état of 1960 echoed widely held views across the country and further fed anti-American sentiment.[65] Finally, in the mid-1960s, after the military regime had ceded power to an elected civilian government in October 1961, negotiations between Ankara and Washington commenced to revise the SOFA treaty, including some secret extensions. These negotiations only concluded in July 1969. The new agreement granted improved powers for the Turkish government to supervise the TUSLOG bases and gave the Turks a share in American SIGINT operations on its soil. The number of American personnel in Turkey was cut from 27,000 to 6,400, and the control of SIGINT bases in Trabzon (TUSLOG Det 3-1) and Samsun (TUSLOG Det 3-2) was transferred to the Turkish military.[66]

In order to understand how mutual distrust between the Turks and the Americans became an essential part of their intelligence diplomacy, it is necessary to analyse both the Turkish and Western approach to the issue. In this regard, the most insightful reflection can be derived from a report submitted to the British Prime Minister, Winston Churchill, based on the views of the retiring Canadian Ambassador to Turkey, General Odlum, in October 1952.[67] According to Odlum, the Turks held the belief that a general war was inevitable, and Ankara perceived itself to be in the front line of a possible Soviet attack that would also include the use of nuclear weapons. The Turks were convinced that the initial Soviet attack would target the Bosporus, the Persian Gulf and Suez Canal rather than being directed towards Western Europe. Although Turkish forces would fight to the death, the possibility of a Soviet nuclear attack in combination with conventional forces would leave the Turks helpless without any external support. Ankara was aware that the British commitment of forces to the region, even with the assistance of the Commonwealth, was not sufficient. The Turks had serious doubts that the British could deploy enough strength to maintain their assurances in the region. Therefore, Ankara wanted to obtain American assistance and the allocation of American forces to the region. The TUSLOG bases, and the authorization to host risky operations from them, can be explained with respect to this strategic worldview.

However, both the Turkish Foreign Ministry and the civilian leadership were frequently bypassed when it came to the use of TUSLOG bases. For instance, when the United States wanted to deploy additional reconnaissance planes at the Incirlik base, Ambassador Warren wrote to Washington that 'the Turks will welcome such an indication by USAF desire to use Adana'.[68] However, what he meant by 'the Turks' was not the civilian leadership of the country, for he added that 'JUSMATT have already made all necessary arrangements with Turkish Air Force. Turkish Foreign Office has not been consulted and instructions to Embassy to approach Foreign Office seem unnecessary and might even prove counter-productive under circumstances'.[69] Moreover, consultation about the U-2 overflights was also mostly conducted with the Turkish military and not the Turkish Foreign Ministry.

Once Ankara had accepted the American presence in Turkey, it was anxious to gain as much as possible from her relations with the West, including taking control of the several US-constructed bases and posts. However, unaware of Ankara's multi-layered efforts to obtain Western aid, Whitehall also wanted to convince the Turks that more British forces would be forthcoming to defend the region; the British thought that, by doing so, they would find the Turks more cooperative in joint defence plans. GCHQ bases in Turkey, alongside American posts, constituted a portion of the 'forthcoming' British assurance and commitment to Ankara.[70] This was not the sole reason for having the British and American posts alongside each other in Turkey. Apart from the British and Commonwealth operations, which had to be kept secret from the Americans, there was also an important difference of perception between the British and Americans concerning the 'missile gap'. The British did not overestimate Soviet capabilities of production and delivery of ICBMs, as the Americans did. Thus, having their own sources would make Whitehall less prone to American errors in this respect.[71]

## The Turks' trial with atoms

Turkish planners acutely realized their lack of capabilities to pursue any kind of independent research and analysis on nuclear matters. Menderes' foreign minister, Fuat Köprülü, informed parliament in February 1956 that the government was well aware of possible impacts of nuclear developments on the military, economic and social arenas.[72] However, he added that forming a nuclear research unit in Turkey would exceed the nation's capabilities. For this reason, he signed the Agreement for Cooperation Concerning Civil Uses of Atomic Energy between the government of the United States of America and the government of the Turkish Republic on 10 June 1955, which paved the way for a greater Turkish role in the nuclear field. Köprülü stated:

> Our government contributes to all efforts to form an international cooperation on atomic energy. Concurrently with our contribution to these efforts, we carefully handle our most important strategic priority of training our national experts. Therefore, we have already sent several of our scientists to gain expertise while being resident at the United States Atomic Energy Commission Centres in the USA.[73]

By this agreement, Turkey was promised a small research reactor and given promises that it would soon obtain further knowledge and technology. Moreover, seeking external aid for nuclear development, such as training Turkish experts on nuclear matters, became a strategic priority for the Menderes government. Beside the technological assistance envisaged in the agreement, it had symbolic importance as a further step in the American commitment to Turkey. Adnan Menderes told an Istanbul-based reporter:

> It is noteworthy and significant that the United States' very first agreement with a foreign state for cooperation in the peaceful uses of atomic energy has been signed with Turkey. The fact that we are the first to conclude such an agreement with the United States is a new an auspicious manifestation of the close cooperation that exists between our friendly and allied nations.[74]

Only a few months after Köprülü's speech, the Parliament voted, in August 1956, to establish the Atomic Energy Commission (much resembling its American counterpart) under the direct supervision of the office of the prime minister. The core duties of the commission were defined as, 'Promoting, coordinating and monitoring the scientific, economic, technical and administrative works on the Atomic energy in order to protect the nation's high interests and elevate the welfare of the country'.[75] Consecutive clauses of the law empowered the commission to establish liaisons with partner countries, and work with other government agencies in matters related to nuclear security. Thus, it was not surprising to see Fuat Alpkartal (an MP from the governing Democrat Party, but formerly a military attaché in Turkey's Washington embassy and liaison officer to JUSMATT, with strong ties to the Turkish intelligence community) giving an explanatory statement in support of the law. He stated:

> We are at the beginning of an important and ambiguous issue that will create an utmost serious problem for whole world. For now, only feasible solution for this problem is to take a part in international cooperation to foster peaceful use of atomic energy. [Apart from international cooperation] With this propitious initiative, it is also important to be prepared for the measures that would prevent the use of nuclear and thermonuclear powers as military forces.[76]

However, although the Turkish government had high hopes of acquiring the necessary technical infrastructure and knowledge on nuclear matters, Washington was sceptical about Ankara's motives on such issues. There is a peculiar case that illustrates this point. In April 1951, even before Turkey's admission to NATO, Bedii Karaburcak, the first secretary of the Turkish embassy in Washington, was authorized to purchase nuclear radioisotopes from the US Atomic Energy Commission. Indeed, the Turkish embassy had previously made another failed attempt to purchase nuclear material from the United States in March 1950.[77] However, having received such a peculiar request from the Turks, the State Department consulted with the American embassy in Turkey, which reported:

> There are no publications in Turkey concerned with atomic energy developments. A careful investigation conducted in cooperation with the Service attachés at this post leads to the conclusion that neither the Turkish military or civilian authorities are engaged in any activity in the field of atomic energy.[78]

The American embassy concluded that there were no publications or development regarding a nuclear programme in Turkey. However, the available records in the Turkish archives indicate that at least by 1955, the Turkish military was preparing studies regarding the use of nuclear weapons in the event of a war. In particular, a classified report prepared in the Turkish War Academy indicates that the Turkish military perceived a Third World War between the Communist and Western bloc to be inevitable. Moreover, the same study concluded that the use of atomic weapons would be the determining factor in the approaching Third World War.[79] The report concluded that, given developments in the nuclear field, it was imperative for the Turkish military to overhaul its tactics and strategy by integrating new defensive and offensive military doctrines, so as to prepare the country for nuclear confrontation.[80]

Although the Turkish military was making its own studies on nuclear warfare, the lack of specialized officers who could comprehend the full implications of nuclear weapons hampered efforts to adapt to the nuclear age. For instance, when the Turkish Colonel Eray was sent to Maralinga, Australia to observe Operation Antler, the British hydrogen bomb tests in 1957, he complained that he had not travelled all the way from Turkey just to see a 'big explosion' from a long distance![81] The British Foreign Office rejected Eray's complaints by stating that, aside from the explosion, he was shown Health Physics Caravans, the Operational Control Desks, the Meteorological Section, the Radiochemical Analysis and the Radioactive Measurement Laboratories in addition to some excursions to the Weapons Research Establishment. Also, Eray's request to see the explosion site after the test was impossible due to obvious health and safety reasons. The British suspected that Eray was making his complaint 'to cover difficulties he had with his government over money', since he was provided with insufficient funds for his visit.[82] But, either way – whether it be limited funds or the lack of trained personnel that was the key issue here – there were clearly real problems with Turkish efforts to obtain an insightful knowledge of the nuclear question.

There was also undesirable institutional competition in Turkey between the newly established Atomic Energy Commission and the

Ministry of Foreign Affairs' NATO department, which dealt with nuclear affairs. The Atomic Energy Commission was chaired by Dr Nûri Refet Korur, a prominent chemist, previously the scientific advisor to the TGS on nuclear and chemical warfare matters. The Ministry of Foreign Affairs' NATO department was led by Hüveyda Mayatepek, a senior diplomat from a prominent family. The competition between these two senior figures, based largely on personal rivalry, hampered Turkey's bid to develop its nuclear capabilities by seeking external aid. A detailed letter from the British embassy in Ankara, sent to the Foreign Office's Atomic Energy department, reveals the negative consequences of this internal feud: it reported on talks between Minford, a First Secretary of the British embassy in Ankara with both figures, concluding that these threw 'an interesting and rather disquieting light on the shortcomings in administration, and the lack of co-ordination in the Turkish Atomic Energy programme'.[83]

Menderes's dependency on external aid to prolong his rule resulted in unnecessary duplication and ambiguity leading to the failure to prioritize areas of development, and in a lack of clarity when it came to developing a solid nuclear research plan. There was also a time-consuming debate over choosing the university that should focus on nuclear training and research, namely between the Middle East Technical University and Ankara University. Moreover, Mayatepek did not hesitate to openly condemn and criticize Dr. Korur in his talk with Minford, stating, for instance, that Korur was not competent enough to pursue such an important project. For his part, Korur revealed a similarly poor opinion of Mayatepek, claiming that the Turkish Foreign Ministry was taking decisions and actions on nuclear matters without even informing the Atomic Energy Commission, thus wasting time and money to little result. To illustrate the disquieting nature of the Turkish nuclear programme, one particular incident is worth noting. When talking with Minford, Dr. Korur told him that the Turkish Foreign Ministry did not provide him with the reports on Nuclear Research and Development they received, even the ones from the International Atomic Energy Agency or the CENTO Institute of Nuclear Science.

Thus, Korur asked Minford if the British could 'draw his attention to papers like this in the future if they thought he ought to know about them'.[84] The head of the Turkish Atomic Energy Commission thus had to request necessary documentation from a foreign emissary because of a personal feud he had with the Turkish Foreign Ministry! Inefficiency caused by this personal feud in the early stages of the Turkish nuclear programme, followed by the military coup in May 1960 and subsequent political chaos caused by inefficient coalition governments until the mid-1960s, meant that more than a decade was lost at the start of the Turkish nuclear programme.[85]

Ankara's knowledge of nuclear matters was also harmed by American reluctance to share the results of its spying against the Soviets. For instance, the US Air Force Technical Applications Centre (AFTAC) Long Range Detection System, under the US Atomic Energy Detection System, started to collect data on the Soviet nuclear programme through the means of acoustic and seismic techniques from the early 1950s. These particular detection methods included Surface-Based Particulate Sampling and Surface-Based Whole Air Sampling. Turkey's capital city, Ankara, provided a suitable location for AFTAC operations: AFTAC's Ankara unit, Team 301 (codenamed Slipstream) was operational as winds from the Soviet test site at Kaspustin Yar carried the debris of nuclear fallouts towards Turkey.[86] However, the Turkish government was not kept fully aware of Team 301's activities and findings. Some items in these units were not even declared in the inventory list. Washington wanted to keep tight secrecy over its technical intelligence methods and prevent a possible leak to 'interested parties' in Turkey, which was felt to be under heavy espionage infiltration from the Soviet bloc. Also, revealing the nature of technical intelligence activities to the Turkish authorities had the potential to startle them due to the 'alien' ways of US intelligence.

On the last point, Wilbur Chase, the political officer in the US embassy in Ankara between 1955 and 1959, states:

> All of a sudden we were becoming very much interested in the study of clouds [in 1956], and we started putting up big balloons in the

air. And we were flying them so they were drifting across the Soviet Union. What we had was all sorts of camera and this stuff, hoping that the balloons would carry way over into the Philippines or China or someplace where we could recover them. And the Soviets objected to this strenuously–these crazy guys. These balloons were being floated from Turkey, and we got a couple of them brought back. They never got across the border, and we picked them up and brought them in and put them in the parking lot back of the embassy. And so here were these damn things laying out there. And you could walk over and see the lenses that they had. These were very definitely spy jobs. What made us have trouble with the Turks was that all of a sudden, out of Washington, we apologized to the Russians and we said we wouldn't do it anymore–and we didn't tell the Turks until afterwards.[87]

Chase's recollection points to a crucial parameter in the characteristics of the technical intelligence liaison between Turks and Americans. The TGS and Atomic Energy Commission simply did not have the scientific background needed to understand the American methods of nuclear spying. Moreover, the Americans were not eager to inform them about their capabilities. Ankara could easily recognize the U-2 project as a reconnaissance exercise. Balloons that looked like 'alien' technology, and top-secret Operation Centres with radar and listening bases were totally outside the experience of Turkish decision makers at that time. However, for the American intelligence community the usefulness of SIGINT and radar bases formed an indispensable part of their spying on Soviet nuclear capabilities. For instance, the US Defence Intelligence Agency reported in March 1962 that their knowledge of the Soviet test sites was derived primarily from other sources rather than U-2 photography.[88]

Alternative sources to the U-2 flights were radar bases and listening posts. Due to the declassification process on the American side, and memoirs of SIGINT operatives gradually surfacing in recent years, it is now possible to form an account of how successful these activities were and what proportion they formed of intelligence diplomacy between the Turks and Americans. For instance, a major ground-based radar system was constructed in the south-eastern Turkish village of Pirinçlik, near Diyarbakır, in late 1955, under the cover of TUSLOG Det-9 as a US Air Force base. A study evaluating the role of the Pirinçlik radar base appeared in the CIA's confidential *Studies in Intelligence* journal in 1964, stating:

> The first installation at Diyarbakir was originally intended to provide mere surveillance of the USSR's missile test range at Kapustin Yar south of Stalingrad-that is to detect missile launchings. The data it came to produce, however, transcended surveillance, permitting the derivation of missile trajectories, the identification of earth satellite launches, the calculation of a satellite's ephemeris (position and orbit), and the synthesis of booster rocket performance.[89]

Apart from the radar bases, the SIGINT posts also provided indispensable help for American spying missions. These bases, most of them not very large, were scattered throughout Turkey, but with a concentration in the Black Sea region and Turkish Straits, under the cover of logistic support units. They were operated by the security agencies of the three main branches of the military, with Air Force, Navy and Army members being present according to their specifications.[90] Officers sent to these bases were trained by the NSA at Fort Meade in linguistics (Turkish, Russian, Bulgarian and Romanian being the main languages), cryptology and electronic systems engineering. Once they were stationed in these bases, they were instructed to limit their contacts with Turkish soldiers and officers, who were usually based outside the perimeter fences of the units responsible for physical security and liaison.[91]

The operations within these (at the time ultra-secret) bases have come to the surface via the recollections of their former officers. For instance, James Baker, who served as an ASA Traffic Controller in TUSLOG Det-4 Diogenes Station in Sinop between 1957 and 1959, states that they were able to detect three Soviet missile test ranges in detail: Kapustin Yar Missile Test Range (codename: KYMTR), which had surface-to-surface missiles with a range of up to 1,000 nautical miles; Tyuratam Missile and Space Complex (codename: TTMTR), which had Intercontinental Ballistic Missiles and Space Launches; and the Vladimirovka – Lake Balkhash Test Range (codename: VLBTR), which fired air-breathing missiles and naval missiles into the Barents Sea.[92] When necessary, the intelligence gathered from these remote posts was transported to the US embassy in Ankara with a top-secret courier. Although it was forbidden by Turkish law for US personnel to carry arms outside of their bases, these couriers were armed with guns to defend the dossiers with their lives if any interruption occurred to their mission. The evidence suggests that, at least until the SOFA agreement and its secret extensions were amended in 1969, Ankara was not provided with a substantial share of information from the US intelligence bases. Moreover, the operational control of all these deployed units was retained in the hands of US military authorities, implying that neither Turkish nor NATO military authorities could control them.[93]

It is apparent from known top-secret Turkish intelligence reports between the mid-1950s and 1960s that the methods, knowledge and sources that Ankara possessed regarding Soviet weapon capabilities and the Soviet nuclear programme were not capable of providing any meaningful intelligence. For instance, a top-secret intelligence report in August 1955, focusing on the extent of the USSR's natural resources used in the weapons industry, stated that uranium production was non-existent and that the Soviets were even struggling to balance their economic development programme with war production.[94] Again, a top-secret intelligence report produced in November 1955, focusing on Soviet weapons production and development (including locations of the sites of production), did not refer at all to nuclear weapons or to intermediate-range missiles that could target Turkish territory.[95] But this lack of information on the Soviet nuclear programme became a spur to the development of Turkish intelligence diplomacy. First, Turkey aimed to gain more from multilateral cooperation with partners who possessed more information on Soviet nuclear matters, in exchange for the Turks helping with further intelligence operations. Second, as seen above, Ankara pressed for the transfer of some TUSLOG posts to Turkish control in the late 1960s, allowing Turkish intelligence to start producing its own intelligence on the Soviet nuclear programme.

## Conclusion

The development of nuclear weapons posed a serious threat to Turkey, which sought to acquire its own eyes and ears on the Soviet nuclear threat while co-operating with its Western allies. However, even as the Turks sought a greater US commitment to their security, Ankara was sceptical about Washington's reliability when it came to sharing intelligence or confirming Anglo-American support in the event of a Soviet invasion. Ankara utilized intelligence diplomacy to acquire the necessary technical know-how and infrastructure for gathering nuclear information; and it had a valuable tool in its readiness to 'run' human agents in joint efforts with the MI6 and CIA. The SOFA agreement potentially marked an important step forward. But the continued lack of Turkish intelligence personnel capable of comprehending nuclear matters and electronic intelligence analysis meant Ankara had to rely for many years on the estimates produced by her Western friends. And the intelligence passed to the Turks by Washington remained limited in its scope and content. For instance, although Soviet missile sites in the Caspian region (which posed a serious threat to Turkey) were detected through SIGINT bases in Turkey, the Americans did not share the intelligence on them with Ankara. Moreover, the inadequacy of intelligence personnel, the problems caused by inter-departmental feuds between the Foreign Ministry and the Atomic Energy Commission, economic weaknesses and the political turmoil around 1960, all hampered Turkish efforts to build its own capabilities.

The episode on intelligence cooperation highlights a major characteristic of Turkish intelligence diplomacy. The existence of a major external threat does not necessarily provide flawless intelligence cooperation among allies. In this case, a Soviet Union capable of a nuclear strike on major Turkish targets did not stimulate a more cautious approach from Turkish decision makers. Moreover, domestic considerations, such as the survival of the then political regime in Turkey, triumphed over Cold War security considerations. Intelligence diplomacy was seen as a means of leverage by Turkey, a minor partner, over the major allies, the United States and the United Kingdom, to sustain economic aid, and which would only be effective if it served the interests of the incumbent government. Therefore, also due to the hybrid nature of the regime in Turkey, a fragmentation among government structures emerged. This particularly affected American aid to Turkey, since Washington was becoming increasingly concerned that the politicisation of the Turkish bureaucracy was damaging its economic and military capabilities.

Such characteristics of Turkish intelligence diplomacy with the West prevailed regarding cooperation on Cold War subversive threats, where the allies could not create a consensus and national (sometimes even domestic political) concerns shaped intelligence diplomacy more than the Cold War itself. The next chapter examines the key features of Turkish intelligence diplomacy on counter-subversion matters.

## Notes

1. Sudoplatov, et. al., *Special Tasks*.
2. For an earlier account of the Soviet atomic spies, please see B. Newman, *Soviet Atomic Spies* (London, 1952).
3. P. Hennessy, *The Secret State: Whitehall and the Cold War* (London, 2003), 33.
4. Sudoplatov, et. al., *Special Tasks*, 183.
5. Grey, *New Spymasters*, 45.
6. Hennessy, *The Secret State*, 31.
7. NARA: RG59: Box 3744: 782.5612/7-259: 'Memorandum of Conversation: Zorlu's Visit to the Secretary', 2 July 1959.
8. NARA: RG59: Box 3744: 782.5612/4-1659: 'Memorandum: IRBMs for Greece and Turkey', 16 April 1959'.

9   Sudoplatov, *Special Tasks*, 181.
10  Hennessy, *The Secret State*, 31.
11  For detailed accounts on decision making regarding the Berlin Blockade and the use of nuclear weapons, please see R. K. Betts, *Nuclear Blackmail and Nuclear Balance* (Washington, DC, 1987), chapter 2; and also see, A. Shlaim, *The United States and the Berlin Blockade, 1948–1949: A Study in Crisis Decision-Making* (Berkeley, CA, 1983).
12  Sudoplatov, *Special Tasks*, 210–211.
13  Grey, *New Spymasters*, 55.
14  K. Kirisci, 'Refugees of Turkish Origin: "Coerced Immigrants" to Turkey since 1945', *International Migration*, 34:3 (1996), 385–412.
15  B. Page, et.al., *Philby: The Spy Who Betrayed a Generation* (London, 1977), 191.
16  The Joint Intelligence Bureau was a new post-war civilian intelligence organization formed to focus on military affairs in 1946 by three wartime agencies, the Ministry of Economic Warfare (MEW), the Inter-Service Topographic Department (ISTD) and the Intelligence Section (Operations) (IS(O)). For more information on the JIB and its activities please see H. Dylan, 'The Joint Intelligence Bureau: (Not So) Secret Intelligence for the Post-War World', *Intelligence and National Security*, 27:1 (2012), 27–45.
17  Following information released under the author's FOI request, see 158/15/48G: Telegram: FO to Ankara, 13 April 1948; 158/16/48G: Telegram: Ankara to FO), 30 April 1948.
18  K. Philby, *My Silent War: The Autobiography of Kim Philby* (London, 1989), 126.
19  TNA: DEFE 60/127: JIB 4/A/104: 'British Intelligence Survey: USSR Defences (Plans) Detailed Defences (by Areas) Black Sea, Transcaucasia and Caspian Sea, July 1951'.
20  NATO: SGWM-024-59: 'Inadequacy of the Early Warning System in Turkey', 13 January 1959.
21  Eisenhower Presidential Library and Archives: National Security Council Staff Papers, Registry Series: Box 12: 'Report on the Mutual Security Program in Turkey', Bureau of Budget, July 1957.
22  Ibid., 4.
23  Ibid., 5.
24  Ibid., 4.

25  NARA: RG59: Box 16: 'Letter from Lampton Berry to Flecther Warren', 1 August 1957.
26  Ibid.
27  NARA: RG59: Box 16: 'Letter from Fletcher Warren to Lampton Berry', 13 August 1957.
28  ADST: Foreign Affairs Oral History Project: Anthony D. Marshall, Interviewed by Richard L. Jackson, 20 February 1998.
29  W. C. Eveland, *Ropes of Sand: America's Failure in the Middle East* (New York: 1980), 263.
30  See Chapter 6 for this discussion.
31  L. Petkova, 'The Ethnic Turks in Bulgaria: Social Integration and Impact on Bulgarian-Turkish Relations, 1947–2000', *The Global Review of Ethnopolitics*, 1:4 (2002), 44.
32  A. Zhelyazkova, 'The Social and Cultural Adaptation of Bulgarian Immigrants in Turkey', in A. Zhelyazkova, ed., *Between Adaptation and Nostalgia: The Bulgarian Turks in Turkey* (Sofia, 1998), 2.
33  Emigres in Turkey from various ethnic backgrounds were also used in various CIA–MI6 operations. One notable example of the use of Albanian emigres in Turkey is the unsuccessful Operation Valuable to overthrow Enver Hoxha in October 1949. Please see Y. Totrov, 'Western Intelligence Operations in Eastern Europe, 1945–1954', *Journal of Intelligence History*, 5:1 (2005), 71–80.
34  For the Turkish minority in Bulgaria, see J. W. Warhola and O. Boteva, 'The Turkish Minority in Contemporary Bulgaria', *Nationalities Papers*, 31:3 (2003), 255–279.
35  NATO: SG 007-35: Standing Group: 'Final Security Surveys in Greece and Turkey', 13 February 1951.
36  NATO: SG 007-30: Standing Group: 'A Report by the Security Coordinating Committee on the Security Surveys in Greece and Turkey', 9 January 1951.
37  NATO: C-M(59)94-Part 2-TU: 'Report on 1959 Annual Review: Chapter on Turkey', 3 December 1959.
38  NATO: SGM-0341-53: 'Report on the Visit of the Intelligence Committee to National Staffs in Ankara, Turkey, Athens, Greece and Rome, Italy, London, United Kingdom and the Supreme Headquarters Allied Powers Europe', 9 March 1953.

39  Author's Collection: TC.MMV. Erkaniharbiyeyi Umumiye Riyaseti İstihbarat Başkanlığı 1.Şube 1.Kısım, no: 218/1187, 'Düşman:İktisadi-Sovyetler Birliğinde madenler, stratejik ana hammaddeler ve gücü', 20 August 1955.
40  Wilson Center Digital National Security Archives: 'Information on Turkish Intelligence Interest on the Uranium Mine Buhovo', 25 March 1955, History and Public Policy Program Digital Archive, Archive of the Ministry of the Interior, Sofia, Fond 2, Record 1, File 1968. Obtained by the Bulgarian Cold War Research Group.
41  M. S. Goodman, *Spying on the Nuclear Bear: Anglo-American Intelligence and the Soviet Bomb* (Stanford, CA, 2007), 41.
42  Ibid., 103.
43  Ibid., 137.
44  Wilson Center Digital National Security Archives: 'Information from Romania on Turkish Intelligence Interests towards Bulgaria', 9 April 1960, History and Public Policy Program Digital Archive, Archive of the Ministry of the Interior, Sofia, Fond 2, Record 1, File 2124. Obtained by the Bulgarian Cold War Research Group.
45  TNA: FO 371/128652: G1692/1: Mr. Speaight to FO, 'Trial of Turkish Spies', 16 March 1956.
46  Petkova, 'The Ethnic Turks in Bulgaria: Social Integration and Impact on Bulgarian-Turkish Relations, 1947–2000', 44.
47  This paragraph was published as a blog post by the author. Archive files can be found in the text. See E. Bezci, 'Ankara's Hidden Hand: Turkish Covert Ops Then and Now', *War on the Rocks*, 1 January 2016.
48  Aldrich, *GCHQ*, 5.
49  Ibid., 103.
50  Goodman, *Spying on the Nuclear Bear*, 102.
51  National Security Agency/Central Security Service, 'Information Paper: TOP SECRET//SI//NOFORN:NSA Intelligence Relationship with Turkey – Turkish National Intelligence Organization (MIT) and the Turkish SIGINT Intelligence Directorate (SIB)', 15 April 2013.
52  5 U.S.T. 1465 TURKEY: STATUS OF UNITED STATES FORCES IN TURKEY: TIAS 3020 5 U.S.T. 1465: 23 June 1954.
53  NARA: RG59: Box 4069: 782.5/10-2753: 'Top Secret Telegram from USCINCEUR to Department of Army', 27 October 1953.

54 NARA: RG59: Box 4056: Telegram from Kohler to Secretary of State, 13 August 1954.
55 Ibid.
56 M. Gönlübol, 'NATO and Turkey' in K. H. Karpat, ed., *Turkey's Foreign Policy in Transition: 1950–1974* (Leiden, 1975), 37.
57 NARA: RG59: Box 3739: 782.5/11-2056: 'Memorandum for Acting Secretary', 20 November 1956.
58 NARA: RG59: Box 3739: 782.5/11-2056: 'Top Secret Telegram from Ankara to Secretary of State', 24 January 1957.
59 Peter J. Roman, *Eisenhower and the Missile Gap* (Ithaca, NY, 1995), 25–26.
60 Ibid., 45.
61 ADST: Training Foreign Affairs Oral History Project, Anthony D. Marshall, Interviewed by Richard L. Jackson, initial interview date: 20 February 1998.
62 NATO: C-M(58)141-PART 2: Report on the 1958 Annual Review, Chapter on Turkey, 6 December 1958.
63 D. Brugioni, *Eyes in the Sky: Eisenhower, the CIA, and Cold War Aerial Espionage* (Annapolis, MD, 2011), 143.
64 B. K. Yeşilbursa, 'The "Revolution" of 27 May 1960 in Turkey: British Policy towards Turkey', *Middle Eastern Studies*, 41:1 (2005), 128.
65 A. A. Holmes. *Social Unrest and American Military Bases in Turkey and Germany since 1945* (Cambridge, 2014), 59–63. Also see A. Güney, 'Anti-Americanism in Turkey: Past and Present', *Middle Eastern Studies*, 44:3 (2008), 471–487.
66 Gönlübol, 'NATO and Turkey', 40.
67 TNA: PREM 11/298: C.(52) 362: 'Note by the Secretary of State for Foreign Affairs: Situation in Turkey', 24 October 1952.
68 NARA: RG59: Box 3744: 782.5411/4-1058: 'Telegram from Warren to Dulles', 10 April 1958.
69 Ibid.
70 See H. Dylan, 'Britain and the Missile Gap: British Estimates on the Soviet Ballistic Missile Threat, 1957–61', *Intelligence and National Security*, 23:6 (2008), 777–806.
71 Ibid.
72 TBMM Tutanakları: 10. Dönem, 10. Cilt, 36. Birleşim, 13 February 1956.
73 Ibid.

74  Eisenhower Presidential Library: Papers as President: Dulles-Herteg Series: Box 12: Turkish Information Office, News from Turkey, 12 May 1955.
75  TBMM Tutanakları: 10. Dönem, 13. Cilt, 91. Birleşim, 15 August 1956.
76  Ibid.
77  NARA: RG59: Box 4069: 782.5611/4-1051: 'Letter from Turkish Embassy in Washington to the Secretary of State', 10 April 1951.
78  NARA: RG59: Box 4069: 782.5611/6-651: 'Telegram from Ankara to Department of State', 6 June 1951.
79  Milli Savunma Akademisi Konferanslari, Nukleer Siyaset, Harp Akademileri Basimevi, 5 January 1956, p. 36.
80  Ibid.
81  TNA: FCO 1/12: FCO/C/7/53: 'Hyers to Hainsworth', 24 November 1957.
82  Ibid.
83  TNA: FO 371/149581: IAE 444/1: 'Turkey's Nuclear Programme: Telegram from Ankara to FO', 27 January 1960.
84  Ibid.
85  For a brief but informative history of the Turkish Nuclear Programme, please see A. Stein, *Turkey's Nuclear History Holds Lessons for the Future* (Monterey, CA, 2013).
86  M. Welch, 'AFTAC Celebrates 50 Years of Long Range Detection', *The AFTAC Monitor* (October 1997), 12. Also see, Goodman, *Spying on the Nuclear Bear*, 104.
87  ADST: Foreign Affairs Oral History Project: Wilbur B. Chase, interviewed by Charles Stuart Kennedy, 24 July 1990.
88  Defence Intelligence Agency: DIA Intelligence Summary 51-62, 2 March 1962.
89  S. G. Zabetakis and J. F. Peterson, 'Diyarbakir Radar', *Studies in Intelligence*, 8:4 (1964), 41.
90  T. Bazzett, *Soldier Boy: At Play in the ASA* (Reed City, MI, 2008), 130–131.
91  Ibid., p. 132.
92  Jim Baker, ASA Traffic Controller Det-4 Sinop between 1957 and 1959, Days of Our lives: Recollections from ASA in Turkey.
93  NARA: RG59: Box 3739: 782.5/12-2856: 'Top Secret Telegram: Dulles to Moscow', 28 December 1956.

94 Author's Collection: TC.MMV. Erkaniharbiye Umumiye Riyaseti İstihbarat Başkanlığı 1.Şube 1.Kısım: Düşman, 'Sovyetler Birliğinde madenler, stratejik ana hammaddeler durumu ve gücü', 20 August 1955.
95 Author's Collection: TC.MMV. Erkaniharbiye Umumiye Riyaseti İstihbarat Başkanlığı 1.Şube 1.Kısım: Düşman, 'Sovyetler Birliğinin Silah Endüstrisi ve Gücü', 23 November 1955.

5

# Counter-Subversion: Our Common 'Enemies'

The domestic dimensions of intelligence work during the Cold War played a major role in the Middle East. In the Turkish case, both the political police and the secret intelligence agency MAH became involved in counter-subversion activities, especially communist penetration of Turkey and Kurdish secessionist activities. The MAH, which acted in practice as both a domestic security service and a foreign secret intelligence service, was the leading agency to conduct intelligence activities both at home and abroad.

Beginning with Ankara's decision to align itself with the West against the Soviets during the Cold War, the country sought to synchronize intelligence activities with its British and American counterparts through bilateral relationships, and through multilateral alliances such as NATO and CENTO. Ankara's growing worries about Soviet subversion were reflected in both its bilateral and multilateral intelligence diplomacy. Soviet intelligence 'believed they had an in-built advantage in the struggle with the Main Adversary [US] and its allies for power and influence in the Middle East'.[1] This was due to the USSR's geographical proximity to the region, and its ability to exploit the special relationship between Israel and the United States, which made the Arab states in the region 'natural Allies' of the Kremlin.[2] Given these assumptions, Turkey stood as a solid ally of the West, yet Turkey's concerns about Soviet subversion in the region did not necessarily overlap with her Western Allies.

This does not mean that Turkish decision makers were concerned only with communist activities. The Kurdish question was often a more serious concern for Turkish intelligence. Thus, the Turks needed to persuade their Western allies that Kurdish activities posed a serious threat to the Western Alliance if they wanted to obtain support for anti-Kurdish counter-subversive operations. Ankara's intelligence diplomacy at a bilateral and multilateral level was partially successful in this regard. In order to analyse the characteristics of Turkish-Western intelligence diplomacy regarding counter-subversion operations, it is first necessary to track the development of Turkish threat perceptions concerning subversive activities, before we reveal the key features of Turkey's bilateral and multilateral relationships.³

## Intelligence-made enemies: Communists and Kurds

In the literature, Turkey's strong feelings about the Kurdish question tend to be attributed to Ankara's obsession with the maintenance of its territorial integrity.⁴ This is also the case regarding communist activities in Turkey – owing to the country's firm anti-communist stance and its strong measures against them, the communist movement and influence in Turkey has often been dismissed as an insignificant movement throughout the Cold War, though there is still a communist movement in the country even after the end of the Cold War.⁵ Moreover, one study of the Turkish Communist Party (TKP) claimed that it had a negligible presence among the Kurdish community in Turkey because the TKP's cadres perceived the Kurdish nationalist movement as feudal and backward.⁶ This was not what the Turkish authorities believed during our period, at least until the 1960s.

A common theme in the literature is that Communism was an insignificant movement in Turkey and that the TKP was unsuccessful in penetrating Turkish society until the late 1960s.⁷ Above all, Turks were traditionally anti-Russian anyway. One study notes that Communism 'might have taken hold' in Turkey 'if it had originated in the West', but that the TKP was seen as 'simply a modern Russian instrument for achieving an old Russian goal'.[8] In hindsight this assessment sounds reasonable enough, but this was not the Turkish view at the time.

It is worth mentioning here George Harris's classic work on the origins of Communism in Turkey. He demonstrates that the communist movement in the early twentieth century was not only controlled by a small émigré group in Baku, but had deep roots in Turkish society. Similar to manifestations of the Kemalist movement led by Mustafa Kemal Atatürk, the TKP also promised rapid and radical social reform. Harris noted that 'as an intellectual movement, as a vision of historical development', communism had 'a considerable fascination for Turks'.[9] The fundamental difference between them was that, whereas the Kemalists looked to the West, the TKP looked to the East, which was about to triumph over the 'decadent' West.[10] It is therefore natural that, in November 1920, Mustafa Kemal decided to accept the establishment of the People's Communist Party of Turkey, an 'official' Turkish Communist Party independent from Moscow, to forestall potential danger from the Bolshevik-backed TKP.[11]

Studies published in Turkish have shown that, while maintaining some diplomatic channels with the Soviet Union, which supported Mustafa Kemal's government in the Turkish War of Independence (1919–23), and while showing good will towards the Bolshevik regime by recognizing the 'official' Communist Party, Kemal ordered the Secret Police chief, Hafiye Teşkilatı, to start monitoring his own military and civil officers with any possible connections to the Bolsheviks from September 1920 onward. Bolsheviks were also believed to have been instigating a communist uprising in the Kurdish provinces.[12] During the interwar period, the Turkish authorities maintained the same position: while keeping some diplomatic communications with the Soviets, and temporarily collaborating with them in certain respects, it did not hesitate to suppress signs of domestic communism.[13] The TKP was forced to go underground from 1925, as it was outlawed by the Turkish authorities.[14] Despite an insistence by the Comintern that the Soviet Union must cut its links with the Kemalists, who were repressing the

TKP as well as most other left-wing movements, Moscow also adopted a dual approach in its foreign policy towards Turkey.[15] In the post-war period, the relationship between Turkey and the USSR became more antagonistic.

Some accounts of clandestine activities by the Soviet Union have begun to appear in recent years. Based on declassified records of the People's Commissariat for Internal Affairs (NKVD), recent works show that the Soviets indeed 'planned to stir up disturbance among the Kurdish tribes to thus to pressure Iran, Turkey and the oil regions of Iraqi Mosul'.[16] According to Hasanlı, in October 1945 local NKVD officers wrote to Lavrenti Beria, head of their organization, that they had recruited twenty-one experienced NKVD and People's Commissariat for State Security (NKGB) officers and seventy-five militants from local residents who were closely linked to the NKGB. These recruits were capable of creating armed guerrilla units from the local population and arranging operations to 'annihilate people and organizations'.[17] TGS was alarmed by a report, prepared by the MAH, on recent military manoeuvres of the Soviet armed forces in regions adjacent to Turkey, in Caucasia and the Balkans. The head of the TGS, Kazım Orbay, met with the US military attaché in October 1945 and shared intelligence on Soviet activities in the region.[18] Nevertheless, the Soviet ambassador, Vladimir Vinogradov, rejected claims by his Turkish, American and British counterparts regarding Soviet aggression at a meeting in Ankara on 2 November 1945. He implied that Turkey should not expect a friendly attitude from the Soviet Union, since Turkey had failed to join their efforts to fight against Nazi Germany during the war.[19] A 'most reliable source' of the MAH, perhaps from a circle of exiled communist members in Bern, Switzerland, noted that Soviet tactics would involve ending their threats over Turkey's eastern provinces and access through the Dardanelles before the scheduled conference of foreign ministers, with the British and Americans, in Moscow in March–April 1947. However, 'after the Moscow Conference, the Soviets would again increase their aggression since they perceived their claims on Eastern Turkey and Straits as a matter of national prestige'.[20]

As tension over Soviet demands in the Turkish Straits reached its height, Ankara became more concerned about communist infiltration in the country. The minister of the Interior, Şükrü Sökmensüer, explicitly stated his concern in parliament about communist infiltration in the country's labour unions, the armed forces, and the military high schools and colleges.[21] His concern was indeed well grounded, for Turkey's newly established MAH identified communist cells and networks within the army.[22] A series of raids on these cells and networks in 1946 and 1947, led by the MAH, proved that the outlawed TKP was financed by and received logistical support from the Soviet Consulate in Istanbul. Kitai Goridoski, a secretary at the Soviet Consulate who was in contact with the TKP, provided the party with US$1,000 every three months.[23]

The Turks were concerned not only by communist activities in the country; but they were also active in trying to eliminate external links with the TKP. Based on information obtained through the TKP, from 1950 onward Turkey monitored the activities of exiled TKP members in Paris.[24] In early 1951 there was a series of debates in the Turkish parliament concerning communist activities in the country. When asked about the exiles in Paris, the foreign minister, Fuat Köprülü, responded that there was clear evidence that these were being funded by Moscow and other communist states.[25] Some Turkish politicians called for stronger and firmer actions against the communists, even for laws that ensured the 'death penalty for being a communist' in the country.[26] It was estimated that communist propaganda publication materials, printed and directed from abroad, appeared 'even in the remote villages in Bursa'.[27] Later in October 1951, a series of investigations by the MAH also led to a number of arrests of communist military officers in Istanbul, who were then brought before Ankara's high military court and convicted.[28]

Turkey never became complacent about enforcing its anti-communist measures. The hunt for underground TKP members continued throughout the post-war period. According to one account, the TKP was virtually eliminated in 1953, when 131 of its members were convicted and imprisoned.[29] The extent to which the Turkish security service successfully contained the spread of communist movements in the country is noteworthy. Indeed, a document released under the Freedom of Information Act – a threat assessment prepared by the British Security Service, MI5, in July 1958 – confidently stated that, despite the anxieties of the Turkish authorities, 'the problem [of Communism] does not exist in organised form' in Turkey.[30] An assessment produced by the CIA in 1960 came to the same conclusion, stating that 'Turkish Communists remain virtually neutralised by the security forces'.[31] The report also noted the effectiveness of Turkey's anti-communist propaganda measures, claiming that 'the small flow of foreign propaganda is believed to be effectively blocked' and that '[Eastern] Bloc broadcasters have been unsuccessfully trying to exploit Turkey's chronic economic difficulties'.[32]

Yet although the MAH successfully rounded up a number of communists in the country, communists or fellow-travellers sometimes penetrated government offices. For instance, the MAH discovered in 1958 that a Turkish diplomat named Saim Polat was passing classified military and diplomatic papers to the Bulgarian Intelligence Service through their embassy in Ankara. MAH agents tailed Polat for several months and caught him red-handed. Polat was sentenced to death for treason, but his sentence was later commuted to fifteen years hard labour. When reporting on the Polat 'Spy' Case, US consular officer John Goodyear states that 'the calibre of both the culprit and the materials he is said to have sold were at a very low level, but the Government of Turkey is not disposed to treat any evidence of disloyalty, no matter how innocuous, with leniency'.[33] However, the Turkish government did not disclose to the public that the diplomat was spying for the Bulgarians. Moreover, Ankara did not even take any action against the Bulgarian Legation in Turkey. In public statements and even in the court ruling, it was stated that the diplomat was spying for an undisclosed country. Since this was a relatively minor issue, Ankara did not want to create additional problems with her north-western neighbour. However, it made sense for Ankara to use examples like the Polat case as 'proof' that a communist threat existed in Turkey and that Ankara needed help from its allies in other counter-insurgency operations against domestic targets by trying to frame all the dissidents as part of a communist conspiracy to oust the current regime. Not all of these dissidents were necessarily communists. Some were Kurdish. Since Kurdish nationalism did not necessarily fall into the framework of 'shared threat' of communist subversion in the region, Ankara had to convince its allies that Kurdish nationalism was a part of the Soviet intrigues in the region. However, Turkish intelligence diplomacy did not really succeed in doing so.

## Do Kurds have no friends but the mountains?

The political position of Kurds is well described by the famous Kurdish proverb: they 'have no friends but the mountains'.[34] Kurds had frequently been scattered among neighbouring powers, previously in the borderlands between the Ottoman and Safavid Empires, and during the Cold War between Turkey, Iraq, Iran and Syria. Indeed, Turkey's primary concern regarding internal subversion in that latter period was not communist infiltration in society, but the Kurds, who constituted more than 10 per cent of the population. Ankara showed no tolerance to Kurdish independence movements from the outset. Soon after the establishment of the Republic in 1923, Turkish authorities brutally suppressed a series of Kurdish uprisings.[35] Dan Kurzman claimed, when discussing subversive activities in Turkey, that 'the main "potential" threat from the Soviet Union was not about Communism but from "the Turkish Kurds", who would seek "an independent Kurdistan – a project that Russia has long sponsored as a means of fostering chaos in the Western-influenced Middle Eastern heartland"'.[36] In the Turkish case, the decision makers themselves were convinced that their traditional enemy, Russia, was using the Kurdish card to weaken the Turkish state. It was a similar rhetoric used by the British in their Cold War colonial struggles to frame any independence movement against them as communist.[37]

Some accounts of clandestine activities by the Soviet Union have begun to appear in recent years. They demonstrate that the Kremlin strategically supported postcolonial liberation movements from the 1950s onward, to help win the Cold War.³⁸ In the case of the Middle East, supporting anti-Western movements was part of Soviet attempts to undermine Western influence in the region.³⁹ This was because there was no prospect of the emergence of a major communist regime 'which would act as a model for the Arab world and spread revolution through the region'.⁴⁰ More importantly, the influential Iraqi-Kurdish leader, Mulla Mustafa Barzani (often called Mulla Mustafa by his colleagues), whose activities had been at the centre of concerns of the Turkish, Iraqi, Iranian and even Syrian governments, was actually a long-running KGB agent (code-named RAIS) from the end of the Second World War.⁴¹ According to Vladislav Zubok, in July 1961, by which time Barzani had returned to Baghdad from his exile in Moscow after the Iraqi Revolution, the KGB Chairman, Aleksandr Shelpin, suggested to the Soviet leader, Nikita Khrushchev, that 'old KGB connections' with Barzani, who was now the chairman of the Kurdish Democratic Party (KDP), should be used to 'activate the movement of the Kurdish population of Iraq, Iran and Turkey for the creation of an independent Kurdish' state.⁴² Thus, it is clear that the Soviets adopted a dual approach to achieve their end, supporting communist and also minority movements in the region at the same time.

The latter was especially the case as communist movements in the Middle East were ineffective – Middle Eastern governments were mostly anti-communist and adopted strong measures against communists. In 1965, Abdul Rahman Ghassemlou, a prominent Kurdish politician from the KDP's Iranian branch, reflected the Soviet point of view when advocating Kurdish self-determination: 'At present the struggle of the Kurdish people assumes, first of all, an anti-imperialist character, imperialism constituting the enemy number one. Political independence and liberation remain incomplete and insecure unless the political influence of imperialism is destroyed, unless imperialist pacts and military bases are abolished.'⁴³ The CIA estimated in 1959 that 'the USSR, while not neglecting to build up its assets among the Kurds, would view them primarily as a means of harassing and undermining Iran, probably in conjunction with following other moves to create trouble for the Shah'.[44] However, CIA analysts also estimated that 'there is little likelihood of the establishment of an independent Kurdistan … The security problem posed by the Kurds is minimal in Turkey, where the government and army have long exercised firm control and have had some success in encouraging assimilation'.[45] Again, this was not what Ankara believed at that time.

Turkey's attitudes towards the Kurdish community and a possible alignment of the Kurds with Russian/Soviet subversion activities can be traced back to the period of the Ottoman Empire. For Tsarist Russia, too, had seen Kurdish uprisings as possible subversive tools against the Ottomans.[46] After 1945, Turkey's concern was very much focused upon the potential link of the Kurds with the Soviets and considered both international and regional contexts. First, as an example of international concerns, when a delegation of Kurds was invited to the San Francisco Conference in 1945, which discussed the establishment of the United Nations, the Turks carefully monitored its activities.[47] Secondly, so far as the regional level was concerned, key developments included Kurdish activities in two neighbouring countries in 1946: the establishing of the Mahabad Republic of Kurdistan in Iran and the founding of the KDP in Iraq. This momentum continued with the establishment of three active propaganda centres, one located in Beirut, a second at Sauj Bulagh in western Iran and a third within the Communist Party of Iraq. It was also at this time that the Soviet Union officially announced its support for the Kurdish independence movement in the region.[48] Again, these developments were closely monitored through MAH's human agents in the region. The Turks soon discovered Soviet officials meeting with Kurdish tribal chiefs and arming 100,000 Kurdish fighters in the northeast of Iran.[49]

The Turkish authorities saw them as a potential domestic threat that the Soviets might exploit. A confidential report submitted to President İsmet İnönü, in 1946, suggested that the Soviets expected to expand their influence beyond the Iranian border.[50] In addition, the treatment of Kurds in the Soviet Union was believed to have influenced the Kurdish independence movement throughout the region. It included the settlement of Kurds in local *kolkhozs* since the 1920s; the establishment of Kurdish-speaking local schools; the training of Kurdologists and Kurdish propagandists at the Lenin Institute in Yerevan (the numbers of which exceeded 30,000); and conflict resolution between south Caucasian people, namely Kurds, Azeris, Armenians and Georgians in the South Caucasus.[51] Moreover, wartime Soviet propaganda, which had already tried to instigate a Kurdish independence movement in northern Iran, was noted.[52] In order to avoid similar developments in Turkey, the authorities closely monitored the eastern border to try to ensure that no agents could infiltrate across it.[53]

The MAH continued to monitor the activities of the Kurds and their links with the Soviets very closely. In response to a question raised, in 1953, in the Turkish parliament about the threat of a possible Kurdish separatist movement in the south-eastern parts of Turkey, the minister of the Interior, Ethem Menderes, stated that, despite the constitutional change from single-party rule to multi-party elections, 'our government is potent, careful and wise to strictly monitor even the smallest clandestine activities in the country'. He then confidently responded to the question, saying 'no one, whatever their backgrounds and treasonous their intentions might be, could dare to launch an uprising'.[54] Due to the nature of its activities, the methods and sources of the MAH remain secret. However, there is evidence to indicate that the MAH employed the following methods to monitor the activities of the Kurds: surveillance; wiretapping of communications and bugging of premises; mail interception; and agent infiltration.[55] By employing such varied methods, the MAH was able to obtain a clear picture of the organizational structure, key personnel and internal differences within the Kurdish groups in the country.[56]

Based on intelligence obtained from interrogation and foreign sources, the MAH placed eavesdropping devices in the premises of suspects, through which the links of the Kurds with the Soviets and also communists became clearer. One of these findings, for instance, led to the arrests of forty-nine Kurds and sympathizers, known as *49'lar*, who conspired for independence of the Kurds with other Kurdish groups in Iran, Iraq and Syria in 1959. The lead came from eavesdropping the home of Şevket Turan, a retired military colonel of Kurdish descent, who revealed his frequent meetings with Sabih Battalgazi, a military captain, who was in contact with other Kurdish groups in the region, including the Soviet-backed Barzani group in Iraq. Apart from the MAH, the CIA also reported that Barzani, at that time, was not well liked by other Kurdish groups, and that even some from his own tribe were against him. The CIA concluded that, if only to keep his political career alive, 'Barzani continued to espouse Kurdish independence and to avail himself of the organizational advantages of a close relationship with the Soviet Union'.[57] The MAH also found that the group's contact with the other Kurds was channelled through underground communist networks.[58] It was further discovered, from the interrogation of one of the conspirators, a contact for the Turkish group of the Europe Kurdish Student Association (EKSA), that the EKSA was acting in accordance with Soviet foreign policy aims in the region.[59] A report by the MAH noted that an Iraqi Kurd, Reşit Arif, who also attended the EKSA 4th Congress in Vienna, visited Moscow in the same year and met other activists to assess the strength and capabilities of the Kurds in the eastern part of Turkey.[60]

Based on such intelligence, the Turkish government unleashed precautionary security measures, often excessively, against the Kurds. For instance, shortly after Adnan Menderes's government was overthrown by Turkish army officers in May 1960, a group of Kurds began to demand Kurdish autonomy. The new military government moved fast and arrested 248 Kurds who were 'believed to have supported agitation for a free Kurdish State'.[61] Ankara's obsession with its Kurdish minority was at least in part justified by the inflow of alarming intelligence about Soviet relations with the Kurds. Thus, the government's fear of Communism merged with its fear of Kurdish independence. It is important to state here that Turkish intelligence were aware of the fact that the Kurdish problem predated the Cold War mostly stemming from domestic and regional problems after the fall of the Ottoman Empire. Moreover, now Ankara was concerned that the question could develop into an ethnic insurgency with the support of the Soviets.

In order to counter these threats, the Turks needed the support of their Western allies to enhance the MAH's capabilities at home and abroad, and to engage in psychological warfare against the Soviets and thereby counter their anti-Turkish propaganda. However, while the Turks were successful in obtaining the necessary support against the communists through intelligence diplomacy, they were not so successful when it came to getting Western help against Kurdish subversion. Also, even though they were allies, Ankara tried to conceal from Western countries that the Kurdish question was its weak spot. All these factors restricted the effectiveness of Turkish intelligence diplomacy on the Kurdish issue.

## Convincing allies

Turkey willingly shared her concerns about the subversive activities of the communists and the Kurds with the Americans and British, both of which were well aware of Soviet links with the communist and Kurdish independence movements in the region. The potential danger of Soviet exploitation of the Kurds was noted early by Washington's intelligentsia, in an article in the highly influential journal *Foreign Affairs* dated July 1946. It stated that the Kurdish independence movement in the Middle East was then the most dangerous of all in the region, since a successful Kurdish movement would carve out chrome-rich territories in Turkey and oil wells in Iraq and Iran, all with Soviet support.[62] The United States approached the Kurdish question in a similar way. Archibald Roosevelt, then a US army intelligence officer in Iraq in 1946, notes in his diary that a large group of Kurdish students from Istanbul University were visiting Iraq to meet Barzani's followers to discuss the Free Kurdistan movement.[63] An intelligence assessment report produced by the CIA, in June 1947, stated that Qazi Muhammed, the founder of the short-lived Mahabad Kurdish Republic in Iran in 1946 and 1947, 'permitted himself to be used as a Soviet "stooge" in his desire to further the Kurdish cause as he conceived it'.[64] The newly established CIA also stated, regarding the Soviet intentions and capabilities in Turkey:

> Communism has little appeal to the Turks, who are traditionally fearful of Russian intervention. The Soviet Union could achieve limited results in Turkey through continuing the war of nerves which imposes on Turkey the economic burden of continued maintenance of large military forces. The Soviet Union could also exert pressure on the Turkish Government by raising the question of the 'historic Georgian and Armenian lands' in Eastern Turkey, or fostering the movement for Kurdish autonomy.[65]

However, the Kurds' potential threat in the Middle East and their subversive potential in Turkey were perceived rather differently by Ankara on one side, and the Americans and British on the other. For the British and Americans, the Kurdish question was closely related to the defence of the Eastern Mediterranean in the event of a Soviet military attack against the region. It was not felt that the Kurds in Turkey possessed the potential or capability to influence Turkish politics according to Soviet desires. Also, Turkish Kurds were evaluated differently from the ones in Iraq, Iran and Syria, which were believed to be more vulnerable to Soviet penetration. This difference in the perception of the Soviet link with Kurdish activities was apparent in staff talks between American, British and Turkish military officers in Ankara in December 1950. The Turkish COS, General Yarmut, informed the Americans and British that access to the resource-rich area that began in northern Iran, and extended southwards to Mosul in Iraq, was of utmost importance in case of potential Russian military action. Thus, in the event of a possible military conflict, the Soviets were likely to use the Kurds in Iran, Iraq and Syria to seize an area in the vicinity of the oil fields and routes to the Middle East. When the US ambassador, George Wadsworth, asked General Yarmut about the possible contribution of Kurds in Turkey to the Soviet plans to seize these areas, Yarmut 'informed him that a small number near the border areas may participate, but for most part those who did would be relatives of the Syrian and Iraqi Kurds, but even they did, the number participating would be of no significance and are a Turkish problem'.[66]

Decision makers in Ankara were quite sensitive about foreign involvement in Turkey's Kurdish problem. So far as they were concerned, Kurdish secessionist activities and a growing Soviet interest in the Kurds were to be countered independently in Turkey and seen as a solely Turkish problem. But, while Ankara did not want any involvement regarding Kurds in Turkey, they still needed support from their allies to gather intelligence about Barzani's Soviet-supported Kurdish groups in the wider region. For this reason, the Turks often raised concerns about Barzani and his activities. However, both London and Washington had their own policies on the Kurds, which did not necessarily align with the ones pursued by Ankara.

The British became concerned about Soviet subversive activities among Turkey's Kurds as early as 1946. The British embassy warned that the Soviets were agitating Kurds in Turkey to rise up in the event of a Soviet incursion into eastern Turkey, and to unite with other Kurdish tribes in the region to found a 'Greater Kurdistan' which would carve out territories from Turkey, Iraq, Iran and Syria. The Soviet propagandists, whose centre was in Kalezava in Iran, penetrated Turkey from across the Turkish-Iranian border. However, the MAH employed strict measures to detect and apprehend Soviet agents. Two incidents reported by the British provide a remarkable demonstration of the British awareness of the situation, and of the Turks' rigorous measures. In late 1945, three Soviet propagandists were caught near the region of Van; they were gathering intelligence on Turkish routes of communication, food stores, telegraph lines and also were agitating amongst the Kurdish population in the region against the Turkish government. All three men were captured and executed. At the same time, the Soviets used the relatives of Turkish Kurds to contact and plant the seeds for a Kurdish uprising against the Turks. For instance, Soviet agents in 1945 instructed Mehmet Misto, the chief of the Mimighian tribe, to send some of his men to contact certain influential Kurdish local leaders in the Van region to organize an uprising. Mehmet Misto and his tribe had been part of the Zeylan uprising against the Turkish government in 1930. At that time, Ankara had fiercely suppressed the uprising, and forced Misto and his tribe to flee to Iran. His mission to contact his kinsmen in Turkey in 1945 and organize a Soviet-backed uprising against the Turks was prevented by the MAH.[67]

The Turks remained vigilant and proved capable of preventing Soviet infiltration among the country's Kurds. The British military attaché became convinced, by September 1946, after a tour of eastern Turkey, that the Turkish army was able to 'fight like a tiger' if a Soviet-supported Kurdish uprising occurred in Turkey's mountainous and Kurdish-populated eastern region.[68] While Ankara dealt with its own Kurdish problem (following what the British defined as an assimilation policy) the Turks asked their American and British allies to counter communist/nationalist activities in Iran, Iraq and Syria. Both Colonel Behçet Türkmen of the MAH, and the secretary-general of the Turkish Foreign Ministry, Feridun Cemal Erkin, passed intelligence obtained by the MAH on communist infiltration among the Syrian Kurds to the British military attaché in February 1946.[69] The Turkish consulate in Aleppo also passed more intelligence to their British counterparts in July 1946, about a meeting between Kurdish political and tribal leaders, with the support of the Soviets, to settle tribal differences and organize a Kurdish national movement.[70]

However, although the Turks regularly passed intelligence regarding the Soviet-Kurdish link in its adjacent countries to the British and Americans, these powers were not convinced about the nature of the threat. For instance, Mr Dennett, an attaché from the US legation in Syria, toured the Kurdish areas in Syria in November 1946 and reported that the Soviet infiltration among the Kurds in Syria was negligible, adding that most of the Kurds in Syria were not politically conscious at all.[71] Meanwhile, the British embassy in Tehran was also trying to influence the Kurds in the region, this time through Qasim

Agha of the Dekbhuri tribe in Iran, against Qazi Mohammed's Kurdish National Movement.⁷² The British and Americans were thus aware that the Kurdish national movement in the region was not entirely the product of Soviet propaganda and genuinely held the goal of national independence. The Turks ultimately failed to convince their British and American counterparts that Kurdish independence movements were nothing more than communist fronts.

In the 1950s, the issue of the Kurds and links between the Kurds and the Soviets were often raised by the Turks in the Baghdad Pact for discussion relating to anti-communist measures. The Turkish representative reported on the activities of the Kurds, including, in 1957, the confession of a Soviet agent, revealing that the Soviets instructed him to contact a group of Kurds to instigate subversion against the Turkish government for Kurdish independence; he also confessed there were links between communists and the Kurdish Youth Association based in Europe.⁷³ Nevertheless, the dynamics of the Pact prevented serious discussion on the issue, and the British rejected Turkish intelligence requests on the grounds that they were unreliable and politically motivated. When the Turks insisted that Kurdish nationalists were supported by the Soviets, the British response was 'nonsense'.⁷⁴ The British representatives in the region were encouraged not to bring unnecessary attention to the Kurdish issue with the Iraqi, Iranian and Turkish governments unless there was any specific request from the regional governments, on the grounds that they were 'extremely sensitive about the Kurdish minority'.⁷⁵ Amongst the three, the Turks were considered the most sensitive on this matter.⁷⁶

In the second half of the 1950s, when stability in the region began to deteriorate, the Turkish, Iraqi and Iranian governments were more concerned about Mulla Barzani and his influence on the Kurds in their respective countries. In the wake of the Iraqi Revolution in 1958, when a rumour was spread that the Iraqi Kurds were fighting against the revolutionary government in Baghdad, both the Turkish and Iranian governments sought to 'expropriate' Iraqi Kurdistan in order to hold on to the Kurds in their own countries.⁷⁷ Once Mulla Barzani had returned from the Soviet Union to Baghdad, after the revolution, the Turkish and Iranian governments kept a close eye on him and there was intelligence sharing between them, aided by the influx of refugees from anti-Barzani Kurdish tribes to both Turkey and Iran. They agreed bilaterally to set up a 'Turco-Iranian bureau' to work on the matter and to share any intelligence on Barzani's activities in Baghdad.[78] The MAH also observed Soviet involvement and its infiltration into Iraqi society, working closely with the Iraqi authorities.[79] Once Barzani was in full revolt against the Iraqi government in 1961, Turkish Prime Minister İsmet İnönü and Iraqi ambassador in Ankara, Talip Mushtaq, confirmed that Turkey and Baghdad would work closely against the Barzani threat, and monitor its activities in the border region.[80]

Turkish intelligence reports during the later period took a predominantly anti-Soviet and anti-communist slant. They periodically stated regarding the situation in Iraq, for instance, that the Soviet Union was pursuing a policy to establish a communist Kurdish state under the leadership of Mulla Barzani.[81] The existing literature makes clear, however, that, although Barzani was closely aligned with the Soviets, he was never a communist. A recent study on the CIA and the Kurds also shows that Barzani was flexible in choosing his allies and methods – all in order to achieve his objective of Kurdish independence. In the early 1960s, while he was fighting against the Iraqi government, Barzani, via his representative, first asked the United States for support and reminded the Americans that he was also prepared to approach the Soviets for assistance.[82] In Turkey's eyes, because of his association with the Soviets, Barzani was seen as a communist, but he was considered more like a puppet of the Soviets. In fact, Turkey was always likely to claim that internal threats had foreign roots. In June 1963 the minister of the Interior, Hıfzı Oğuz Bekata, reported to the Turkish parliament:

> Upon the investigation and arrests made by the National Security Service, we succeeded in bringing an extreme leftist group in front of justice ... this extreme leftist group is *commanded by foreign countries* which have particular interest in the Kurdish activities in Turkey ... Our government is following these activities very closely and taking

necessary steps against them. Again, these people [referring to the rounded-up Kurdish activists] have *their roots in foreign countries* and these people are *mostly Communists*. Our investigation has revealed that all provocative, separatist and subversive activities in the country are *commanded by foreign countries*.[83]

Turkish intelligence diplomacy concerning the Kurds thus aimed to convince its Western partners that Kurdish nationalist activities were a product of Soviet agitation. However, both the British and Americans considered that the Kurdish issue was more deep rooted than that. The British Foreign Office noted, in a report in 1958 on Soviet propaganda among the Kurds, that the Turks had long faced uprisings from the Kurds. They had tried to suppress them by assimilation, but the Kurds always resisted and would continue to do so in the future.[84] The CIA made a similar estimation regarding the Kurdish question. According to Sherman Kent, the CIA's legendary assistant director for Estimates:

> The Kurds will continue to have considerable nuisance value as rebels – or potential rebels – at least for some years to come. As a traditionally war like and still largely nomadic or semi-nomadic people who occupy relatively remote areas and have a long history of bad blood with the authorities of their host countries, the Kurds could fairly readily be aroused if given arms and funds from outside. Even in the absence of an acknowledged over-all leader, enough tribes might be stirred up to make considerable trouble for a weak host country, especially if it had other security problems to contend with at the same time.[85]

The CIA was convinced that the Kurdish movement was not necessarily subordinate to the Soviets. The decentralized nature of Kurdish tribes, and the lack of a single leader uniting the Kurds, meant that any number of outside powers could engage some Kurds for their own purposes. As a result, Ankara could not persuade the Americans and British of its perception of the Kurdish national movement. Nonetheless, Turkey was able to use intelligence diplomacy effectively when it came to communist subversion activities and the use of psychological warfare against the communists and the Soviet Union.

## Our common enemy

Ankara efficiently countered its domestic communist threat, even during the Second World War. The MAH paid particular attention to communist propaganda among university students and workers, and managed to compile a very detailed picture of communist networks in Turkey. The intelligence service was able to eliminate the communist movement in Turkey, even during the war period when that movement was in its infancy.[86] But, despite such Turkish successes, starting from the end of the war, the Soviets increased their propaganda activities in Turkey.

The memoirs of Oleg Penkovsky, a GRU agent in Ankara during the mid-1950s, reveal that Soviet intelligence established special intelligence and propaganda posts in Batumi, Sukhumi, Leninakan and Sevastopol to conduct operations against Turkey.[87] The main Soviet aim was to create Turkish opposition to the Western alignment of the Turkish government after the war. Alongside the Soviets, Turkish communists in exile also criticized their government as a tool of US imperialism. Communist propaganda was not only directed against the government, but also against NATO and CENTO. Trying to undermine NATO and CENTO was in line with Soviet subversive aims in the region.[88] For instance, at the EKSA 4th Congress, held in Vienna in July 1959, it was agreed to condemn CENTO as a bulwark of Western imperialism, and to work together with the Soviet and Iraqi Communists for the independence of the Kurds in the region.[89] Thus, both Turkish and Western interests merged when it came to producing counter-subversive propaganda. CENTO and NATO acted as effective mechanisms for the conduct of intelligence diplomacy.

CENTO was a platform to discuss subversive activities in the region. It has been dubbed by one researcher as a 'failed alliance', since 'there was no real threat to be deterred in the first place'.[90] But CENTO was not without its uses for Turkey. Since the regional member states, Turkey, Iraq, Iran and Pakistan, were above all eager to tackle subversive activities in their countries, it was therefore natural that the idea of forming 'joint anti-subversion machinery' was discussed at the inaugural meeting of the Pact Council, in Baghdad, in November 1955.[91] While the formation of the regional defence pact against the aggression of the Eastern bloc was received with scepticism by many Turks, Prime Minister Adnan Menderes enthusiastically supported the idea, since it would enable Turkey to enhance its capabilities to tackle subversive activities in the region.[92] Turkey sent representatives from the MAH, the TGS and the Foreign Ministry to work with their regional counterparts.[93] However, this working relationship was rather difficult, since every member state had a different conceptualization of the definition of 'subversive elements' until they reached a broader agreement on the subject later in the 1960s.

One aspect of these secret counter-subversion organizations under CENTO is particularly noteworthy.[94] As an example of multilateral intelligence and security cooperation, these organizations were tasked from the outset to tackle communist movements in the region.[95] Their purpose was to 'facilitate the exchange of information relating to Communist subversive activities and Soviet bloc espionage', and 'recommend ways and means by which security services can best fulfil their tasks'.[96] One of the advantages of intelligence sharing under CENTO was that the members shared their knowledge of communist activities, the link between communist movements and the Soviets, and their subversive activities in the Pact area, which then enabled them to obtain a wider picture of the threats posed by international communism in the region. The subjects of their information exchange included, for instance: the strength and activities of the Communist Parties in each signatory country; propaganda broadcasts by various radio stations of the Eastern bloc countries aimed at the instigation of subversive activities in the Pact area; and any scheduled communist-sponsored international meetings.[97] The exchanged information also included a list of known communist members in the region; a 'watch list' containing forthcoming communist and non-communist meetings; and action needed to be taken by relevant authorities against them.[98]

Alongside CENTO, NATO had its own mechanism for cooperation in counter-subversive measures. Immediately after the ratification of the Atlantic Pact, an agency called the North Atlantic Treaty Information Service (NATIS) was founded within the organization to facilitate the exchange of ideas among member states and so improve their ideological defences against Cominform propaganda.[99] The agency was responsible for the creation and dissemination of NATO propaganda material. Until the late 1950s, the US Information Agency and the British Information Research Department (IRD), provided the bulk of the staff, budget and expertise behind it.[100] In 1955, Britain's Lord Ismay, the first NATO secretary-general, sent a memorandum to the permanent national representatives to explain the alliance's non-military activities under article 2 of the treaty; he put special emphasis on counter-subversive activities and explained their role as 'exchanges of information in the Council and Information Committee on the trends and devices of Soviet propaganda leading to the adoption of common attitudes towards certain Soviet inspired propaganda moves or projects'.[101] This exchange of experience and information within the NATO context helped Ankara to improve its own methods for countering domestic communist activities. For instance, when the French delegation informed the Council about the evident usefulness of the 'Paix et Liberte' movement, Ankara was asked by NATO to allow a Turkish branch of the movement to operate in Turkey to counter communist propaganda.[102] However, the level of intelligence diplomacy in this multilateral context did not exceed the bilateral level of intelligence diplomacy developed through Ankara's respective ties with London and Washington. The secret nature of the psychological warfare conducted in Turkey against Communism meant that the Turks, British and Americans engaged in more informal bilateral activities. It is also apparent in the declassified NATO archives that NATO was not informed about these activities. This episode demonstrates that intelligence cooperation in the multilateral setting was not suitable for the minor powers, in this case Turkey, to conduct intelligence diplomacy. The multilateral intelligence cooperation was bound up more with the formal agreements, and there were associated risks due to the involvement of many stakeholders, giving only a limited space for the minor power to drag the cooperation in its direction. Therefore, the joint operations conducted bilaterally were not necessarily shared within NATO. It was also useful for the Americans and British to do this, since they could avoid 'free-riders' within the alliance, and have more freedom in their operations by not risking a leak of their sources and methods.

The British Foreign Office propaganda unit, the IRD, was well embedded within CENTO's Counter-Subversion Office. Operations carried out by this office were planned in large part by IRD officers. Peter Joy, the IRD officer in Ankara during the late 1950s, was especially well experienced in anti-communist measures, and he shared his experience with his Turkish counterpart, Mr. Halil of the MAH. Counter-subversive activities in the CENTO region were generally slow to develop, due to a lack of experience and of trained writers. However, Joy reported in the Turkish case that the 'Turks were doing quite well'.[103] The MAH established a special relationship with the IRD in the British embassy, and both agencies engaged in the translation of IRD material and its insertion into mainstream Turkish newspapers. Both the IRD and MAH also arranged a special tour for the 'respectable variety of Turkish journalists' to the UK, so that they could be briefed on trends regarding communist propaganda and anti-communist measures. The cooperation between IRD and MAH proved very valuable: when it became known that NATO anti-communist propaganda was not very successful, mostly due to the lack of effective structure within NATO to conduct this propaganda, cooperation between the IRD and MAH, and MAH and CIA filled that gap.[104]

This cooperation proved particularly effective when it came to assessing the Turkish political scene. Anti-communist propaganda stories, for instance, were inserted in newspapers that were critical of the ruling Menderes government as well as in pro-government media outlets. A considerable amount of the IRD's anti-communist material was published in newspapers such as *Dünya* and *Yenigün*, which were critical of the right-leaning Menderes government. Pro-government newspapers such as *Zafer* and *Son Havadis* also published IRD's anti-communist material.[105] By inserting such items into newspapers on both sides of the political spectrum in Turkey, the MAH–IRD joint endeavour sought to divert both sides from any sympathy to the Soviet narrative. To take one example, CENTO's Counter-Subversion office in Ankara reached out to well-known leftists in the country to implement anti-Soviet propaganda. For instance, Bulent Ecevit, a well-known centre-left figure who later became the country's prime minister with the Republican People's Party in the 1970s, and again in the late 1990s with the Democratic Left Party, was one of the contacts that the Counter-Subversion Office used to publish anti-Soviet materials in his newspaper column.[106]

The MAH's knowledge of the domestic situation, and its ability to reach out to the editors and writers in newspapers across the range of the political spectrum, was supported by the IRD's capacity to produce propaganda material. Bilateral counter-subversion cooperation between the Turks and the British thus became successful and satisfying for both parties. However, the Turks still wanted to direct the IRD's activities in Turkey according to Ankara's foreign policy aims. But, once the IRD–MAH joint counter-subversive activities proved to be effective and successful, the Turks started to get nervous. Turkish foreign policy aimed to avoid direct confrontation with the Soviet Union. Thus, Fahmi Oral, the Turkish representative from MAH, asked Peter Joy 'what would happen if the Russians, having monitored the Press Service, accused the Turkish government of permitting Ankara to become a base for anti-Soviet radio propaganda and use this argument as an excuse for jamming the transmissions'.[107] Ankara wanted to raise concerns with the British that they would not want their success to attract an undesired confrontation with the Russians. To address these concerns, IRD–MAH joint efforts decided to avoid any direct attack on communist countries and concentrate defensively on reporting communist propaganda claims and exposing communist aims and tactics.[108] As it transpired, the Turks were able to secure IRD support to fight against communists at home without attracting undesired attention from the Soviets.

However, Turkish desires to use joint IRD–MAH propaganda work in an offensive manner do not appear to be genuine in light of declassified documents from the CIA. Before 1959, the CIA was partially involved in IRD–MAH efforts. However, by late 1959, the US representative declared that he would not attend these meetings, and instead left a deputy to attend to CIA cooperation with the Turkish and British agencies. Peter Joy reported to the Foreign Office that the American withdrawal from the Counter-Subversion Office presaged less CIA involvement in their efforts and more concentration on exclusively American activities.[109] Concurrently with the US withdrawal from joint IRD–MAH efforts, the CIA accelerated its own psychological warfare campaign against the Soviet Union and Communism in general. In an operational guide dispatched from CIA headquarters to all stations around the world, their stated objective was:

> to uncover identities and activities of Bloc clandestine assets (organizations, groups, press media, individuals) used in covert political action and/or psychological warfare against non-Communist countries, and to produce operational aids setting forth whatever international operational patterns may emerge as the study continues.[110]

Indeed, the CIA was quite forthright in its new approach to counter communist subversion. Its scope expanded beyond the production and dissemination of counter propaganda, and extended to the agency's paramilitary (KUCAGE) and foreign intelligence (KUTUBE) branches.[111] The CIA targeted official Russian bodies such as SOVEXPORTFILM, which the agency believed to be one of the main institutions abroad that hosted Russian agents supporting local groups in their subversion efforts. Turkey was not immune from the CIA's operations, but such aggressive methods against communists and the Soviet Union did not raise concerns in the MAH. Indeed, the Turks preferred to be involved in offensive intelligence operations led by the Americans, rather than the British. Allowing the CIA's counter-subversive actives to be based in Turkey meant that the Turks could alleviate Washington's concerns about the effectiveness of American security assistance to Turkey – whereas the diminution of British power in the Middle East, after the Suez crisis of late 1956, led Ankara to avoid any confrontation with the Soviets as a result of Anglo-Turkish cooperation. Instead, the Turks sought US participation in any intelligence operation that would directly target the Soviet bloc. However, even during the joint MAH–CIA operations, Turkey's own strategic imperatives created problems for Turkish intelligence diplomacy.

## Radio debacle

In 1951, the US government took major steps to intensify its propaganda efforts. As a result, the Psychological Strategy Board (PSB) was formed within the National Security Council to monitor, coordinate and determine the effectiveness of US psychological operations. It was immediately concluded that 'existing National Security Council Policy Papers are inadequate for PSB planning purposes'.[112] The main areas of operation were initially the Soviet Union, China and Korea, with Soviet satellite countries as secondary targets. There was also a growing 'recognition in the US Government of the need for strengthening their psychological position in the Middle East'.[113] On this basis the US government launched a Psychological Offensive in the Middle East.[114]

In order to wage an effective propaganda campaign, the PSB initially sought to answer what elements affected individuals' attitudes, such as satisfaction of needs (vital things such as food, shelter, clothing) and their desire for freedom.[115] Soviet émigrés sought to answer these questions and assist the Americans in conducting their operations. One of the methods of psychological warfare was to set up radio broadcast stations. To find émigrés to staff these and to establish the additional stations needed to conduct an effective propaganda effort, the CIA had to find appropriate local partners. Turkey became an eager and suitable partner; the Americans planned to operate a Ring Plan Station in Turkey (Project East),[116] which targeted the Caucasus, Turkestan, the European USSR, Bulgaria, Czechoslovakia and Poland; and a large number of emigres versed in the language and culture of these places resided in Turkey. A diary entry from 1952, by the CIA's Istanbul station chief, Archie Roosevelt, sheds light on these efforts. Roosevelt wrote that in order to create a more efficient Counter-Subversive campaign, he needed to compile a list of defectors, deserters and MAH contacts.[117] Moreover, he also exploited the MAH's contacts with influential Soviet emigres in Turkey, such as Zeki Velidi Togan, a prominent scholar on Turkic nations under the Soviets, in order to craft an effective means of reaching Turkic people living in the Soviet Union.[118]

Even before Turkish admission to NATO in 1952, the US embassy in Ankara concluded that, if the Turks demonstrated their willingness to cooperate in these propaganda campaigns, the State Department would be better able to show Congress that the Turks were not only traditional security partners but also indispensable allies in American Psychological Warfare efforts.[119] However, the Menderes government had another agenda. For Ankara, this liaison, as with other aspects of intelligence diplomacy, created two distinct opportunities. The first was material gain. In order to allow the US government to establish propaganda bases in Turkey, the Turkish government asked the United States to extend its mutual security funds for immediate reconstruction and the development of Turkey's own radio broadcasting and communication systems.[120] While the US government agreed on the additional funds, Ankara had another, deeper goal that became apparent with the cessation of propaganda operations in 1955.

After initial negotiations, US propaganda stations started to operate in Turkey. To set them up, a considerable amount of funds, personnel and logistics were diverted from the Munich station to Istanbul. The propaganda activities were monitored by a joint board consisting of representatives from the two countries. However, towards the end of 1955, the Turkish authorities requested the exclusive right to control all broadcasts from stations in Turkey. It is safe to assume that once the MAH had acquired the necessary logistics and capabilities, it was pragmatic for Ankara to use the propaganda missions to push forward Turkish interests concerning the Caucasus, Balkans and Central Asia, interests that were not necessarily embedded in the Atlantic Alliance. However, the Americans found the Turkish proposal unacceptable and moved all their overt propaganda missions based in Turkey back to Munich![121] Thus, while Turkish intelligence diplomacy tried to get greater American commitment through joint counter-subversion operations, the result was rather the opposite.

## Conclusion

Counter-subversion was an integral part of the MAH's activities during the Cold War and thus became a major feature of intelligence diplomacy with Washington and London. Decision makers in Ankara insisted that Turkey was vulnerable both to Kurdish nationalist activities in the region and to communist penetration within Turkey. Ankara saw these issues as points where the Soviets could conduct a war of nerves against the Turks and instructed the MAH to be extremely vigilant against these two subversive streams. However, Turkey was still a weak country, compared to its key allies, lacking the resources and methods necessary to conduct counter-subversion, especially when it came to psychological warfare. By synchronizing Turkish with Western foreign policy, Ankara aimed to obtain that support from the British and Americans, through bilateral relationships as well as in multilateral settings such as CENTO and NATO. But this synchronization had its limits. For instance, Ankara avoided becoming the IRD's regional base of operations against the Soviets since such a development would have led to undesired confrontations with the USSR, and the Turks did not believe that the British would have enough power to protect Turkey from the Soviets. The Turks therefore drew on British help largely for domestic anti-communist measures, and on American help when it came to more aggressive anti-Soviet operations. However, that

American help also backfired, when it became apparent that the Turks and Americans had major differences of opinion regarding the nature of threats in the region and foreign policy aims more generally.

Cooperation between the Turks and their British and American partners against communist movements and Soviet propaganda did not extend to the Kurdish nationalist movement. Although Ankara constantly underlined the link between communism and Kurdish nationalism, both the United States and United Kingdom disregarded Ankara's claims and did not provide the support it needed to suppress the Kurdish movement. Washington and London instead developed their own approach to the Kurds, and contacted and supported certain factions in the Kurdish movement. Ankara's obsession with the Kurds, in other words, was not echoed through its bilateral relationships or through multilateral bodies such as CENTO. This suggests that Turkish intelligence diplomacy worked well when the Turks and their allies agreed on who constituted an enemy. When they did not agree, national imperatives triumphed over mutual aims and tactics. As we will see in the next chapter, the issue of covert operations further illustrates how these divergent national imperatives could create undesired frictions among the allies.

## Notes

1   C. M. Andrew and V. Mitrokhin, *The World Was Going Our Way: The KGB and the Battle for the Third World* (London, 2005), 139.
2   Ibid.
3   Excerpts from this chapter are published in Hashimoto, and Bezci, 'Do the Kurds Have "No Friends but the Mountains"? Turkey's Secret War against Communists, Soviets and the Kurds', 640–655.
4   A. L. Karaosmanoğlu, 'The Evolution of the National Security Culture and the Military in Turkey', *Journal of International Affair*, 54:1 (2000), 199–216; Ü. Cizre, 'Demythologyzing the National Security Concept: The Case of Turkey', *The Middle East Journal*, 57:2 (2003), 213–229; E. Bezci and G. G. Öztan, 'Anatomy of the Turkish Emergency State:

A Continuous Reflection of Turkish Raison d'état between 1980 and 2002', *Middle East Critique*, 25:2 (2016), 163–179.
5 W. Laqueur, *Communism and Nationalism in the Middle East* (London, 1956).
6 B. Gökay, *Soviet Eastern Policy and Turkey, 1920–1991: Soviet Foreign Policy, Turkey and Communism* (London, 2006), 41.
7 Ö. M. Ulus, *The Army and the Radical Left in Turkey: Military Coups, Socialist Revolution and Kemalism* (London, 2010); J. M. Landau, *Radical Politics in Modern Turkey* (London, 2016).
8 Quoted from D. Kurzman, *Subversion of the Innocents: Patterns of Communist Penetration in Africa, the Middle East, and Asia* (New York, 1963), 198.
9 G. Harris, *The Origins of Communism in Turkey* (Stanford, CA, 1967), 7.
10 Ibid.
11 W. Laqueur, *The Soviet Union and the Middle East* (London, 1959), 27–28; Harris, *Origins of Communism in Turkey*, 84–85.
12 Akal, *Moskova-Ankara-Londra Üçgeninde İştirakiyuncular,Komünistler ve Paşa Hazretleri*, 191–196.
13 Kurzman, *Subversion of the Innocents: Patterns of Communist Penetration in Africa, the Middle East, and Asia*, 199.
14 Harris, *Origins of Communism in Turkey*, 136–138.
15 Laqueur, *The Soviet Union and the Middle East*, 28–29, 50–52, 87–88, 104–107.
16 Hasanli, *Stalin and the Turkish Crisis of the Cold War, 1945–1953*, 126.
17 Ibid., 139.
18 Ibid., 140–141.
19 Ibid., 144.
20 BCA: 30.10.0.111.700.3/İ: Encrypted telegram by Turkish Consulate in Bern, to COS, 25 March 1947.
21 TBMM Tutanakları, 8. Dönem, 4. Cilt, 37. Birleşim, 29 January 1947.
22 Ibid.
23 Author's Collection: Erkanıharbiyei Umumiye Riyaseti İstihbarat Başkanlığı, Ankara, Untitled, *c.* 1947.
24 BCA: 30.1.0.41.242.10/B2: 'Paris to Ankara', 31 July 1950.
25 TBMM Tutanakları: 9. Dönem, 4. Cilt, 31. Birleşim, 17 January 1951.
26 Ibid.

27 Ibid.
28 TBMM Tutanakları: 9. Dönem, 25. Cilt, 9. Birleşim, 9 November 1953.
29 Kurzman, *Subversion of the Innocents: Patterns of Communist Penetration in Africa, the Middle East, and Asia*, 198.
30 OL.101/P.2: Draft report, 'The Indigenous Communist Parties and Their Relationship to Subversive Activity in the Baghdad Pact Area', presented by Philip Kirby-Green of MI5, the British representative to the Liaison Committee of the Pact Top Secret, p. 1, 14 July 1958. A document released under the FOIA (REF: 1145–11). Credit of this source is to my late friend Dr Chikara Hashimoto who went through bureaucratic hurdles to get this document released. Moreover, he was kind enough to share this document with me.
31 CIA: 0005757344, 'Sino-Soviet Bloc Activity in Turkey', 2 May 1960.
32 Ibid.
33 NARA: RG59: Box 3744: 782.5269/7.3439: 'Turkish Foreign Office Employee Convicted of Spying: From Goodyear to Warren', 11 July 1959.
34 *Passim.*
35 A detailed study of these uprisings was prepared and published by the Turkish General Staff in 1946: *Doğu bölgesindeki geçmiş isyanlar ve alınan dersler* (Ankara, 1946).
36 Kurzman, *Subversion of the Innocents: Patterns of Communist Penetration in Africa, the Middle East, and Asia*, 198.
37 S. Onslow, ed., *Cold War in Southern Africa: White Power, Black Liberation* (London, 2009); L. S. Carruthers, *Winning Hearts and Minds: British Governments, the Media and Colonial Counter-Insurgency, 1944–1960* (Leicester, 1995).
38 This point was raised by C. Andrew, et al., *The Mitrokhin Archive II: The KGB and the World* (London, 2005), 9.
39 V. Zubok, *A Failed Empire: The Soviet Union in the Cold War from Stalin to Gorbachev* (Chapel Hill, NC, 2007), 110.
40 Andrew and Mitrokhin, *The World Was Going Our Way: The KGB and the Battle for the Third World*, 141.
41 C. Andrew, et al., *The Mitrokhin Archive II: The KGB and the World* (London, 2005), 175. See also P. Sudoplatov, et al., *Special Tasks*, 259–264.
42 V. Zubok, 'Spy vs. Spy: The KGB vs. the CIA, 1960–1962', *Cold War International History Project Bulletin*, 4 (1994), 29.

43 A. R. Ghassemlou, *Kurdistan and the Kurds* (Prague, 1965), 235.
44 CIA-RDP79R00904A000500010091-8: 'The Kurdish Problem', 8 April 1959.
45 Ibid.
46 M. A. Reynolds, 'Abdürrezzak Bedirhan: Ottoman Kurd and Russophile in the Twilight of Empire', *Kritika: Explorations in Russian and Eurasian History*, 12:2 (2011), 411–450.
47 Toplumsal Tarih Vakfı BBM: Necmetttin Sahir Sılan Evrakı, report by Kadri Kemal Kop, Ankara, to İsmet İnönü, 'Türkiye ve Kürtler yahut Doğu Anadolu'ya "politik bir bakış"', 6 March 1946.
48 W. L. Westermann, 'Kurdish Independence and Russian Expansion', *Foreign Affairs*, 24 (1945), 675–686.
49 Toplumsal Tarih Vakfı BBM: Necmetttin Sahir Sılan Papers, report by Kadri Kemal Kop, Ankara, to İsmet İnönü, 'Türkiye ve Kürtler yahut Doğu Anadolu'ya "politik bir bakış"', 6 March 1946, pp. 3–8.
50 Ibid.
51 Ibid., 71–72.
52 Ibid., 73.
53 TNA: FO 195/2595: 'Minutes: Kurds', AKH to EW, 5 February 1946.
54 TBMM Tutanakları: 9.Dönem, 25. Cilt, 5. Birleşim, 16 November 1953.
55 Author's Collection: Genelkurmay Başkanlığı Askeri Mahmekesi, Sayı:964-27 Esas:964-6 Karar:964-36, Ankara, 30 April 1964.
56 Ibid. One of the detainees, Örfi Akkoyunlu, stated at one of their meetings in the Istanbul Messerret Hotel on 27 October 1959 that as long as the Americans supported Turkey and continued having a presence in Turkey, the Kurdish liberation movement would not succeed in the country.
57 CIA-RDP63-00314R000200180010-2: 'The Kurds', January 1960.
58 Ibid. The convicts spent the years between 1959 and 1964 in prison until they were released by a general amnesty; and *Milliyet*, 29 June 1963, p. 7.
59 *Milliyet*, 29 June 1963, p. 7 the detainee was Gazi Dizey (born in Erbil), the Interior Minister Oğuz Bekata stated in 1963.
60 Ibid., born in Kirkuk fluent in Turkish, Kurdish, Arabic and English, who was under the disguise of a civil engineer based in Baghdad.
61 TNA: FO 371/153093: Press cutting from the *Daily Telegraph*, 'Turks Release Tribesmen', 23 November 1960.

62  Westermann, 'Kurdish Independence and Russian Expansion', 675–686.
63  Library of Congress: Archibald Roosevelt Papers: Box 1: Diary Entry, 15 June 1946.
64  Central Intelligence Group, Document No: 0000257305, 'Developments in Azerbaijan Situation', 4 June 1947.
65  CIA: Document No: CIA-RDP86B00269R000300040009-5, 'Soviet Capabilities and Intentions', 15 November 1950.
66  Foreign Relations of the United States, Vol. V (1950): 'Memorandum by the Special Assistant, Joint Military Mission for Aid to Turkey: World Situation', Ankara, 28 December 1950.
67  TNA: FO 195/2595: 'Kurds and Kurdistan: no.18/2256: Soviet Propaganda in Eastern Turkey', 24 January 1946.
68  TNA: WO 106/6069: 'Report of Tour of Eastern Provinces, Turkey by MA', 16 September 1946.
69  TNA: FO 195/2595: 'Minutes: Kurds', 5 February 1946.
70  TNA: FO 195/2596: 'Kurds and Kurdistan: no.14/29/46', 23 July 1946.
71  TNA: FO 195/2596: 'Kurds and Kurdistan: no. 95/5/46', 11 November 1946.
72  TNA: FO 195/2596: 'Kurds and Kurdistan: no. 850/645/A-7/46', 11 September 1946.
73  TNA: FO 371/127861: VB1692/9: 'Report by the Turkish Delegation on Communist Activities in Turkey', 23 May 1957; TNA: FO 371/149746: 'Report by the Turkish Delegation to the Liaison Committee's 8 Session', 6 February 1960.
74  TNA: FO 371/170252: 'Minutes: 'CENTO Liaison Committee (Washington, 21–25 January)', by deGourcy Ireland, 14 January 1963.
75  TNA: FO 371/144805: RK1822/1: 'Letter by L.M. Minford, Ankara, to E.J.W. Barnes of FO', 29 January 1959. McDowall, *A Modern History of the Kurds*, 169.
76  TNA: FO 371/144805: 'Letter by L.M. Minford, Ankara, to E.J.W. Barnes of FO, London', 29 January 1959.
77  Telegram (classified SECRET) by the British embassy, Istanbul, to FO, 18 July 1958, in M. Barzani, *Mustafa Barzani and the Kurdish Liberation Movement, 1931–1961* (Basingstoke, 2003), 167–168.
78  TNA: FO 371/132747: E1821/1: 'Letter by Chancery in Ankara to FO', 15 August 1958.

79 Author's Collection: Report by Erkanıharbiyei Umumiye Riyaseti İstihbarat Başkanlığı (Classified SECRET), Ankara, 'İktisaden Geri Kalmış Memleketlere Sovyet Blok'unun İktisadi, Teknik, Ticari ve Askeri Yardım Faaliyetleri', c. 1962, p. 12.
80 *Milliyet*, 14 June 1963, 1.
81 Author's Collection: Report by Erkanıharbiyei Umumiye Riyaseti İstihbarat Başkanlığı (Classified TOP SECRET), Ankara, '1961 Eylül : 1962 Mart Ayları Arasında Sovyetler Birliğinin dünya devletleriyle olan Siyasi, İktisadi ve Askeri Münasebetleri', c. May 1962, p. 10.
82 Little, 'The United States and the Kurds: A Cold War Story', 68.
83 *Milliyet*, 29 June 1963, p. 7, the Minister of Interior Hıfzı Oğuz Bekata. Emphasis added.
84 TNA: FO 371/136521: 'Minutes: Soviet Propaganda on Kurds', 20 January 1959.
85 CIA-RDP79R00904A000500010091-8: CIA – Office of National Estimates: 'Kurdish Question', 8 April 1959.
86 BCA: 30.0.10.0.0.209.427.8: 'Süleymaniye Camii'ne afiş asmaktan tutuklu komünist Tahsin Berkmen hakkında alınan bilgi', 8 February 1944. For a detailed report on communists in the universities and unions, see BCA: 490.1.0.0.1191.176.2: 'Üniversite talebeleri hakkında yapılan tahkikat ve Komünist Partisine dahil olanlar', 14 February 1947.
87 Penkovsky, *Penkovsky Papers*, 82.
88 CIA-RDP78-00915R000900090011-1: 'Assessment of the Threat of Communist Subversion in Baghdad Pact Area: US Submission', 15 July 1959.
89 Author's Collection: Genelkurmay Başkanlığı Askeri Mahmekesi, Sayı:964-27 Esas:964-6 Karar:964-36, Ankara, 30 April 1964.
90 P. Dimitrakis, *Failed Alliances of the Cold War* (London, 2012), 4.
91 TNA: PREM 11/1938: V1073/1361: Report by Sir Michael Wright, Baghdad, to Harold Macmillan, 'First Meeting of the Council of the Baghdad Pact', 22 November 1955. Academic literature, nevertheless, maintains silence on this aspect of the Pact activities. Only two exceptions are a collection of declassified documents cited by R. Aldrich, ed., *Espionage, Security and Intelligence in Britain, 1945–1970* (Manchester, 1998), 223–225; and C. Hashimoto (ed. by R. Cormac), *The Twilight of the British Empire: British Intelligence and Counter-Subversion in the Middle East, 1948–63* (Edinburgh, 2017).

92 Hale, *Turkish Foreign Policy, 1774–2000*, 128–129.
93 BCA: 30.0.18.1.2/147.54.17: Başvekalet, 'Bağdat Paktı Milli Emniyet Makamı teşkil edilmesi', 24 October 1957.
94 CENTO was comprised primarily of four major working committees below the highest body, the Council of Ministers. These were the Military Committee, the Economic Committee, the Counter-Subversion Committee and the Liaison Committee. See N. Stack, 'CENTO – The Unknown Alliance', *The RUSI Journal*, 177 (1972), 51.
95 TNA: FO 371/121283: V10710/8: Telegram by Sir R. Stevens, Tehran, to FO, 5 April 1956. Also see Aldrich, *Espionage, Security and Intelligence in Britain, 1945–1970*, 223–225.
96 TNA: FO 371/121283: V10710/6: Telegram by Sir Michael Wright, Baghdad, to FO, 15 December 1955; FO 371/121283: V10710/1: Telegram by M Wright to FO, 27 January 1956.
97 TNA: FO 371/127861: VB1692/9: Report by the Turkish Delegation on Communist Activities in Turkey, 23 May 1957.
98 TNA: FO 371/149746: EB1691/2/G: 'Draft Report of the UK Contribution to the CENTO Liaison Committee Papers by MI5, "Special Study 1: The Iraq Communist Party"', 3 March 1960. TNA: FO 1110/1353: PR146/20: Monthly report on the CSO (January) by Peter Joy of FO, 5 February 1960. These actions, for instance, were making recommendations to their own authorities to refuse any applications of any individuals for exit visas in order to participate in the events.
99 L. Risso, *Propaganda and Intelligence in the Cold War: The NATO Information Service* (London, 2014), 36.
100 Ibid.
101 NATO: PO(55)985: 'Some Thoughts on the Non-Military Activities of the North Atlantic Community with Special Reference to Article 2 of the Treaty', 6 December 1955.
102 NATO: AC/24-D/26.6 : 'NATO Information Conference – February 1953 – French Activities in Countering Anti-NATO Propaganda', 4 February 1953; Paix et Liberte was a French anti-Communist movement operating transnationally during the 1950s. The organization had local committees in various European capitals, and engaged in propaganda campaigns against Communism. Allegedly, the movement had support from the CIA and was used in covert operations as well. See B. Ludwig, 'Paix et

liberté: A Transnational Anti-Communist Network', in L. van Dongen, ed., *Transnational Anti-Communism and the Cold War* (London, 2014), 81–95.
103 TNA: FO 1110/1251:1689/4/2: 'Monthly Report on the Counter-Subversion Office', 3 December 1959.
104 For NATO Information Service, see: Risso, *Propaganda and Intelligence in the Cold War: The NATO Information Service*, 30–59.
105 TNA: FO 1110/1251: 'Turkish Writers' Panel Articles', 3 December 1959.
106 TNA: FO 1110/1426:10523/7: 'Counter Subversion Committee Monthly Report', 10 May 1961.
107 TNA: FO 1110/1251: 'Turkish Writers' Panel Articles', 3 December 1959.
108 TNA: FO 1110/1251:1689/1/53: 'CENTO Press Service', 24 October 1959.
109 TNA: FO 1110/1251:1689/4/2: 'Monthly Report on the Counter-Subversion Office', 3 December 1959.
110 CIA: Dispatch no. 1242 from KUDEST to all: 'Clandestine Subversive Activities by Sino-Soviet Bloc Representatives in Public Information Media', 1 May 1959.
111 Ibid.
112 Truman Archives: PSB Files: Box 10: 'Role of PSB regarding Psychological War Plan for Middle East', 19 October 1951.
113 Ibid.
114 Truman Archives: PSB Files: Box 10: From McGhee to Barret: 'Psychological Offensive in the Near East', 31 October 1951.
115 Eisenhower Archives: NSC Series: PSB Central Files: Box 10: 'Indication of Psychological Vulnerabilities and of Propaganda Effectiveness', 10 January 1953.
116 NARA: RG59: Box 3: 5503.0100: 'Kohler to Delgado', 15 July 1951. Ring Plan refers to a strategy for the encroachment of the Soviet periphery to ensure an efficient transmission into the Soviet lands.
117 Library of Congress: Archibald Roosevelt papers: Diary Entry from 1952.
118 Ibid.
119 NARA: RG59: Box 3: 5503.0100: Kohler to Micocci, 'Turkey', 21 November 1951.
120 NARA: RG59: Box 3: 5503.0100: From Morton to Macknight, 2 December 1951.
121 NARA: RG59: Box 3: 5503.0100: Richards to Kohler, 14 November 1955.

# 6

# Covert Action: The Turks' Hidden Hand in Syria

Covert action has long been an appealing tool for Turkish decision makers. As defined by Richard Aldrich, covert operations are used 'to influence the world by unseen means – a hidden hand'.[1] As a minor power with great foreign policy ambitions, Ankara often deployed these unseen means to influence areas removed from Turkish control after the collapse of the Ottoman Empire. The deniability of covert action was a key feature for Ankara as it strove to avoid direct confrontation with its neighbours and, more importantly, with the Soviets. Moreover, deniability also created an opportunity to avoid repercussions under international law, notably at the United Nations. Ankara's target areas of influence mostly concerned former Ottoman territories in the Balkans and the Middle East. Therefore, it is important, as Len Scott warns, not to fall into the trap of seeing every covert action carried out during the Cold War in the context of East–West rivalry.[2] Yet in the Turkish case, covert action was not used as part of the colonial struggle as was the case for some Western countries during the Cold War.[3] For Turkey, covert action was rather a means for revising the conditions imposed by the fall of the Ottoman Empire, and by doing so obtaining the support of its Western allies for Turkish endeavours in the Cold War context.

## Making sense of Turkish covert operations

A special focus was therefore given to Ankara's covert aims concerning the Turkish-speaking and Muslim communities left outside Turkish borders after the Treaty of Lausanne in 1923, which defined most of modern Turkey's borders – except for Hatay, which was left to the French mandate of Syria.[4] As seen in Chapter 2, Hatay was annexed by Turkey in 1939 through a combination of covert action and diplomacy. Ankara's deployment of covert action was not, however, limited to issues around the Treaty of Lausanne and its aftermath. During the Second World War, as also seen in Chapter 2, the MAH was deployed to collaborate with MI6 in several operations in the Balkans and the Middle East, and to conduct its own solo operations, in particular to hamper Axis manoeuvres in and around Turkey. These experiences before and during the war increased the MAH's ability to conduct covert operations, and to use its joint operations with Western counterparts to further its own strategic aims where possible. For instance, at the end of 1949, as very early endeavours began to create stay-behind guerrilla units against a possible Soviet advance towards Turkey, the MAH formed three large units of this type. These were to be supported by the British parachuting two battalions of sappers to sabotage lines of communication and provide transportation to support the Turks against the Soviet advance.[5] As British power retreated after the debacle at Suez, the Menderes government in Ankara sought more American cooperation, including the organization of stay-behind units. Although the exact nature of these CIA–MAH stay-behind units is still not available in detail, declassified records tell us that the Greek military attaché in Turkey was aware of their existence in 1957, and asked the American embassy whether classified Turkish military outposts were used as training-grounds for Turkish guerrillas to be sent to Cyprus to counter the Greek-Cypriot EOKA insurgency's Enosis campaign. The American ambassador assured the Greeks that the US embassy was fully aware of their existence and that these units had nothing to do with Cyprus.[6]

Yet the Greek attaché's concerns still raise questions, due to the fact that the Turkish underground movement in Cyprus, the Turkish Resistance Organization (TMT), was also founded in the same year. MAH's collaboration with her Western partners for forming stay-behind guerrilla units had different motivations, methods and aims vis-à-vis the cases of covert operation abroad, especially in the territories of the former Ottoman Empire. However, it is not plausible to examine the Cyprus case in this study since Turkish covert operations in Cyprus were not executed in collaboration with Ankara's Western partners. These were independent Turkish operations, conducted more via the informal Turkish nationalist networks within the Turkish military and intelligence services. This episode, which can be the topic of another study, shows that former Ottoman territories were frequently a covert action target for Turkish intelligence. It also shows that Turkish covert action has not necessarily needed a Western security umbrella to operate in. However, both in Turkish joint operations with the West and in its solo operations, these overt operations could easily turn into overt military intervention. It was the case with Syria in the late 1950s (and the current ongoing episode that began in 2016), as well as with Cyprus in 1974. The reason for this escalation is that the covert action falls short as a means to achieve Turkish policy goals, which are usually regime change or annexation of a territory. Thus, the military action replaces the covert action when means and goals do not coincide.

The issue of Turkish domestic politics and foreign policy endeavours were mutually entangled when covert operations were at stake. Turkish intelligence diplomacy, conducted for Ankara's secret intelligence relations with its Western partners, was also applicable for joint covert operations. Yet Turkey faced more severe outcomes from joint covert operations than its partners, which not only hampered the country's national security but also created lasting effects that are even visible today. In particular, the balance of civil–military relations was upset, leading to a military coup. Also, during the rest of the Cold War, the Turkish image in the Middle East was severely damaged. Why was this the case?

As outlined in Chapter 4, even in crucial matters such as nuclear weaponry and spying on the Soviet nuclear programme, Ankara did not hesitate to deceive the CIA and MI6 when it found it pragmatic to do so. Particularly concerning nuclear weapons the MAH utilized human agents from the ranks of Turkish émigrés from Bulgaria for joint espionage missions concerning uranium production and the location of missile ramps. However, the experience and capabilities gained in these operations by the MAH were later used in subversive covert action in Bulgaria to encourage a revolt by the Turkish minority against the Bulgarian government.[7] This also illustrates a characteristic of Turkish intelligence. The intelligence and covert action, as they were conducted by the same organization, had a connotation that is embedded together. However, this created some deficiencies in Turkish intelligence diplomacy. These deficiencies are demonstrated below in the episode on Syria. Since Turkish-Western relations have been security focused at their core, the volatility in the Turkish role in joint covert operations is profoundly affected by its relations with the West, namely the United States and the United Kingdom.

Therefore, the characteristics of the Turkish covert action may be explained by using the ladder of escalation metaphor. Loch K. Johnson argues that covert operations have four distinct thresholds when it comes to the 'ladder of escalation for covert operations, one based on a rising level of intrusion abroad as policy makers climb upward from low-risk to high-risk activities'.[8] The ladder metaphor entails a spectrum ranging from routine intelligence operations, such as daily intelligence gathering abroad, to the extreme options of coup attempts and arms supplying that would seriously infringe the target nation's sovereignty. Johnson further argues that political leaders with nationalist views, where accountability mechanisms are not in place, could easily climb the ladder upwards for escalation since they would only pay attention to the results of their actions without any ethical and legal consequences.[9] The ladder metaphor provides a framework by which to explain the Turkish approach to covert operations. The first stage of Turkish covert action displayed a rather hesitant pragmatism from the Foreign Ministry, and merely created 'minor disturbances' in the region. The second stage was mostly embedded in the Western Alliance and its focus lay in playing a role in larger operations taking place in the surrounding region. In the third stage, when Turkish covert action was not synchronized with its Western allies, the nature of the action was an incompetent pro-activism that might escalate into a major armed conflict with the target country. This incompetent pro-activism, which has its implications even today, is the result of a mismatch between Turkish policy goals, means used to achieve these goals and overall Turkish capabilities to carry out such operations.

Following the first Gulf War in 1991, for instance (to take a much later example), Turkey's southern flank was exposed to additional security threats due to the US-imposed no-fly zone above the traditionally Kurdish region in Iraq. The Kurdish insurgent group, the Kurdistan Workers' Party (PKK), found safe haven in that region outside the control of the Turkish and Iraqi governments. As the PKK stepped up its attacks on Turkish territory it began to pose a critical threat to Turkey.[10] After the doomed 1991 Iraqi uprisings in the country's predominantly Shi'a and Kurdish regions, respectively in Iraq's southern and northern regions during Operation Desert Storm, Ankara decided it had to mobilize its Turkmen kinsmen in the regions of Mosul and Kirkuk as a counterbalance to Kurdish influence. With backing from Turkish intelligence, several Turkmen groups merged together and formed the Iraqi Turkmen Front (ITF). Indeed, the ITF had success at least in projecting Ankara's policy preferences in the region. Due to the Turkmen presence in the strategic and oil-rich regions of Kirkuk and Mosul, US officials had to negotiate with Iraqi Turkmen officials on issues spanning from logistics to reconnaissance.[11] Therefore, Ankara managed to open a new channel via the ITC to influence developments on its southern flank, at the potential cost of a contest for influence with the United States. However, the United States still neglected Turkish concerns regarding the PKK, and merely watched as the insurgent group settled in mountainous areas of Iraq which were out of Turkey's reach. This is a clear example of a mismatch between policy goals and means. While Turkey's initial aim was to remove the PKK from northern Iraq by negotiating with the Americans, what Turkey achieved in the end was a thaw with the Americans, and a front organization that Turkey had to foster for the coming decades. Means had become the goal itself.

To remove the PKK from northern Iraq, Turkey again, on numerous occasions, has had to conduct military operations. However, these operations have not achieved conclusive results.

This Turkish strategy of using covert action, risking friction with allies and a major war with the target country, was not just a post–Cold War phenomenon. Even at the height of the Cold War, the Menderes government used covert action in adjacent regions in an even riskier way than its successor in 1991. In particular, the case study of Turkish covert action in Syria during the early Cold War demonstrates profound differences in aims, methods and capabilities between London, Washington and Ankara. Moreover, the Syrian example also shows how Turkish intelligence diplomacy incurred rather heavy costs for the Turkish government.

## Turkey's struggle for Syria

The American Ambassador Fletcher Warren interrupted a Turkish cabinet meeting in April 1957.[12] He was there to prevent it from deciding to intervene militarily in Syria. He told the Turkish Prime Minister Menderes that Washington would not like to see the Turks go beyond their borders. To do so would be a great disservice to their alliance. The prime minister nodded his head and said that Ankara 'is deeply grateful and thankful to the American government for the interest it is taking to preserve peace in the area'.[13] As a result of this exchange, Turkey refrained from moving into Syria.

Warren's intervention happened at a crucial time in the history of the region, for Syria had fallen into the anti-Western camp as a result of a coup in 1954. Both the Turks and Americans perceived further communist penetration into Syria as a serious threat to the containment of communist expansion in the region. The Menderes government considered a military intervention to prevent total communist control of Syria. By doing so, Menderes also hoped to keep Turkish military officers, who were becoming increasingly resentful of his regime, busy with Syria.[14] However, Washington had different methods in mind. Warren did not want Turkey to intervene in Syria because Washington was at that time in the midst of trying to remove Syria's leftist government from power by covert action.[15] The Turkish military threat to Syria was already helping to consolidate the influence and power of Syrian leftists, putting the success of that action in jeopardy. There were wider strategic considerations for the Americans as well, for the United States also wanted to avoid Turkey dragging it into a major East–West confrontation in the Middle East.

Long before the Cold War began, Syria occupied an important place in Ankara's strategic worldview. Cold War rivalries, however, meant that Syria posed more risks and opportunities for Turkish planners. Most of these concerned the province of Hatay, rather than the ramifications of political and economic rivalries between the West and the Soviet bloc in the Middle East. But the American government, and particularly American officials charged with carrying out covert action, saw Syria in a rather different way. Due to the release of previously classified archives, it has become apparent that since the late 1940s, Syria was acting as a testing ground for the CIA's early covert operations. Growing instability and Soviet influence there gave the CIA added incentives to conduct covert action. Moreover, as Little argues, the strategic location of the country – on the shores of the Levant, neighbouring Turkey to its north and Israel to its south and its ability to disrupt the flow of Middle Eastern oil to the Western world – lay behind US efforts to keep Damascus from falling under Soviet influence, and to thereby safeguard President Truman's containment strategy. CIA agents further emphasized the fact that the active leftist parties and groups operating within the Arab Republic made the country more prone to dangerous instability.[16] Therefore, the CIA supported Syrian Army Chief of Staff Husni Zaim's military coup in March 1949.[17]

The Turks, however, did not see the need to align their aims in Syria with those of the Americans. This contention between Turkish and American policies concerning Syria, and tactical differences between Ankara and Washington, brought Turkey to the brink of war with her southern neighbour in the very midst of American covert action to stimulate a regime change in the country. In order to fully grasp this situation, it is important to identify various elements in Turkey's Syrian policy, and how these policy priorities diverged from the American policy.

## Early approaches

After the annexation of the Hatay by Turkey in 1939, the ceding of territory from an Arab country encouraged the development of an Arab nationalist movement in Syria. Being aware of these developments, Turkey's policy on Syria was to delay Syrian claims on Hatay from the proclamation of the independence of Syria in 1941 until the San Francisco Conference, which founded the United Nations, in 1945. However, coinciding with the San Francisco Conference, Arab nationalism emerged as a notable force influencing the post-independence development of Syria.[18] Hinnebusch points out:

> Arab nationalism was the most successful ideology in filling the post-Ottoman identity vacuum because it best bridged the Syrian 'mosaic', bringing together the Arabic-speaking minorities, most significantly the Alawis and Christians, with the Sunni majority, albeit excluding non-Arabs such as the Kurds.[19]

In order to consolidate the Arab nationalist mobilization at home, and to cement a new post-independence Syrian national identity, Syrian foreign policy also took an Arab nationalist turn. By considering Hatay as stolen Arab territory, Damascus sparked several initiatives to regain it from Turkey by diplomatic means. The legal *raison d'etre* was to claim that the previously ruling French mandate government was not in a position to make territorial compromises of this kind with Turkey on behalf of the Syrian people. Therefore, the Committee for Defence of Alexandretta, formed prior to the San Francisco Conference in 1945, appealed to the Arab League and to the San Francisco Conference for the return of the territory to Syria.[20] The attainment of Syrian independence enabled Damascus to gain full control of its foreign policy as well. The issue of Hatay meant that Ankara refused to give diplomatic recognition to Syria. Turkey's friendly relations with Iraq and Jordan – the Hashemite Arab Kingdoms – forced Damascus to ease its whipping-up of domestic nationalistic sentiment and to manoeuvre itself carefully due to pressure from its powerful neighbours. However, for Ankara, the fragmentation of post-independence Syrian domestic politics created a suitable environment for Turkish agents to engage in minor operations in the newly established country. A remarkable example occurred as early as September 1946, when a former Turkish jurist, Said Haydar Bey, formed a foundation named 'ŞARK' in Damascus. This example is illustrative of the way Turkey endeavoured to influence Syrian public opinion and decision makers through front organizations and by having news inserted into the Syrian media.

Said Haydar Bey, a Syrian national and former chief judge at the Syrian Court of Appeals, was a graduate of the Istanbul Law Faculty. However, when the French mandate government in Syria ordered his execution, he escaped to Turkey, and lived there between 1927 and 1938. During his exile in Turkey, Said Haydar Bey established close contacts with top-level Turkish politicians and bureaucrats. Another of his roles, as a correspondent for the Egyptian newspaper *Al-Belagh*, gave him access to the higher echelons of Turkish political life. During his time in Turkey he also married a Turkish woman and considered Turkey as his second home. In short, his entire background convinced the Turkish embassy in Damascus that he was a strong Turcophile who could run their front operation to expand Turkish influence in Syria, and to rebuild the image of Turkey among the Syrian political elite and in Syrian public opinion.[21]

The Turkish embassy in Damascus held great hopes for this front organization, both in terms of Said Haydar Bey's ability to influence the Syrian cabinet and in the accuracy of the intelligence he provided regarding Syrian attitudes towards Turkey.[22] In particular, the Turkish ambassador to Syria, Abdulahat Akşin, reported to Ankara that all the intelligence flowing from Said Haydar Bey was in accordance with the embassy's own estimates, and was thus deemed to be correct.[23] His intelligence stated that anti-Turkish sentiment in Syria was a result of French colonial rule, and that it was fading away. Moreover, according to the embassy, both the Syrian President Shukri Quwatli and his deputies were looking to develop friendly relations with Turkey and Bey's front organization could facilitate suitable public opinion in Syria.[24] These estimates proved overly optimistic, however, and the embassy's unfounded belief in Said Haydar Bey's capabilities rendered the front organization less useful than it otherwise might have been. In 1947, Syria held national elections and the anti-Turkish card again became a useful propaganda tool for the competing nationalist parties, who did not hesitate to accuse each other of being friendly to Turkey and thus acting against the Syrian national interest. And even as the Turks attempted to influence Syrian public opinion they faced competition in that respect from the CIA, not to mention Britain and France.[25] They did at least learn from their first mistake, and tried to develop a more comprehensive approach to influence Syrian public opinion, and even to influence the outcome of the Syrian elections.

Ankara's initial approach was to feed pro-Turkish pieces to the Syrian newspapers. For instance, in March 1947 Turkish Foreign Minister Hasan Saka informed the prime minister, Recep Peker, that an influential newspaper in Aleppo, titled *Al-Jihad*, had already started to produce news and opinion pieces advocating close cooperation between Syria and Turkey. The foreign minister further suggested that Ankara should invest substantial money into this newspaper to expand its coverage within Syria.[26] The years 1946–7 witnessed the brewing of a new, rather more radical, version of Syrian Arab nationalism. As shown below, Ankara's efforts to create a Turkish sphere of influence were not successful. The most important reason for this was that Turkish intelligence reports reaching Ankara were highly politicized and lacked a firm grasp of political realities on the ground. For instance, an intelligence report on the 1947 Syrian elections claimed that the Aleppo-based The People's Party (al Hizb al Ahrar) was under attack for being supported by the Turkish government and claimed that the party's chairman Rusdu Kahya was an ethnic Turk. The other leading political force, The National Party (al Hizb al Watani), which also included well-known nationalist figures in Syria, such as then president Shukri Quwatli, was accusing the Ahrar party of acting as a Turkish stooge. Moreover, the report also quoted the aims of the National Party as (1) reinstating Syrian control over Hatay, (2) objecting to Turkish friendship with the Hashemite Kingdoms in the region (which advocated unity with Syria to form a Greater Syrian Arab state in the Levant) and (3) refusing to act as a watchdog for the Turks or any other state. However, Turkish intelligence concluded that this party was under the control of the Cabiri family in Syria, and all their anti-Turkish rhetoric was due to the elections, and did not reflect long-term anti-Turkish sentiment.[27]

Although Turkish intelligence possessed detailed knowledge concerning the tribal/family politics behind each respective party on the Syrian political scene, it failed to grasp the importance of Arab nationalism in that milieu. It was true that family politics played a major role in the National Party, and that leading figures of the party, such as Shukri Quwatli, Jamil Mardam, Faris al-Khuri, Lutfi al-Haffar and Sabri al-Asali, enjoyed considerable personal support due to their role in the Syrian national uprising against French rule, as well as to the power of their families.[28] Growing up in the post-war environment, young Syrians were being introduced to more radical 'emancipatory' ideas in the political cafes of Damascus, which led to further fragmentation of the political scene into different political, religious and ideological camps.[29] Further polarization between Damascus and Aleppo during the election campaign did not help the process. For instance, the Damascus-based People's Party was supported by the traders, merchants and bankers of Aleppo who were profoundly affected by being isolated from Turkish and Iraqi markets after the dissolution of the Ottoman Empire in 1922. Aleppo's political elite saw wider possibilities in the abolition of formal borders with Iraq and Turkey since they perceived that Syria as currently constituted was too small for them to expand their business and market. However, the People's Party was not a pro-Turkish or a pro-Hashemite party. As Patrick Seale points out, they were loyal to the Arab nationalist institutions of the Syrian republic, yet they saw opportunities to develop closer relations with Turkey and the Arab Hashemite Kingdoms in the region.[30] Initial Turkish covert operations all failed because Turkish intelligence agencies did not properly account for these nationalist motives when they assessed the People's Party, its leadership and its programme. The main underlying reason behind these misperceptions was the deep politicization of the intelligence services.

As demonstrated in Chapter 1, the Turkish intelligence service suffered from political appointments and the politicization of its personnel. When estimating Syria's internal political situation, for instance, the intelligence agency went out of its way to praise the Turkish government, due to its relatively relaxed approach to Islamic rhetoric, especially compared with previous years, and further claimed that the government's approach to Islam had a positive impact on the image of Turkey in Syria.[31] However, such a simplistic reflection of the complex political, religious and ethnic landscape in Syria did not help efforts to influence Syrian politics. Moreover, following the elections, the People's Party and the Ba'ath party joined forces and cemented in embryonic form a coalition that would influence Syrian politics for years to come, but not in a way that Turkey desired. As Ba'ath Party leader Michel Aflaq put it when they joined forces with the People's Party, 'it was a rather revolutionary force that grasped the young Syrian's dissent toward the regime, and demanded a further nationalistic course that encompassed the whole Arab Spring rather than just the streets of Aleppo'.[32] However, Turkish intelligence neither grasped this nationalist trend nor anticipated the coups and American covert actions in the region in the years to come.

After the fiasco of the 1948 Palestinian war, when newly founded Israel defeated the Arab League armies, both Syrian Army officers and the Syrian people grew increasingly discontented with the mishandling and corruption of the Syrian Cabinet. The Syrian prime minister was scapegoated for these failings and replaced in December 1948 by the independent, though not especially nationalist, figure of Khalid al-Azm. Al-Azm tried to secure deals with France and the United States to increase the flow of funds to the Syrian treasury. However, growing nationalist discontent reflected itself inside parliament through the People's Party, and through the Muslim Brotherhood and the Ba'ath Party in street demonstrations. However, Al-Azm signed the French-Syrian agreement in February 1949 to solve any financial problems remaining from the French mandate. Also, in the same month he signed an agreement with ARAMCO for the construction of a pipeline to carry Dhahran oil to the Mediterranean. Both these agreements were to be ratified by parliament, but the ghosts of the recent colonial past haunted the Syrian scene. The parliamentarians reacted to the agreement by claiming it would bring back French influence and open the country to future American interventions.[33]

## Beginning of the coups

While al-Azm was trying to convince the other parties to ratify the agreements, the country's right-wing Chief of Staff, Husni Zaim, had already started planning a coup with Miles Copeland, CIA's Middle East Specialist, to overthrow Quwatli's government.[34] Amidst the political stalemate in the Syrian parliament, Zaim requested that Fort Meade foster internal disturbances and channel the necessary funds deemed 'essential for coup d'état'.[35] When the demonstrators hit the street to protest government corruption, Zaim had enough excuses to overthrow the government on 30 March 1949. Turkey, preoccupied with its own internal politics as it made the transition to multi-party elections in the late 1940s, did not pay sufficient attention to Syria at the time. Even the Turkish Foreign Ministry was dragged so deep into Ankara's internal political debates that they did not provide consular services at this point to Turkish citizens in Syria, as confirmed by the many letters of complaint that flooded into the ministry.[36]

Six months later nationalist officers headed by Colonel Sami Hinnawi overthrew Zaim and executed him in August 1949. Four months later, in December 1949, Colonel Shishakli overthrew Hinnawi. In February 1954, Colonel Adnan Malki overthrew Shishakli. And in April 1955, a pro-Shishakli group from the Syrian Social Nationalist party assassinated Colonel Malki. Nationalist President Quwatli was re-elected in August 1955. After that the Turkish interest in Syria made a reappearance, this time with Turkey as a NATO member country working jointly with her powerful American and British allies. Turkish membership of NATO in 1952, and soon after that the formation of the Baghdad Pact, created grounds for Ankara to re-ignite plans for Syria. Especially through American training and military aid, Ankara rapidly boosted its military capabilities and reached a false conclusion that it could independently show its muscle in Syria to execute the Turkish plan, as long as the Americans deterred the Soviets from interfering. Also, the Baghdad Pact facilitated further grounds for the Turks to establish a tighter influence on the regional members. However, again this episode illustrated the mismatch between Turkish capabilities, policy goals and the means to achieve these goals. Why, again, was this the case in Syria?

## Back in Aleppo

It should be noted that anti-Turkish sentiment in Syria provided much of the backbone for the country's competing political parties. For instance, in 1953 the Arabian Liberation Movement in Damascus boldly published maps as guidance for Syria's geopolitical plans, and these maps included the southern Turkish provinces of Hatay, Mersin, Adana, Kahramanmaraş and Gaziantep.[37] Moreover the official Syrian Information Bureau published leaflets in 1954 embracing these aspirations and even going further to include Cyprus as a Syrian territory 'which sooner or later must return to Syria'.[38]

However, the ouster of Shishakli in 1955 gave new impetus to anti-Western nationalist groups in Syria, such as the Ba'ath Party and the

People's Party. Moreover, the previously underground communists sought new ways to support and combine forces with anti-Western nationalists in Syrian politics.[39] The formation of the Baghdad Pact in the same year between Turkey, Iraq and Britain, with American encouragement, sparked further anti-Western and anti-Turkish sentiments and open hostility between Israel and Syria. As a result, James Moose, the American ambassador in Syria, wrote to Washington in January 1956 saying 'Orthodox diplomatic procedures to improve [the] US position in Syria' necessitates 'other methods' such as an 'anti-Communist coup' in the country.[40] This time, the initial plan to remove the anti-Western nationalist groups from power, Operation Straggle, required greater cooperation as it meant more complication in the planning and implementation process. The CIA operative in charge of the plans, Wilbur Eveland, outlined the plan in the following way: 'Turkey would create border incidents, Iraqis would stir up the desert tribes and the *Partie Populaire Syrienne* in Lebanon would infiltrate the borders until mass confusion justified the use of invading Iraqi troops.'[41]

Turkey started this border incident on 23 June 1956 by claiming that the Turkish army was merely chasing 'sheep smugglers' into Syrian territory.[42] This minor 'customs protection' assignment soon evolved into a major crisis, both within Turkish state institutions and in a row with Syria that went as far as the United Nations. When the Turkish army stepped inside the Syrian border, an exchange of fire occurred between the smugglers and the army. Moreover, Syrians from surrounding villages opened fire on the Turkish soldiers. As a result, three Turkish soldiers were killed on the spot, yet the Turkish army was able to detain thirty-five Syrian nationals three hundred yards inside Syrian territory and bring them back to Turkey as prisoners.[43] As they withdrew from Syria with their prisoners, the Turkish military left the bodies of their fallen soldiers in Syria. While the Syrian government returned the bodies of the soldiers to the Turkish authorities, Ankara did not return the Syrian prisoners to their country.[44] The available sources indicate that the United States did not ask Ankara to penetrate deep into Syrian territory to take Syrian citizens hostage. However, it is likely that since the military was conducting these operations, the scale of Turkish intervention got out of hand and led to a major diplomatic crisis between Syria and Turkey at the United Nations. Moreover, since the military's excursion into Syria and reluctance to release the hostages was not coordinated with the Turkish Foreign Office, there was only a limited area of manoeuvre for Turkish diplomats to exploit the situation in Turkish intelligence diplomacy.

This incident highlighted deep cracks in the Turkish state's foreign policy and intelligence structure. Orhan Eralp, the head of the political department of the Turkish Foreign Ministry, immediately told the British ambassador in Ankara that the 'Turkish gendarmerie and authorities were primarily to blame for what might become a serious matter between Turkey and Syria'.[45] Moreover, the Syrians threatened to take the case to the UN Security Council unless the Turks immediately returned the prisoners. The British were also concerned that Ankara's mishandling of the situation, and the possibility that the Syrian incident might appear before the Security Council, would allow the Soviets to exploit the situation and encourage Syrian leftist and nationalist groups to more successfully advocate a political union with Egypt.[46]

Sir James Bowker, the British ambassador in Ankara, asked the secretary-general of the Turkish Foreign Ministry, Muharrem Nuri Birgi, at the Pakistani president's dinner reception in Istanbul on 21 July whether Ankara could release the prisoners to resolve the situation. Birgi, however, repeated Eralp's previous remarks that 'there was a difference of opinion between the Turkish military and civilian authorities regarding the crisis'.[47] The Turkish army, which also dominated the Turkish security service, apparently desired an escalation of the conflict which would indeed create plausible grounds for Turkey to launch a large-scale operation into Syria and seize the opportunity being created by Operation Straggle. However, the Turkish Foreign Ministry did not approve of the maverick activities of the army and almost echoed a Soviet version of the story that cast all blame on the Turkish army. After pressure continued to increase from the British, Americans and the Turkish Foreign Ministry, the army eventually released the prisoners on 25 July before the issue was taken up at the United Nations.

This was more than just a question of internal differences in Turkey. Every single foreign actor in the Syrian theatre had their own agenda, and tried to pull the intelligence operations in their own direction. For instance, the deputy of the British Secret Intelligence Service, George Kennedy Young, told his American counterpart, Wilbur Eveland, that 'Egypt, Saudi Arabia and Syria threatened Britain's survival. Their governments would have to be subverted or overthrown. Iraq – central point of British support – and Iran and Turkey as allies might be help in any British action'.[48] Operation Straggle presented the British with suitable grounds with which to achieve these objectives, and they tried to align it with larger British top-secret plans for intervention in Egypt.[49] In order to do so, the Americans felt that the British deliberately kept them in the dark.[50] Indeed, British secrecy concerning their plans in Egypt would later lead to the Suez Crisis, and to the aborting of Operation Straggle when the plot was foiled by Syrian Intelligence, that claimed there was a Western and Iraqi coup attempt in Damascus in October 1956.[51]

It was not only the British who deceived their partners over Operation Straggle. The French, too, had their own national agenda, which was not necessarily included in Washington's plan for the Middle East. For instance, for the French ambassador in Syria, a greater expansion of American, British, Iraqi or Turkish influence in the Levant, a traditional French area of influence, was a greater danger than the region falling into the orbit of the anti-Western bloc.[52] Even the CIA noted in April 1955, after Shishakli's ouster, that France, as well as Egypt, Saudi Arabia and Israel, 'have continually operated against the Syrian government developing closer ties with Baghdad and Ankara'.[53] The Soviet Union also started to exploit the row between Syria and Turkey, directing its subversive propaganda campaign against Turkey and 'emphasizing its connection with imperialist designs' in the region.[54] Moreover, the Turkish Prime Minister Adnan Menderes's pro-Western attitude at the 1955 Bandung Conference created a serious reaction around the nonaligned world; and his stance further enabled the Soviet propaganda campaign against Turkey.⁵⁵

At the same time, the Iraqi premier, Nuri al Said, was concerned that Ankara would use the instability that Baghdad was creating in Syria as a pretext for a Turkish military intervention there. The special intelligence committee set up in Beirut between the Iraqis, Americans and British thus made sure that the Turks would not go beyond their borders in November 1956.⁵⁶ In light of the available sources, it is safe to suggest that Iraqis were aware of the Turkish involvement in Operation Straggle. However, Baghdad's concern could be explained by worries that the Turks would try to exploit the whole scheme and try to regain the lands that the Ottomans had lost only three decades before. This was also a reflection of anti-Turkish sentiment in the minds of the Arab rulers. Both in Turkey and in the Arab world memories of the Ottoman past were still vivid. Moreover, Nasser's Arab nationalist propaganda was strengthening anti-Turkish feeling in Arab public opinion.⁵⁷ At the same time, while Turkey saw the Suez Crisis as an opportunity to diminish Nasser's influence in the Arab world, an increased French presence in the Levant created additional obstacles to Turkish endeavours there. The Turkish charge d'affaires in Damascus, 'expressed disgust at French machinations in the Levant detrimental to Western interests', in a conversation to his American counterpart, and promised to support anti-French groups in Syria.⁵⁸

Existing literature regarding Operation Straggle does not pay sufficient attention to Turkey's own ambition to increase its influence in former Ottoman territories, particularly in Syria, due to its strategic geographical and political location in the eastern Mediterranean.⁵⁹ The literature on the operation focuses more on the Anglo-American plan to use Iraq, and right-wing elements in the country itself to install a pro-Western regime in Syria. It is particularly important to examine the Turkish role in the covert action in Syria to reveal that even after Operation Straggle was aborted in October 1956, when the main conspirators were arrested by the Syrian authorities for the coup attempt and tried in Damascus, the Turks saw it not as an obstacle to advancing their plans, but as an opportunity to exploit friction between the United States and the British, and also to exploit the vacuum created by the British retreat after the Suez Crisis. Yet again, Turkish endeavours to execute their own plans in Syria, particularly after the end of Straggle, resulted in further friction among the allies, and possible military confrontation with the Soviets. Why has it always been the case?

Turkish covert action, and overt military intervention when necessary, became important tools to achieve these goals, in spite of the various Western governments trying to exercise power in the country. The Turkish consul in Damascus informed his British counterparts in 1956 that 'Ankara would have preferred to see its jurisdiction revived in parts of Arab world, but was ready to accept some sort of confederation there under British influence. Syria, however, was an exception, and should be awarded to Turkey as a trusteeship.'[60] Yet, it is also important to note that Turkey's Democrat Party government was propagating the Turkish right to intervene in Syria, both in the domestic and foreign arenas. For instance, the pro-government newspaper Zafer 'was building up moral and political case for Turkey's involvement in Syria – to counter Cairo's intrigues'.[61]

However, Turkey's desire to seize the opportunity to expand its influence in Syria was subject to both internal restrictions and the external ones from her allies. Adnan Kural, the Turkish consul in Aleppo, believed that 'any Iraqi and Turkish intervention would push Syria more towards Russia and create excuses for Syrian leftists to seek closer ties with Russia'.[62] While Kural himself did not believe that a potential external intervention in Syria would work, his voice did not make it to the upper echelons of the Turkish political system. Especially after Turkey and Iraq jointly formed the Baghdad Pact in 1955, both the Turkish Foreign Ministry and the ruling Democrat Party overemphasized their role in the Middle East and dissenting views, such as Kural's, became less popular than ever in Ankara.[63] However, Kural was right. Operation Straggle failed, concurrently with the Suez debacle, following the Iraqi plot in late 1956 to oust the regime in Damascus as well as the expulsion of three American officials from Syria in August

1957 on the grounds of being part of the coup plot. The outcome was the opposite of that intended. As the CIA noted, 'external pressures have probably helped knit the [anti-Western] coalition together and have considerably strengthened its position within the country, as well as among the other Arab states'.[64] The CIA also concluded:

> The Turks are probably inclined to favor active and forceful means to solve the Syrian problem, but they are unlikely to act without assurance or support from the US and they are probably aware of the difficulties of making a military action in Syria politically successful without extensive Arab participation, which now appears unlikely.[65]

The CIA memorandum, prepared by Sherman Kent, the assistant director for National Estimates, was accurate and further outlined how Arab nationalism fostered anti-Western sentiment. Washington thus became careful not to further alienate regional governments and push them more towards Moscow, whose image in the region was becoming increasingly positive. Moreover, this highlights the fact that the divergence between Turkish capabilities and aims, in addition to the regional enmities preceding the Cold War, profoundly shaped Western intervention in the Middle East.

## Ankara does not give up

Ankara continued its own agenda in Syria independently of this East–West confrontation. As demonstrated at the beginning of this chapter, American Ambassador Warren interrupted a Turkish cabinet meeting to openly warn the government not to intervene in Syria anymore. There were several reasons for this attitude from Washington. First, as CIA operative Eveland says, Washington was concerned that 'Turkish intervention in Syria could provoke a global war'.[66] President Eisenhower was also convinced that 'Turkey was truly serious about a showdown in Syria', and as a reaction, 'the Soviets might very well move against Turkey'.[67] Warren's intervention also coincided with increasingly negative attitudes towards Turkey in Washington, as we saw in Chapter 5, yet they could not completely abandon a NATO ally lest they leave the Middle East open to further communist influence. Thus, the Eisenhower administration endeavoured to manage possible setbacks from an aborted CIA covert action in the Middle East.

However, the Menderes government still tried to seize the opportunity. Michael Ilyan, a former Syrian foreign minister previously used in Operation Straggle to fund pro-Western groups in Syria, told CIA operative Eveland that he was 'working with Turkey to spark a revolution in Syria'. Ilyan admitted he prepared plans at Turkey's request and saw no reason why the United States should want them halted.[68] Meanwhile, the Turkish ambassador in Washington was trying to align the American government with Turkish intentions, and moreover convince them that the Turkish position and Baghdad Pact policies on Syria were indeed in accordance with the Eisenhower doctrine, which the president authorized in early 1957 for US assistance if a country requested its help against an external aggressor, particularly concerning the Middle East.[69] As a way to convince Washington, Turkish Ambassador Suat Hayri Ürgüplü (who was himself born in Damascus in 1903) emphasized to Owen T. Jones, Director of Greek, Turkish and Iranian Affairs, that when Ürgüplü was the Turkish ambassador in London between 1955 and 1957 he had a primary role in the failed Iraqi plot to overthrow the regime in Damascus.[70] Ürgüplü also tried to convince the Americans that they needed to end their indulgence of Nasser, who could betray them, and focus on supporting the agenda of their reliable ally, Turkey.

Indeed, some results of these plans leaked to the Turkish newspapers. *Cumhuriyet*, for instance, reported on 11 February 1957 that 'The Islamic Society for the Salvation of the Homeland from Russian Oppression' was founded in the Turkish city of Hatay. The daily newspaper also stated that the Turkey-based organization was conducting many subversive activities, including propaganda and sabotage to overthrow the Syrian government in Aleppo, Hama and Homs.[71] Similar stories also surfaced in Lebanese and Turkish newspapers, including arson and bomb attacks against certain Ba'ath Party officers' houses in Aleppo, as well as armed clashes between Turkish-backed Arab tribes and Syrian government forces. These clashes led to the deaths of several Syrian soldiers, and allegedly some Russian ones as well.[72]

Following the set-up of proxy organizations to conduct subversive activities in Syria, in particular using a number of Syrian refugees that arrived in early 1957, the Turkish military concentrated military forces along the Syrian border and made several incursions into Syrian territory with a small number of troops to create disruptions.[73] Indeed, John Morris, American Consul in the Turkish port city of Iskenderun, near the Syrian border, held a meeting with Brigadier General Cevdet Yamanoğlu, the Iskenderun Garrison Commander, and reported that 'he had never seen the General so open in his remarks. It is possible the General was passing along the information the Turks wanted disseminated.'[74] The news was certainly worth disseminating. Yamanoğlu informed the American diplomat that 'the Turkish troops were in position and prepared to cross into Syria to take Aleppo. He stated that he was "waiting for only one thing – the orders from Ankara to move into Syria".[75] Soon after this conversation, Ankara asked Eisenhower what his attitude would be if the Turks moved alone into Syria.[76] Although Washington did not approve a Turkish action in Syria, Yamanoğlu's surprisingly frank remarks concerning the immediate possibility of a Turkish invasion demonstrated two important aspects of Turkish intelligence diplomacy. First, the Turks were sure that if they created a de facto situation, the Americans would have no other choice but to support them in their campaign in Syria. Secretary of State Dulles also repeated the same concern when informing Senator Mike Mansfield, the Senate Majority whip, who came to the same conclusion.[77] However, as Ivan Pearson states, the potential Turkish campaign had an 'inherent limitation' that came from being a non-Arab state:

> Had the US been associated with a Turkish move, it would have alienated itself from its regional allies, and by doing so strengthened Nasser's position. To the British, had the 'Turkish Alternative' been implemented, this action would have threatened the IPC pipeline that

ran through Syria, and meant that another opportunity to strengthen Iraq's position (and perhaps even destroy Nasser) was lost.[78]

In other words, Ankara was trying to lure Americans into supporting a Turkish campaign in Syria through conventional channels, through the remarks and activities of its military officers. Ankara also tried to create an ambiguity in NATO, and seize the opportunity for dragging NATO members into the Turkish campaign. However, recognizing the risks of implementing the Turkish Plan, the British and Americans also created their own 'Preferred Plan'. This plan, designed to take place in September 1957 and topple the regime in Damascus with only a limited role for the Turks, was never implemented given the rising tension between the Turks and the Soviets at the time.[79]

## Alliance in discord

These events created serious friction among the NATO allies, since Turkey failed to inform NATO of its troop movements in Syria, even when the situation was discussed at the NATO Council in September 1957. Jean Chauvel, the French ambassador to London, noted to his British counterpart that the 'Turks had been unduly secretive, and had not come clean as when the matter was recently discussed in NATO Council'.[80] He further asked whether the British knew anything about the Turkish troop concentration near Syria. Ankara did not share any information with Britain either. The British military attaché in Ankara concluded that 'the Turks have moved a very considerable number of additional troops' to the Syrian border.[81] The attaché also added that 'he might as well have been in Moscow for all the cooperation which he had received'.[82] Michael Stewart, British chargé d'affaires in Turkey, informed the Turkish Foreign Ministry's secretary-general that the Turkish handling of the Syrian situation was creating an atmosphere of disapproval in NATO, which was observed by Paul-Henri Spaak, the NATO secretary-general. Moreover, the Turks also misinformed other NATO members, such as Belgium and Norway, by saying that all Turkish military activities in Syria were carried out with the knowledge of the British and Americans.[83] It is important to note that Ankara tried to deceive NATO by claiming that its troop concentration near the Syrian border was part of a routine NATO exercise named *Deepwater*. However, the American delegation in NATO informed Dulles that 'there is no direct connection between these [Turkish] exercises and Exercise Deepwater'.[84]

In October 1957, Eisenhower, Dulles, British Prime Minister Harold Macmillan and Foreign Secretary Selwyn Lloyd held a meeting at the White House to discuss the situation between Turkey and Syria, and the possible Russian reaction. Dulles informed them that he interpreted the Russian position to the conflict as 'a genuine fear on their part that they might be confronted with either backing down or fighting in the Middle East, and they did not want to fight at the present time'.[85] He further concluded that they would not like to start a 'cycle of challenge and response [with the Russians] and response which would lead to general war'.[86] On the other hand, the situation 'called for the most careful handling' since no action in their part should be 'misinterpreted by Turks as indicating that [they] had lost our [their] nerve or become frightened by the Russian bluster'.[87]

In coordination with the Americans, the British Foreign Office sensed that the Turks had been 'unnecessarily reticent with everyone', possibly for trying to deceive the alliance over the Turks' own strategy in Syria. However, William Hayter, the Deputy Under-Secretary stated that 'in practice this [Turkish reticence] does not mean too much to [the British] as [Britain is in] close touch with the Americans. The Turkish attitude has caused much concern to others'.[88] He concluded, 'The Turks probably have in mind the US message to the Turkish Prime Minister of early September [1957]. This message did not of course suggest that Turkey should take military precautions, but its general tenor could be understood as approving defensive measures on Turkey's part'.[89] However, Turkish measures were not defensive but organized in a way to invade Aleppo. This diplomatic ambiguity among the Western

Alliance was also assisting Turkey's aim of giving its military some time to finalize its invasion plans. As the Turkish intelligence diplomacy was a synchronized approach between the intelligence service and the diplomatic office, it was providing the weaker partner in the alliance with the opportunity to exploit such an ambiguity.

Turkey's Western allies were not the only ones concerned about a possible Turkish military action in Syria. Her Arab partners, as well as Arab public opinion, shared these concerns as well. Indeed, Arab countries such as Iraq and Jordan informed Dulles that they 'were turning away from taking overt military action against Syria. Their thinking, however, was running increasingly along the lines of covert action within Syria ... it was our feeling that, however, if Turkey took military action alone, it could have almost as bad an effect, although not quite, as if the Israelis took military action on their own against Syria.'[90] Dulles noted that 'we had no doubt that the Turks could beat up the Syrian army, but we foresaw a subsequent period of almost unending turmoil in the Middle East as a consequence of Turkish action.'[91]

Apart from their leaders, Arab public opinion was strongly against a possible Turkish intervention too. During the crisis, the Arab Islamic leaders, the Ulema, sent a letter from Baghdad to the Turkish Prime Minister Menderes saying: 'Your conflict with Syria has shaken all the Arab and Muslim world. We urge you to drop your hostile attitude, and your alignment with the infidel powers, otherwise it may result with a catastrophic war, whose initial victims would be Muslim countries.'[92] The possible reaction from Arab public opinion placed another restraint on Ankara, and gave Turkish planners a sign of how their game of deception in Syria could backfire. Therefore, Turkish intelligence diplomacy faced great limitations in pursuing its strategy in Syria. However, at the same time Turkish actions greatly complicated the issue so that, as a result, neither Arab countries nor Turkey's Western partners could pursue an active engagement in Syria either. Syrian unification with Egypt into the United Arab Republic in February 1958 certainly did not accord with Turkish intentions. Again this was a consequence of the divergence in Turkish capabilities, means and goals.

This time, such a divergence was explicitly counterproductive since it brought Nasser to the Turkish border, and hampered American covert action efforts.

An unintended consequence of the Turkish attitude to Syria concerned the weaknesses on NATO's flank between the Turks and the Greeks. This weakness surfaced to great effect when the Syrians took the crisis to the UN General Assembly to ask for an investigation on Turkish troop movements along their border.[93] Surprisingly, the Greek delegation to the plenary defended the Syrian complaint, although other NATO members all voted against it. The Italian delegate, while concerned about Turkish motives in the affair, 'found it particularly shocking that Ambassador Stratos should have taken so anti-Turkish line when the Arabs themselves were so pointedly remaining silent'.[94] Greek-Turkish relations were already under great stress due to the conflict over Cyprus. On a personal note, the Greek delegate Andreas Stratos's father, Nikolaos Stratos, was one of the Greek ministers who were executed for treason and responsibility for the Greek defeat in the Turco-Greek war between 1919 and 1922, an event for which he never forgave Turkey. Therefore, Stratos used the Syrian complaint and rising disapproval around the world towards Turkish behaviour concerning Syria, as his opportunity to strike at the Turks.[95]

This increasing turbulence in the alliance led the Americans and British to restrain Turkish behaviour in Syria. The Soviets also made moves to defuse the crisis. During debates at the United Nations, Soviet Premier Nikita Khrushchev showed up at a Turkish national reception at the Turkish embassy in Moscow. There he made a statement which declared: 'Let him be damned who wants war. Let him fight alone. But why talk about war anyway? There will be no war.' Asked whether his presence at the Turkish reception indicated a lessening of tensions in the Middle East, Khrushchev replied: 'Yes. This is a gesture, a gesture towards peace.'[96] The silencing of the war drums between Syria and Turkey was thanks to two important aspects. Frictions were obviously surfacing within NATO. The allies would not allow themselves to be dragged into a conflict between Turkey and Syria, a conflict which could escalate into a much larger war. For this reason, the Americans successfully focused on restraining Turkey. Khrushchev also did not wish to be dragged into a conflict with the West.[97] The calming of the situation by Washington, by Moscow and by the formation of the United Arab Republic halted Turkish actions towards Syria. But they were only halted for a couple of months.

## Last try

The US marine landing in Beirut in July 1958 – which occurred even as Qassim took power in Iraq and withdrew from the Baghdad Pact – created both external pressures and opportunities for Turkey to utilize covert action once again, and if necessary overt action in Syria, this time with other partners. It is necessary to take a closer look at the regional developments which occurred in 1958, in order to analyse which courses of action enabled Turkey to return to its previous aims in Syria, and this time in Iraq as well. First, the aftermath of the Suez crisis in 1956, and concurrent failed covert attempts in Syria, empowered anti-Western sentiment in the Arab World. Thus, in October 1957, right in the midst of the Turco-Syrian crisis, 'a highly secret Anglo-American working group in Washington prepared a wide-ranging report that emphasised the need for political, economic and propaganda measures in the Middle East'.[98] Political instability in Lebanon starting in May 1958, the bloody coup by Iraqi nationalist officers on 14 July 1958 and the weak position of the Hashemite monarchy in Jordan further encouraged Washington and London to prepare military contingency plans in the Middle East to reverse the anti-Western tide.

In the historical literature that deals with the Middle Eastern side of the Anglo-American relationship, the primary focus is either the British retreat of power in the Middle East, or the American takeover of the leadership of the Free World in the Middle East against the Soviets.[99] There are also works which emphasize the frictions and struggles, and the division of labour when necessary, between the Americans, British and Egyptians for leadership in the Middle East at the height of the Cold War.[100] However, while it is not widely discussed in the literature, regional members of the Baghdad Pact, led by Turkey, also prepared their own covert and overt plans on Iraq and Syria to change the tide in their favour.

Pro-Nasser rebel groups initiated instability in Lebanon in May 1958, on the grounds that the country's Christian president, Camille Chamoun, was thoroughly corrupt and was seeking unlawfully to extend his tenure as president. Washington was alarmed at the instability caused by Nasser's flow of men, arms and subversive propaganda into Lebanon. Dulles, however, was not convinced that a US military intervention in Lebanon would bring stability to the country. On the contrary, he believed that a Western intervention would 'undoubtedly give rise to an intensified wave of anti-Western feeling of which Nasser could capitalize'.[101]

Many of Washington's local partners, however, supported an American intervention. Dulles recognized these points by noting they 'had to take into account the fact that if Lebanon which had been the most independent and pro-Western of Arab States, appealed for help and was refused, the impact of that also would be great'.[102] In this delicate situation, he also noted that 'Turkey and Iraq would precipitate fighting by their own action on the theory that it would compel the United States to come in'.[103]

Meanwhile, Turkish intelligence diplomacy was working to attract US intervention in the Middle East in accordance with Turkish priorities – namely preventing infiltration by Nasser and the Soviets, and expanding Turkish influence in the places from where the British were retreating. As an indicator, the Menderes government even hoped to replace Suat Hayri Ürgüplü, the Turkish ambassador in Washington, with Melih Esenbel in early July 1958, since Ankara hoped that Esenbel would prove more able to convince the Americans of the Turkish position regarding the Middle East, particularly in Syria.[104] Therefore, both to further secure his position and to convey the concerns of

Ankara to Washington, Ürgüplü immediately told William Rountree, Assistant Secretary for Near Eastern Affairs in Washington, that 'a formal discussion of Middle Eastern problems without the presence of Middle East countries – particularly Turkey – is not acceptable to the Turkish government'.[105] Alongside conventional diplomatic endeavours, Ankara's intelligence diplomacy focused on Iraq and Syria, in order to create a possible de facto situation that would force Washington to support Turkish expansion into those two countries.

Immediately following the Iraqi coup, and the US landing in Beirut, the British Foreign Office received growing quantities of intelligence which suggested that the Turks would seize the moment and conduct a military intervention in Syria. Even the British envoy in Lebanon noted on 17 July that President Chamoun 'had received unofficial or private word that Turkey intended to intervene in Syria'.[106] Upon receiving this intelligence, the Foreign Office decided to consult the Americans to find out Washington's 'considered views about the desirability or otherwise of Turkish intervention, and whether or not they feel that anything should be said to the Turkish government on the subject on the present time'.[107] At this point in the summer of 1958, British attention was focused on protecting their influence in Iraq and Jordan.[108] However, Turkey was also keen on exploiting the British retreat from power, even trying to bypass the British presence in the Baghdad Pact, and on directly using the cover of the American military presence in Beirut to execute Ankara's own plan.

First and foremost, Ankara opened its military bases and logistic units, especially the Incirlik airbase, to support the American military mission in Lebanon. By providing these bases, Turkey aimed to nudge Washington further in line with Turkish interests in the Middle East.[109] Apart from providing logistic support to the American mission, Ankara devised a more complicated plan regarding the Middle Eastern situation. This plan was in accordance with the methods of Turkish intelligence diplomacy – namely exploiting frictions within the alliance, using military deterrence, conventional diplomacy and secret intelligence – to achieve Turkish goals.

The Turkish cabinet met late on the night of 12 July to discuss the situation in Lebanon, and the possibilities of a Turkish military intervention into Syria. This meeting happened alongside the mobilization of a large number of troops on the Turkish-Syrian border.[110] At the same time, Turkey introduced intensified security controls on its southern border, and the secretary-general of the Turkish Foreign Ministry, Melih Esenbel, asked the top echelons of the US embassy in Ankara not to leave the city. Ankara needed to coordinate its overt and covert actions with the Americans since Turkish desires exceeded their own capabilities. For an operation of this kind the stakes were incredibly high.

Ankara, for instance, remained afraid of a Kurdish revolt in Iran, the only other remaining Middle Eastern member of the Baghdad Pact. The Turkish foreign minister, Zorlu, told American Ambassador Warren that 'both they and the Shah [were] in a great fear of a possible Kurdish revolt inspired by the [United Arab Republic]'.[111] Turkish officials encouraged the Shah to follow its own line on the Kurdish question, portraying Kurdish movements as anti-Western to its allies in order to legitimize its own repressive policies on the Kurds, and other dissident groups in the Cold War context. Moreover, Warren reported that 'the Turks intend to advise the Shah of Iran to take the strongest possible measures within Iran, in a dictatorial fashion if necessary, on the premise that a show of democratic procedures within Iran would lead to the Shah's replacement by an anti-Western dictator'.[112]

At the same time, Ankara was pushing King Hussein of Jordan to 'assume positive leadership of the Arab Union, as his constitutional right, thereby establishing the ability to act against the rebels in Iraq'.[113] Zorlu 'sent Hussein a plan of Turkish action "to bolster his morale"'.[114] King Hussein informed the Americans that it was a plan for unilateral Turkish military action against Syria. Given the available information from the archives, it is safe to suggest that the Turks knew that their shared plan with King Hussein would be leaked to the British and

Americans as well. By showing their seriousness, Ankara wanted to push the Americans to support the Turkish intervention.

Turkish plans were not only limited to Syria. At the same time, as they meditated a unilateral military intervention in Syria they also considered taking action in Iraq. Turkish intelligence infiltrated tribes in Kirkuk and Mosul to obtain the support of 'these tribes in the event that Turkey should move on Iraq through the Mosul province'.[115] However, Ankara did not plan to move on Iraq on its own. Although there were a considerable number of Turkish-speaking tribes in the region – the American consulate estimated the Turcoman population as around 100,000[116] – Turkey, Pakistan and Iran, as non-Western members of the Baghdad Pact, decided to initiate a joint military action to restore order in Iraq.[117] This military action reflected the desire of the non-Western members of the Baghdad Pact to exclude the British from their military planning and expand their influence in the Middle East by dragging the United States into their plans. In accordance with this plan, Turkey also remobilized its forces along the Syria–Iraq border, and was prepared to go over the border when the political decision was taken.[118] Finally, on 23 July 1958, the Turkish COS, Feyzi Mengüç, forwarded a plan to the US COS, General Randy Taylor, for an invasion of Iraq and Syria to be led by Turkish forces. In this plan, Ankara requested that the 'United States furnish air cover and some technical material assistance'.[119] However, General Taylor did not provide an affirmative answer to his Turkish counterpart, and let diplomatic channels convey a message to Ankara that the United States was not willing to support the Turkish plan.

The Turkish plan in the summer of 1958 also brought the Soviet bloc and the Western bloc to the brink of war. When Turkey mobilized its forces on its southern border, the Soviets concentrated substantial forces on the Turkish-Bulgarian border.[120] The Soviets also concentrated their troops on Turkey's eastern border. Ankara certainly noticed the danger of a Soviet military response to the possible Turkish military action in the south. Thus, the Turkish COS requested the US Air Force to provide

'24 hour aerial reconnaissance of the area extending 100 miles north of the Turkish Black Sea coast'.[121] Finally, there were increasing signs that the Soviets were also channelling paramilitary forces and some submarines towards Iraq and Syria, as well as an increasing propaganda campaign that the conflict could easily escalate into a larger war between the East and West.[122] However, this had an unintended effect in Moscow, causing war hysteria among its residents.[123] At this point, Washington was able to restrain the Turkish endeavours and Moscow, in any case, did not intend to commit to a military intervention in Turkey, from which it could not easily withdraw.[124] The relatively quick and easy success of the US marine landing in Beirut to stabilize the situation in the country, moreover, as well as the prompt withdrawal of the American forces in October 1958, helped to prevent the escalation of the conflict. It also ended the opportunity for Turkey to implement its Syrian and Iraqi plans.

## The coup against itself

There were other considerations that forced Turkey to shelve plans to intervene in Syria. From the middle of 1958, Turkey became increasingly preoccupied with its covert and diplomatic endeavours in Cyprus, to protect the island's Muslim community as well as Turkish interests after the decolonization of the island. Sir Anthony Parsons, the First Secretary in the British embassy in Ankara, also confirmed that the Cyprus problem 'created either major inter-communal strife or even worse an actual inter-state war between Greece and Turkey, both members of NATO'. Cyprus now replaced the wider Middle East as the crucial focus of Turkish foreign policy.[125] Menderes's Democrat Party government faced growing domestic pressure at home, from both the army and the main opposition political party, the Republican People's Party, as well as rising Turkish nationalist sentiment due to the increasingly pressing issue of Cyprus – all of which rendered immediate Turkish action in Syria impossible. For instance, as Parsons noted, the religious-conservative tone of the Menderes government, which wanted to roll back the country's secularization, created major discontent within the army.

As early as late 1957, that discontent led the Menderes government to arrest nine high-level military officers, and forcibly retire two respected generals in the Turkish Armed Forces, namely General Kani Akmanlar and General Cavit Çevik.[126] While some of the discontent between the Menderes government and the military concerned the Syrian debacle and Cyprus, the other bone of contention lay in the increasingly undemocratic and authoritarian tendencies of the government due to its considerable loss of power in the general election of October 1957.[127] For instance, when there were protests by the opposition after the elections, the Menderes government ordered the local military commanders to open fire on the protesters. When the officers refused the orders, the government arrested them on charges of 'instigation to revolt' and 'intrigues'. Moreover, their jail conditions were below an acceptable standard, and even their right to see their families, for instance, was prohibited.[128] Most of the officers were released more than six months later due to pressure from the higher echelons of the army.[129]

The government had to have good relations with the higher echelons of the army, which was the main tool for conducting the government's policies in the Middle East and Cyprus. However, severe damage was done to relations between the Menderes government and military officers after the arrests of 1957, and even the chain of command was not able to prevent discontented army officers from planning a coup. Just months after Turkey's military manoeuvres concerning Syria, the Turkish defence minister, Ethem Menderes, informed Warren that 'if the present repressive tendencies of the democratic regime continue, military leaders will intervene and a dictatorship will result'.[130] Neither the CIA nor the State Department gave the information enough attention because it was focused on Cold War subjects – not on monitoring the Turkish military for possible coup plots. At that time, most of the CIA's energy in Turkey was dedicated to conducting U-2 spy plane operations, organizing stay-behind networks, and waging covert actions and espionage missions against the Soviets. The agency simply did not have the resources to develop an informed view on potential coup leaders or their intentions. The Cold War framework overrode all other considerations. Moreover, as Christopher Gunn brilliantly points out in his recent article:

> By the spring of 1960, the U.S. government was frustrated by Adnan Menderes's policies and his proclivity to ignore U.S. advice. His disastrous economic policies were threatening the stability of one of NATO's most important members. The failure to implement much-needed military reform had caused the Turkish armed forces to become increasingly expensive, inefficient, and incompatible with US security needs. Finally, relations between the Menderes government and the Soviet Union seemed to warm whenever Ankara's pleas for financial aid were ignored by the West. This tendency, particularly after Menderes announced he would make an official visit to the USSR in April 1960, proved to be a major irritant in US-Turkish relations. The increasing friction between the US and Turkish governments, and policy decisions made by the Eisenhower administration, undermined Menderes' position in the months leading up to the coup.[131]

Precisely a year after Ethem Menderes informed the Americans about the possibility of a coup, such an event removed the civilian government from power. The generals behind it executed three leading figures of the government – Prime Minister Adnan Menderes, Foreign Minister Fatin Rüştü Zorlu and Finance Minister Hasan Polatkan, shortly thereafter. Following the coup, it was not only Turkish covert operations that went into hiatus, due to the focus on domestic politics, but the liaison between Turkish intelligence and the CIA was also weakened, an outcome that Washington certainly had not foreseen or desired. For instance, during the Yassıada trials, where Menderes and his co-defendants were accused of treason, the heads of MAH testified to the effect that the Menderes government had made the Turkish security apparatus heavily dependent on American financial help, and alleged that the CIA even occupied one whole floor of the MAH HQ in Ankara.[132] Hence, after the 1960 coup, the MAH was more closely controlled by the Turkish military and the CIA was asked to move their offices from the MAH HQ to an outside liaison office.[133] Turkish intelligence diplomacy thus entered into a new phase, with a more limited focus on covert action abroad and a greater focus on domestic targets.

# Conclusion

Turkey emerged from the First World War as a relatively minor and weak country, with great ambitions as a former imperial power that far exceeded its capabilities. While it could not achieve these ambitions through overt means, it could nevertheless try to attain them through covert means, and a coordinated approach between its diplomatic and security apparatus. While some of these endeavours failed, such as the Özdemir Bey operation in 1922 against the British in Iraq's Mosul province, some of them, such as the operation to annex Hatay from Syria in 1939, proved successful. During the Cold War, however, the bipolar power structure of global politics, as well as the increasing Soviet threat to Turkish sovereignty, meant that Ankara could not successfully conduct operations on its own without integrating them into the larger framework of Western operations. Therefore, one of the main objectives behind Turkish covert operations during the early Cold War was to encourage Washington to share Turkish strategic imperatives, and attract American commitments of various kinds to Ankara's objectives in the region.

The Turkish campaign in Syria was a remarkable example of such an endeavour. Ankara tried to exploit both the retreat of British power in the region and post-Suez friction between the British and Americans, to obtain a larger role for Turkey in the Middle East, and expand its sphere of influence, particularly in Syria. However, Turkish attempts to obtain American support for and commitment to Ankara's plans in Syria not only caused friction among NATO members, who did not wish to be dragged into a larger conflict with the Soviets for the sake of Turkey, but also brought the Soviets and the Western countries close to a large-scale war. Turkish actions in this respect bred growing distrust of Ankara among its Western allies. For these reasons, Turkey failed to gain American support for its campaigns in the Middle East. Moreover, the Menderes government with its authoritarian tendencies tried to use the country's security apparatus in an unaccountable way, so that any plan for Turkish covert action in the Middle East promptly climbed upward in the ladder of escalation, risking a major regional war.

The Turkish security apparatus's operations in Cyprus and Syria, which ultimately proved beyond its capabilities, fuelled ongoing tension between the civil and military leaders of the country. The increasingly undemocratic tendencies of the Menderes government, and its failures with regard to Syria, helped to break the chain of command both in the Turkish security apparatus, and their relations with civilian leaders. The result was the military coup of 27 May 1960. From then on, and for decades to come, the Turkish military, and the country's military-dominated intelligence services, became primarily preoccupied with the search for domestic targets in the midst of continued political instability and turmoil. As a result, Turkish intelligence cooperation with Western countries entered a new phase, where Turkey became more reluctant to cooperate as closely with the Americans as before, or conduct covert operations in its adjacent regions, until the Cold War ended in 1991.

## Notes

1   Aldrich, *Hidden Hand*, 5.
2   Scott, 'Secret Intelligence, Covert Action and Clandestine Diplomacy', 329.
3   Particularly on the role of secret intelligence and covert action in the British decolonization process, please see Cormac, Confronting Colonies; G. Davey, 'Intelligence and British Decolonisation: The Development of an Imperial Intelligence System in the Late Colonial Period 1944–1966', unpublished thesis (King's College, London, 2015); P. Murphy, 'Intelligence and Decolonization: The Life and Death of the Federal Intelligence and Security Bureau, 1954–63', *The Journal of Imperial and Commonwealth History*, 29:2 (2001), 101–130.

4   The Turkish foreign policy focus on the Turks outside of Turkish borders is successfully evaluated in U. Uzer, *Identity and Turkish Foreign Policy: The Kemalist Influence in Cyprus and the Caucasus* (London, 2010).
5   Aldrich, *Hidden Hand*, 155.
6   NARA: RG59: Box 3744: 782.55347C/8-156: Telegram from Warren to the State Department.
7   For an account of the lives of Bulgarian Turks who have been used by Turkish intelligence, please see P. Krasztev, 'Understated, Overexposed. Turks in Bulgaria-Immigrants in Turkey', *Balkanologie: Revue d'études pluridisciplinaires*, 5: 1–2 (2008), 1–23.
8   L. K. Johnson, 'On Drawing a Bright Line for Covert Operations', *The American Journal of International Law*, 86:2 (1992), 284.
9   Ibid., 298.
10  Nihat Ali Özcan, *PKK (Kürdistan İşçi Partisi) tarihi, ideolojisi ve yöntemi* (Ankara, 1999), 68.
11  M. Rubin, 'A Comedy of Errors: American-Turkish Diplomacy and the Iraq War', *Turkish Policy Quarterly*, 4:1 (2005), 120.
12  See Egemen Bezci and Nicholas Borroz, 'The CIA and a Turkish Coup', *War on the Rocks*, 16 September 2016.
13  NARA: RG59: Box 3744: Warren to Dulles, 25 April 1957.
14  P. Mogens. *Military Intervention and a Crisis Democracy in Turkey: The Menderes Era and Its Demise* (London, 2014).
15  A. Rathmell, *Secret War in the Middle East: The Covert Struggle for Syria, 1949–1961* (London, 1995).
16  D. Little, 'Cold War and Covert Action: The United States and Syria, 1945–1958', *Middle East Journal*, 44:1 (1990), 52.
17  Ibid.
18  R. Hinnebusch, 'Modern Syrian Politics', *History Compass*, 6:1 (2008), 264.
19  Ibid.
20  A. K. Sanjian, 'The Sanjak of Alexandretta (Hatay): Its Impact on Turkish-Syrian Relations (1939–1956)', *Middle East Journal*, 10:4 (1956), 382.
21  BCA: 030.10.0.0.265.792.38: 608/343: 'From Damascus to Ankara', 24 September 1946.
22  Ibid.
23  Ibid.
24  Ibid.

25 Anthony Gorst and W. Scott Lucas. 'The Other Collusion: Operation Straggle and Anglo-American Intervention in Syria, 1955–56', *Intelligence and National Security*, 4.3 (1989), 577.
26 BCA: 030.10.0.0.265.792.45: 'Hasan Saka to Recep Peker', 17 March 1947.
27 BCA: 030.01.0.0.65.406.13: 'General Directorate of Security: Special Affairs Branch: 442', 2 July 1947.
28 All these names represent notable local families in the Syrian politics. P. Seale, *The Struggle for Syria: A Study of Post War Arab Politics 1945–1958* (Oxford, 1965), 28.
29 Ibid., 29.
30 Ibid., 30.
31 BCA: 030.01.0.0.65.406.13: 'General Directorate of Security: Special Affairs Branch: 442', 2 July 1947.
32 Seale, *The Struggle for Syria*, 30.
33 Ibid., 36.
34 Little, 'Cold War and Covert Action', 56.
35 Ibid., 56.
36 BCA: 490.01.0.0.607.102.21: Tel to RPP HQ, 28 January 1948.
37 CIA-RDP80-00809A000500800076-7: 'Syrian Territorial Aspirations', 3 February 1954.
38 Ibid.
39 Little, 'Cold War and Covert Action', 62.
40 Ibid., 66.
41 Eveland, *Ropes of Sand*, 171.
42 TNA: FO 371/121868: V/103445(a): 'Official Turkish Statement on the Detention of Syrian Nationals', 23 June 1956.
43 TNA: FO 371/121868: V/10344/8: 'British Chancery in Ankara to FO', 21 July 1956.
44 TNA: FO 371/121868: 'Official Syrian Communique to Levant Department Foreign Office', 10 July 1956.
45 TNA: FO 371/121868: V/10344/8: 'British Chancery in Ankara to FO', 21 July 1956.
46 TNA: FO 371/121868: V/10344/4: 'From Damascus to Foreign Office', 11 July 1956.
47 TNA: FO 371/121868: V/10344/12: 'Istanbul to Foreign Office', 21 July 1926.
48 Eveland, *Ropes of Sand*, 169–170.

49   Little, 'Cold War and Covert Action', 67.
50   Ibid.
51   S. Lucas and A. Morey, 'The Hidden "Alliance": The CIA and MI6 before and after Suez', *Intelligence and National Security* 15:2 (2000), 108.
52   Eveland, *Ropes of Sand*, 125.
53   CIA-RDP91T01172R000300060009-5: 'From Office of Current Intelligence to Deputy Director: The Situation in Syria', 15 April 1955.
54   Ibid.
55   Aydin, 'Determinants of Turkish Foreign Policy: Changing Patterns and Conjunctures during the Cold War', 121.
56   Seale, *The Struggle for Syria*, 273.
57   In the historiography, three major approaches exist to examine anti-Turkish sentiment in Arab nationalism. George Antonius, for instance, argues that from its inception in the nineteenth century, Arab Nationalism was directed against the centuries-old Ottoman domination, see G. Antonius, *The Arab Awakening* (London, 1938). However, Zeine points out that it was the Young Turks' forceful Turkification process that created anti-Turkish sentiment among Arabs. See N. Zeine, *The Emergence of Arab Nationalism: With a Background Study of Arab-Turkish Relations in the Near East* (Delmar, NY, 1973). A more recent study by Kayalı brings a more balanced approach and claims that it was a struggle among Arab and Turkish elites regarding Ottoman administrative reforms for the centralization of the empire that created the anti-Turkish sentiment in Arab nationalism. See H. Kayalı H, *Arabs and Young Turks. Ottomanism, Arabism, and Islamism in the Ottoman Empire, 1908–1918* (Berkeley, CA, 1997). There are still debates on the origins of the anti-Turkish sentiment in the Arab world. However, for the sake of this research, it is important to acknowledge the significance of anti-Turkish sentiment in foreign policy and security matters. c.f. D. Jung, 'Turkey and the Arab World: Historical Narratives and New Political Realities', *Mediterranean Politics*, 10:1 (2005), 1–17.
58   Rathmell, *The Covert Struggle for Syria, 1949–1961*, 96–97.
59   All the existing literature, except Pelts' military intervention and crisis of democracy in Turkey, do not reveal the Turkish motives and plans in Operation Straggle, and in the further episodes in Syria. Thus, their

interpretation of the Cold War in the region falls short of revealing the role of local agency. See N. Ashton, *Eisenhower, Macmillan and the Problem of Nasser: Anglo-American Relations and Arab Nationalism, 1955–59* (London, 1996); S. Blackwell, 'Britain, the United States and the Syrian Crisis, 1957', *Diplomacy and Statecraft*, 11.3 (2000), 139–158; H. Wilford, *America's Great Game: The CIA's Secret Arabists and the Shaping of the Modern Middle East* (Philadelphia, PA, 2013); A. Gerolymatos, *Castles Made of Sand: A Century of Anglo-American Espionage and Intervention in the Middle East* (London, 2010).
60 Mogens Pelt, *Military Intervention and a Crisis of Democracy in Turkey: The Menderes Era and Its Demise* (London, 2014), 39.
61 Pelts, *Military Intervention and Crisis of Democracy in Turkey,* 119.
62 Eveland, *Ropes of Sand*, 186.
63 Ibid.
64 CIA-RDP79R00904A000400010012-6: 'Memorandum for the Director of Central Intelligence: Near East Reactions to Developments in the Syrian Situation', 9 October 1957.
65 Ibid.
66 Eveland, *Ropes of Sand*, 263.
67 Little, 'The Cold War and Covert Action', 76.
68 Eveland, *Ropes of Sand*, 263.
69 NARA: RG59: Box 16: 'Rountree to Dulles', 9 January 1057.
70 NARA: RG59: Box 16: 'Owen to Dulles', 25 September 1957.
71 TNA: FO 371/128221: VY101521: 'Ankara to FO', 15 February 1957.
72 TNA: FO 371/128221: VY101518: 'Ankara to FO', 8 February 1957.
73 NARA: RG59: Box 3744:782.54/5-2057: 'Ankara to State: Turkish Military Manoeuvres on the Syrian Border April-May 1957', 20 May 1957.
74 Ibid.
75 Ibid.
76 Eisenhower Library: Papers as President: DDE Diaries Box 26: 'Memorandum of Telephone Call', 26 August 1957.
77 Eisenhower Library: Dulles Papers: General Correspondence Series: Box 1: 'Memorandum of Conversation', 6 October 1957.
78 I. Pearson, 'The Syrian Crisis of 1957, the Anglo-American "Special Relationship," and the 1958 Landings in Jordan and Lebanon', *Middle Eastern Studies* 43:1 (2007), 50.

79  M. Jones, 'The "preferred plan": The Anglo-American Working Group Report on Covert Action in Syria, 1957', *Intelligence and National Security*, 19:3 (2004), 401–415.
80  TNA: FO 371/128244: VY10344101: 'FO to Ankara', 24 October 1957.
81  TNA: FO 371/128244: VY10344101(a): 'Ankara to FO', 25 October 1957.
82  Ibid.
83  TNA: FO 371/128244: VY1034489: 'Ankara to Patrick Hancock', 25 October 1957.
84  NARA: RG59:Box 3744: 782.54/9-1157: 'Houghton to Dulles', 11 September 1957.
85  Eisenhower Library: Dulles Papers: General Correspondence Series: Box 1: 'Memorandum of Conversation at the White House', 25 October 1957.
86  Ibid.
87  Ibid.
88  TNA: FO 371/128244: VY10344/89G: 'FO to Ankara', 14 November 1957.
89  Ibid.
90  Eisenhower Library: Dulles Papers: General Correspondence Series: Box 1: 'Memorandum of Conversation', 6 October 1957.
91  Ibid.
92  BCA: 030.01.00.00.7.36.35.1/2: 'Tel from Baghdad to Ankara', *c*. September 1957.
93  TNA: FO 371/128244: VY10344/87: 'United Nations General Assembly: Complaint about Threats to the Security of Syria and to International Peace', 30 October 1957.
94  TNA: FO 371/128244: VY10344/79: 'New York to FO', 29 October 1957.
95  TNA: FO 371/128244: VY10344/79(A): 'Washington to FO', 1 November 1957.
96  TNA: FO 371/128244: 2727: 'Immediate Telegram from Moscow to FO and Whitehall', 30 October 1957.
97  Vladislav Zubok and Constantine Pleshakov. *Inside the Kremlin's Cold War: From Stalin to Krushchev* (Harvard University Press, 1997).
98  S. Blackwell, 'A Desert Squall: Anglo-American Planning for Military Intervention in Iraq, July 1958–August 1959', *Middle Eastern Studies*, 35:3 (1999), 3.
99  See R. Ovendale, *Britain, the United States, and the Transfer of Power in the Middle East, 1945–1962* (Leicester, 1996); Ashton, *Eisenhower*,

*Macmillan and the Problem of Nasser: Anglo-American Relations and Arab Nationalism, 1955–59.*

100 R. J. Worral, 'Coping with a Coup d'Etat: British Policy towards Post-Revolutionary Iraq, 1958–63', *Contemporary British History*, 21:2 (2007), 173–199; Blackwell, 'A Desert Squall: Anglo-American Planning for Military Intervention in Iraq, July 1958–August 1959'; N. J. Ashton, '"A Great New Venture"? Anglo-American Cooperation in the Middle East and the Response to the Iraqi Revolution July 1958', *Diplomacy and Statecraft*, 4:1 (1993), 59–89.

101 Eisenhower Library: Dulles Series General Correspondence Series: Box 1: 'Memorandum of Conversation: Participants: Secretary of State, Ambassador Lodge, and Mr. Hammarskjold', 7 July 1958.

102 Ibid.

103 Ibid.

104 NARA: RG59: Box 16: 'Rumours of Possible Replacement of Turkish Ambassador to Washington', 10 July 1958.

105 NARA: RG59: Box 16: 'Appointment with the Turkish Ambassador Urguplu, from Rountree to Undersecretary', 23 July 1958.

106 TNA: FO 371/134392: VY103448: 'From Beirut to Foreign Office', 18 July 1958.

107 TNA: FO 371/134392: VY103441: 'Foreign Office to Washington', 18 July 1958.

108 See S. Blackwell, *British Military Intervention and the Struggle for Jordan: King Hussein, Nasser and the Middle East Crisis, 1955–1958* (London, 2013).

109 NARA: RG59: Box 16: 'Appointment with the Turkish Ambassador Urguplu, from Rountree to Undersecretary', 23 July 1958.

110 NARA: RG59: Box 3744: 782.54/7-1458: 'From Ankara to Secretary of State', 14 July 1958.

111 Eisenhower Library: White House Staff Papers: Defense Series: Box 4: 'Memorandum for Chief of Staff: Situation Report on Lebanon, 0800–1200', 16 July 1958'.

112 Ibid.

113 Ibid.

114 Ibid.

115 Eisenhower Library: White House Staff Papers: Defense Series: Box 4: 'Memorandum for Chief of Staff: Situation Report on Lebanon, 0400 18 July 1958–0400 19 July 1958'.

116 NARA: RG59: Box 16: 'Newberry to Jones: Turkish population in Iraq', 30 October 1958.
117 Eisenhower Library: White House Staff Papers: Defense Series: Box 4: 'Memorandum for Chief of Staff: Situation Report on Lebanon, 0400 18 July 1958–0400 19 July 1958'.
118 Eisenhower Library: White House Staff Papers: Defense Series: Box 4: 'Memorandum for Chief of Staff: Situation Report on Lebanon,1200 16 July 1958–0800 17 July 1958'; Eisenhower Library: White House Staff Papers: Defense Series: Box 4: 'Memorandum for Chief of Staff: Situation Report on Lebanon, 1400 17 July 1958–0400 18 July 1958'; Eisenhower Library: White House Staff Papers: Defense Series: Box 4: 'Memorandum for Chief of Staff: Situation Report on Lebanon, 0400 18 July 1958–0400 19 July 1958'.
119 Eisenhower Library: White House Staff Papers: Defense Series: Box 4: 'Memorandum for Chief of Staff: Situation Report on Lebanon, 0400 23 July 1958–0200 24 July 1958'.
120 Eisenhower Library: White House Staff Papers: Defense Series: Box 4: 'Memorandum for Chief of Staff: Situation Report on Lebanon, 0200 24 July 1958–0200 25 July 1958'.
121 Ibid.
122 Eisenhower Library: White House Staff Papers: Defense Series: Box 4: 'Memorandum for Chief of Staff: Situation Report on Lebanon, 0400 18 July 1958–0400 19 July 1958'.
123 Eisenhower Library: White House Staff Papers: Defense Series: Box 4: 'Memorandum for Chief of Staff: Situation Report on Lebanon, 0200 24 July 1958–0200 25 July 1958'.
124 Ibid.
125 Cambridge University Churchill College Archives: British Diplomatic Oral History Programme: Jane Barder interviewing Sir Anthony Parsons on 22 March 1996 at home in Devon.
126 NARA: RG59: Box 3744: 782.551/4-1458: 'Istanbul to Washington: Army Officers Accused of Conspiracy', 14 April 1958; NARA: RG59: Box 3744: 782.551/5-2658: 'Istanbul to Washington: Trial of Army Officers Accused of Intrigues', 26 May 1958; NARA: RG59: Box 3744: 782.551/5-2758: 'Istanbul to Washington: Trial of Army Officers', 4 June 1958; NARA: RG59: Box 3744: 782.551/7-258: 'Istanbul to Washington: Release of Accused Army Officers', 2 July 1958.

127 Ibid.
128 Ibid.
129 Ibid.
130 Eisenhower Archives: 'Synopsis of State and Intelligence Material Reported to the President', 12 May 1959.
131 C. Gunn, 'The 1960 Coup in Turkey: A US Intelligence Failure or a Successful Intervention?' *Journal of Cold War Studies*, 17:2 (2015), 105–106. c.f. a similar point is recently argued in a comparative study on coups in Turkey and Pakistan. See Ö. Aslan, 'U.S. Involvement in Military Coups d'état in Turkey and Pakistan during the Cold War: Between Conspiracy and Reality', unpublished thesis (Bilkent University, 2016).
132 E. Altaylı, *Ruzi Nazar: CIA'nin Turk Casusu* (İstanbul, 2013), 355.
133 Ibid.

# Conclusion: Keeping up with the Alliance

The military coup d'état of 27 May 1960 transformed Turkish politics on both a domestic and international level. While the putschists intended to introduce a new constitution to change the Turkish political landscape, there were also some unintended consequences, such as increased Turkish nationalism, Kurdish nationalism, a greater involvement of the army in politics through the National Security Council and the emergence of student movements, sometimes armed, from the extreme left and right wings, as destabilizing elements in the country. This instability lasted until another coup d'état, on 12 September 1980. This time, military leaders introduced a more restrictive constitution that limited political and social freedoms in the country.[1] The Turkish Security Service acted as a tool during these periods, under the military and civilian leadership, to suppress dissidents at home.

These developments, of course, limited liaison efforts between Turkish intelligence agencies and the Western Allies. Indeed, the CIA reported to President Eisenhower just three months after the coup that 'the new government is retiring 90% of the general and flag officers of the armed forces, 70% of the colonels, and 15–20% of the majors. This has caused apprehension and shock among the Turks, and will impede our joint activities with them, since many key contact men have been retired.'[2] In accordance with the changing tide in Turkish-American relations, the US National Security Council revised its policies on Turkey and hinted that Turkish decision makers, from then on, would be more 'independent than previous governments in assessing their own interests'.[3] Moreover, after increased Turkish covert action in Syria starting from the mid-1950s, the National Security Council came to the conclusion that 'Turkey's general attitude toward North Africa and Middle East is influenced by the Ottoman Empire's historical position in these areas'.[4] While a member of the North Atlantic Alliance, Turkish foreign policy in its adjacent region was not formulated solely in the context of the Cold War, but was instead derived from a mix of Cold War security threats and the legacy of its imperial background. Yet modern Turkey, lacking the capabilities of its imperial Ottoman past, had to embed its strategic imperatives within the Western Alliance, in order to carefully manoeuvre against threats from the Soviet Union, and to seek opportunities to build up its own capabilities while in the Western Alliance so that it could later pursue its own strategic imperatives, usually through secret intelligence means.

This desire to align Turkish foreign and security policy with the Americans reached such a level that during US President Eisenhower's visit to Ankara in December 1959, the soon-to-be-ousted Turkish PM Menderes told the president that 'since there is no other country is so much in line with the United States as is Turkey, there is really very little to talk about'.[5] Yet Menderes's efforts to present his government as completely aligned with American policy did not prove itself useful. Growing negativism in Washington over Turkey's pragmatic and at the same time manipulative approach to deceive the alliance for Turkish interests, either to obtain military aid or to expand the Turkish sphere of influence in the Middle East, came with great costs for Menderes: even the cost of his own life. Not long, just five months after this conversation, a military coup ousted the Turkish government and Washington did nothing.

It should be noted that the CIA knew about the coming Turkish coup days before it happened, and informed Eisenhower that the Turkish military was making final arrangements in the leadership of the coup to carry out the action against the government.[6] The British Foreign Office was also aware that a coup was brewing within the Turkish army, yet it also stood idle and watched the coup happen.[7] Moreover, the military junta did not satisfy Turkey's Western allies either. How did the United States and the United Kingdom let one of their NATO ally governments be ousted in a coup, when their ally claimed that their policies were so well aligned? A hint to the answer of this question is hidden in the words of then-US Ambassador Warren.

After General Cemal Gürsel became the leader of the coup, the National Union Committee (the executive organ of the coup) appointed Selim Sarper as the minister of Foreign Affairs. Sarper did not hesitate to tell the American ambassador Warren that General Gürsel 'was not a great brain'.[8] Surprisingly, it was not the top Turkish diplomat but the American ambassador who praised Gürsel by reporting to Washington that 'I do not particularly like him but I respect him, consider him to be an intelligent, loyal, patriotic Turk. But he is a Turk, in everything that the word implies'.[9] The word *Turk* implied to the Americans a pragmatic, manipulative and over-ambitious partner, which might drag the Western Allies into undesired adventures in the Middle East, or work behind the scenes to extract financial aid in order to build its national capabilities. It is important to note how the relations unfolded to build up such a distrust. It is especially important to review the chronological unfolding of the relationship between Turkey and the West, given that this book has been organized thematically.

Following the Italian invasion of Albania in April 1939, and Nazi Germany's occupation of Czechoslovakia in March 1939, an Anglo-French-Turkish treaty was signed in May 1939 to seed the origins of the first Turkish security agreement with the West. The treaty of mutual assistance assured that if any of the countries were attacked by a foreign aggressor, the other parties would provide assistance. In addition to mutual defence, France and Britain promised to provide military and economic aid to Turkey to bolster the country's military preparedness. In return, Turkey was tasked to come to the Allies' help in the Balkans. Although the treaty did not last long due to the rapid defeat of France by Germany in June 1940, it provided the initial ground for Turkish security engagement with the West. For instance, Turkey continued to receive British military advisors and military aid for the construction of air fields and radar units. More importantly, the British and Turkish intelligence services established a joint Anglo-Turkish Security Bureau in November 1940 in Istanbul. However, even at the very inception of this relationship, both sides had reservations about the other, partly because Turkey signed a Non-Aggression Pact with Nazi Germany in June 1941 and kept on exporting chrome to Germany to feed the Nazi war machine. The main motivation behind Ankara's intelligence diplomacy was that it was hesitant in trusting British capabilities and doubted it would protect Turkey from the Soviet Union, which was the main threat at that time in Turkish eyes. When the Turkish foreign minister, Şükrü Saraçoğlu, visited Moscow in September–October 1939, he did not find Moscow to be friendly; rather, Molotov made demands for Soviet military bases on the Straits and the yielding of Turkey's eastern provinces to Soviet control. Therefore, during the war Turkey employed a multilayered approach; they would not be dragged into the war, but would exploit as much as possible sources from the British to help Turkey militarily. It was not until the very end of the war in February 1945, that Turkey declared war on the Axis powers since it was a condition to attend the San Francisco Conference that started in April 1945.

However, immediately after the war, the Soviets increased their pressure on Turkey to demand control of the Straits, as well as a revision of the Turkish-Soviet border asking for the ceding of certain eastern provinces of Turkey to the Georgian Soviet Republic. Moreover, the bankrupt British after the war were not able to prolong their security commitment to Turkey (or Greece) beyond 1947. Turkey, hence, found a new ally across the Atlantic, the United States, which was engaged in a growing confrontation with the Soviets over the post-war settlement. In an initial demonstration of the American commitment to Turkish security, on 5 April 1946 the USS Missouri carrying the deceased Turkish ambassador, Mehmet Münir Ertegün, approached the Turkish shores.[10] The battleship was escorted by the cruiser Providence, the destroyer Power, as well as three Turkish destroyers. The mission dropped anchor in the Turkish straits dividing Istanbul while its approach was cheered by a Turkish crowd holding banners saying 'Welcome Missouri'. Enraged by the growing ties between

Ankara and Washington, the Soviets presented a note to Ankara on 7 August 1946 asking for control over the Turkish Straits. This move pushed the United States and Turkey closer together. It was partly as a result of this that President Harry Truman made his speech before Congress on 12 March 1947 committing the United States to protecting the sovereignty and independence of Greece and Turkey.

Concurrently with the American security commitment, Ankara began engaging with joint secret intelligence operations with the West, most of which initially targeted the Soviet Union. These operations, as early as 1948, aimed to infiltrate agents through the Soviet border to spy on Soviet force preparedness. Especially following Moscow's first atomic bomb test in August 1949, these operations accelerated, and in a gradual way Turkish intelligence aligned more with the CIA, turning away from the MI6 as British influence in the region diminished. Moreover, Ankara used these joint operations as leverage that contributed to Turkey's initial association with NATO in October 1950, in addition to a brigade of Turkish soldiers being sent the same month to fight alongside American soldiers in the Korean War.

The first half of the 1950s witnessed further alignment in Turkish-American relations. In February 1952, Turkey became a full member of NATO, despite British doubts, and strengthened its position as an indispensable ally of the West during the Cold War. Moreover, the unique location of Turkey in the proximity of the USSR and the Middle East provided an advantageous opportunity for hosting American and British SIGINT bases to spy on the Soviets. Moscow detonated its first hydrogen bomb in August 1953, making the existence of SIGINT even more necessary. Moreover, the Status of Forces agreement in June 1954 created the legal framework for the foundation of British and American SIGINT bases to operate under the guise of logistics bases. The Menderes government used this opportunity as leverage to maintain American economic aid for an increasingly dependent Turkish economy.

Particularly from the mid-1950s onwards, the Turkish economy stagnated and Western aid was the only choice for the Menderes government to remain in power. Moreover, the rising economic and domestic pressures caused the incumbent government to become more authoritarian, and use 'foreign adventures' to distract public opinion. The formation of the Baghdad Pact emerged in these conditions in February 1955. Through its position in the Pact, Turkey further demonstrated its commitment in the region for the Western cause, which enabled Ankara to have a better leverage over the West, and pursue its independent policies in the region under the cloak of the Western security commitment. However, such a double-layered attitude in Turkish foreign policy, in addition to the growing authoritarian tendencies on the domestic scene, as well as the chronically unstable economy due to the ineffective use of American aid, triggered a growing negativism in Washington as regards Turkey during the same period.

This negativism is apparent in the unfolding of the events following Britain's Suez debacle in late October to early November 1956. After the British and French failed to gain American support for their campaign against Egypt, Ankara recognized that the power of these two traditional powers was rapidly waning, while Nasserist elements were gaining support in the Middle East. This was particularly apparent in the failure of the Western-backed coup in Syria, concurrently in October 1956. Moreover, the Suez crisis showed Ankara that there were frictions in the Western Alliance which it could exploit to pursue its own plan to fill the vacuum in the Middle East instead of the Nasserists. Thus, at the expense of further friction in the Western Alliance, Ankara tried to persuade Washington to provide Turkey with military protection, while Turkey sought to install pro-Turkish elements in Syria throughout 1957. The Turks also drew encouragement from President Eisenhower's declaration of January 1957 that promised American protection for regional countries who faced external aggression against their sovereignty.

Exploiting the reinvigorated American commitment in the Middle East, Ankara hoped to exploit the US intervention in Beirut in July 1958 and take the leadership of Baghdad Pact countries in favour of military action in Syria and Iraq (where, in the same month, nationalist officers ousted and assassinated the pro-Western prime minister, Nuri al Said). However, the Turkish plan to 'deal' with the ongoing problems of the Middle East almost resulted in a military conflict between the Soviet Union and NATO. During the course of these crises, American ambassador Fletcher Warren had to interrupt Turkish cabinet meetings to ensure that the Turks would remain within their borders. However, Ankara was able to use intelligence diplomacy as leverage to manage the growing negativism in Washington. For instance, starting from July 1959 Turkey showed a willingness to host American Jupiter nuclear missiles on its soil, making it an indispensable partner in American nuclear planning. Turkish-based spy plane operations targeting the Soviets from 1954, including U-2 missions, provided further leverage for Ankara. Even after a U-2 was downed over Soviet territory on 1 May 1960, Ankara insisted on continuing the operations from Turkish soil, even though it risked major Soviet retaliation. However, none of this prevented the Americans from standing idly by while a coup was brewing to oust the incumbent Menderes government. Suspicion in Washington caused it to withhold crucial intelligence from Ankara before the coup of 27 May 1960.

## Contributions and further investigation

This research into Turkish-Western intelligence diplomacy not only provides a missing link in the historiography of Turkish foreign policy, but also broadens our understanding of the Cold War and of intelligence cooperation in general. It is demonstrated here that any argument which claims that Turkish foreign policy was completely dependent on the West between 1945 and 1960 does not reflect the true nature of the origins and implementation of Turkish foreign policy, which was often focused on extracting Western support for Turkish strategic imperatives. These strategic aims did not stem solely from the Cold War context, or from rivalry with the Soviet Union, but rather from the prolonged legacy of Turkey's imperial past. These strategic imperatives were (1) building up Turkey's economic and military capabilities by obtaining Western financial aid, (2) increasing Turkey's sphere of influence in the areas adjacent to Turkey, which were previously part of the Ottoman Empire and (3) obtaining security commitments from Washington against Turkey's northern neighbour, the Soviet Union.

From the Second World War onward, Ankara crafted delicate intelligence diplomacy to satisfy these objectives. Intelligence diplomacy did not consist solely of intelligence liaisons or cooperation, as previous literature on the topic has suggested, based simply on intelligence exchange on a quid pro quo basis. Nor was intelligence diplomacy reducible to the domination of Turkey by more powerful members of the Western Alliance.

Intelligence diplomacy required a synchronized approach and understanding among the country's intelligence community, foreign ministry and other decision makers, to either obscure or foster secret intelligence activities between the allied countries and to pursue one's own strategic aims at the expense of the alliance when necessary. For instance, after Turkish admission to NATO in 1952, Ankara did not hesitate to exaggerate the Soviet threat in the Caucasus – and Turkish intelligence reports submitted to NATO were crafted in such a way as to attract more military aid and security commitment from Washington. A similar but more complicated approach was adopted towards regional intelligence cooperation through the Baghdad Pact. In the Baghdad Pact Counter-Subversion Office, Turkey tried to convince the Americans and the British that the Kurdish groups operating in Turkey and the region posed major threats to Western interests because, the Turks argued, the Kurds were all communists. Ankara thus aimed to legitimize Turkish suppression of the Kurds, and if possible to attract Western support for these endeavours. However, it was not only Turkey who used intelligence diplomacy to further their own ends. In response to the Turkish claims on the Kurds, the British and Americans intentionally obscured their exchange of intelligence with Turkey through the Baghdad Pact, as both countries pursued their own multilayered approach towards the Kurds in the regional context. However, Turkish intelligence diplomacy did not only have consequences for intelligence exchange, but also for the building of trust among the allies, as well as for covert action in the Middle East.

Existing literature concerning intelligence liaisons is particularly concerned with the security of the information shared between the various partners. If one of the partners becomes concerned that their secrets are likely to fall into the wrong hands, the trust on which intelligence liaisons are built is jeopardized. Therefore, both NATO and the Baghdad Pact operated independent security committees to inspect the integrity of registries of the respective countries to prevent security leaks. Although these security committees acted as a trust-building mechanism, it does not explain why countries obscured their intelligence sharing, particularly in multilateral settings. This research demonstrates that, even when information security is a prerequisite for effective intelligence sharing, countries still usually withhold information for two main purposes. First, this research shows that, in terms of the British contribution to the Baghdad Pact's military committee, Britain wanted to upset the working of the committee when they saw it moving in a direction that the British did not want. The British, for instance, used intelligence diplomacy to inflate their actual military capabilities in the Middle East in order to convince the regional countries that British arms could defend them in the case of war, when in fact they were not capable of doing so. Second, as this book demonstrates regarding the Turkish attitude towards the NATO Standing Group, Ankara usually obstructed the flow of information regarding Turkish military capabilities and manoeuvres because they were out of alignment with NATO policies in general, particularly in the Middle East. Greco-Turkish rivalries also played a role here: while both allies in NATO, the Turks, and probably the Greeks as well, did not wish to expose their military secrets to each other due to their historical disputes and ongoing conflict over Cyprus. None of the above-mentioned issues are related to the security of information. This book therefore goes beyond the importance of trust in intelligence liaisons, and emphasizes the importance of perceived national interests in the extent and nature of the intelligence shared.

As an illustrative case of the consequences of intelligence diplomacy, this book demonstrates that Ankara wanted to fill the vacuum created by the retreat of the British from the Middle East. For instance, starting from the interwar years, Ankara aimed to spread its influence into Syria. Apart from annexing the province of Hatay from French mandate Syria through covert and overt means in 1939, Ankara also saw Western covert operations in Syria starting from the late 1940s as an opportunity to impose Turkish designs on the British and Americans. Turkish intelligence diplomacy acted, on the one hand, to embed itself within these Western covert operations, such as Operation Straggle. On the other hand, the Turks tried to create a de facto situation on the ground by using both military and covert operations to impose the Turkish plan on the Western Alliance. This 'Turkish plan' aimed to exploit the retreat of British influence in the region, meanwhile diverting possible American military and political support away from Arab countries towards Turkey. As explained by the Turkish ambassador in Washington in the midst of the Lebanon crisis of 1958, the Turks did not want to see any developments in the Middle East where Turkish interests were not taken into account. But the Turkish plan backfired, particularly in the Syrian case, creating greater distance between the Turks and their Western partners, risking a major war with the Soviets and seeding discontent among the country's military leadership with their civilian rulers.

Turkish intelligence diplomacy also encountered problems in other areas where Ankara did not have the adequate expertise. For instance, in matters such as nuclear weapons or military re-organization aligned with NATO standards, the lack of relevant expertise among Turkish government officials raised serious concerns among their allies. Moreover, this lack of comprehension led to a major gap between the country's diplomatic and military leaders, causing further friction within the country's security and foreign policy structure. This friction was also closely related to the differences of approach towards intelligence cooperation between the allies.

In Turkey, which has long been a hybrid regime, mixing features from authoritarianism and democracy, secret intelligence was seen as a tool existing in a politicized realm, to be used in power struggles. Moreover, the line between political police and the secret intelligence service has frequently been blurred, hampering intelligence liaison and diplomatic relations with Western countries, which were stable democracies. As a prominent example, the competition among the various factions within the Turkish security establishment to obtain more resources helped to cripple the liaison process on technical and nuclear matters. Turkey tended to use cooperation on these questions as 'leverage' against the United States and the United Kingdom, rather than developing its own capabilities. As a result, intelligence cooperation in the technological field was rather weak compared to that in areas involving human agents, where Turkey had vast resources. However, even in this last area, there were flaws throughout the 1950s, where Turkish attempts to infiltrate agents over the Soviet border to take part in joint operations resulted in fiasco. One of the main reasons for these failures was the difference in the intelligence cultures and approaches between Turkey and her allies for the mission in question.

The differences and fragmentation within the alliance did not solely depend on cultural and philosophical differences. In intelligence cooperation, particularly after the Suez crisis in 1956, there was a fragmentation of political outlook between the United States and the United Kingdom regarding the Middle East. For instance, while the United Kingdom was more focused on containing the spread of the Nasserite elements, the United States was more focused on the further penetration of the Soviets in the region. These divergences were reflected in the counter-subversion field, where Ankara hoped to exploit the fragmentation to pursue its own ends, especially in Syria. This attempted exploitation backfired, however, because the United States and the United Kingdom patched up their differences after Suez, shared intelligence on the Turkish military moves and were determined that Ankara's regional ambitions should not drag them into an undesired confrontation with the Soviet Union.

While this book explains the character and origins of Turkish intelligence diplomacy during the early Cold War, there are limitations that it cannot yet overcome. First, some of the British prime minister's files dealing with Turkey remain closed to the public.[11] This lack of access limits our understanding as to the degree of Turkish endeavours to manipulate to their own advantage friction between the Americans and the British after the Suez crisis. Furthermore, it is also not known what kind of policies, if any, the British developed to keep Ankara in their orbit to prevent increasing Turkish dependence on America during the early Cold War. It would also be interesting to learn whether the British used any methods of intelligence diplomacy against Turkey to limit the loss of British leverage on the country, including the use of GCHQ SIGINT bases in Turkey, and psychological warfare to counterbalance rising American influence. Another limitation of this research concerns access to Turkish archives. The limited and disorganized public disclosure of the Turkish archives limits this research as regards assessing to what extent the politicization of the Turkish security community hampered its relations with the West, and fragmented the Turkish security community in general.[12] Such access to the relevant archives would reveal the domestic dimension of Turkish intelligence diplomacy to a much greater extent.

In a related manner, but not necessarily depending on access to primary sources, this book has only limited insight into how domestic politics and leadership in Turkey, the United States and the United Kingdom affected intelligence diplomacy. There are valuable studies focusing on how security and intelligence policies related to decision makers on both sides of the Atlantic.[13] Yet the scope of this book is limited as regards providing an in-depth investigation of the effect of domestic politics and the character of political leadership on the conduct of intelligence diplomacy. Moreover, this book does not set out to provide a comprehensive contribution to theories concerning international relations and foreign policy analysis. However, this book nevertheless provides historical insights regarding contemporary developments in Turkey.

Recent developments demonstrate that the importance of intelligence diplomacy was not limited to the origins of the Cold War, but instead has been embedded into Turkish foreign and security policy. Intelligence diplomacy has continued, even as it complicates the task of keeping the alliance together, as confirmed by recent developments surrounding Turkish involvement in Syria since the eruption of the Arab Spring in 2011.[14] After Turkish F-16s downed a Su-24 Russian tactical bomber over the region where Turkmen anti-Assad groups are based, Turkish President Erdogan tacitly confirmed Turkey's covert support for Syrian rebels fighting against Damascus, stating that 'anyone who bombs that area attacks our brothers and sisters – Turkmens'.[15] In the case of the current Turkish government's policies in Syria, Ankara is playing a maverick role, its policies deliberately out of line with its traditional Western Allies. Covert action, such as arming rebel groups in Syria, has been the main pillar of Turkey's recent Middle East policy, and involves great risks.[16] Ankara is distrusted by its Western Allies. Even more than during the late 1950s, such tensions have called future intelligence liaison between Turkey and the West into question, a disturbing element being Turkey's readiness to work closely with Moscow.[17] But those who study the earlier period will see that differences of objectives between Ankara and its allies in intelligence diplomacy are far from new.

# Notes

1   See Bezci and Öztan. 'Anatomy of the Turkish Emergency State: A Continuous Reflection of Turkish Raison d'état between 1980 and 2002', 163–179.
2   Eisenhower Library: White House Staff Papers: Office of Staff Secretary: Alphabetical Series: Box 14: 'Synopsis of State and Intelligence Material Reported to the President', 10 August 1960.
3   Eisenhower Library: National Security Council: Policy Series Box 29, 'NSC 6015/1: US Policy towards Turkey', 5 October 1960.
4   Ibid.

5   Eisenhower Library: White House Staff: Office of Staff Secretary: International Series: Box 14: 'Memorandum of Conference with President', 6 December 1959.
6   Eisenhower Library: White House Staff Papers: Office of Staff Secretary: Alphabetical Series: Box 14: 'Synopsis of State and Intelligence Material Reported to the President', 25 May 1960.
7   See Gunn, 'The 1960 Coup in Turkey: A US Intelligence Failure or a Successful Intervention?'.
8   Eisenhower Library and Archives: Office of Staff Secretary: International Series: Box 14: 'Warren to Jones', 11 August 1960.
9   Ibid.
10  See G. İnanç and Ş. Yilmaz, 'Gunboat Diplomacy: Turkey, USA and the Advent of the Cold War', *Middle Eastern Studies*, 48:3 (2012), 401–411.
11  For instance, numerous Freedom of Information Requests and Appeals to the Public Records Office to release 'PREM 11/279: Prime Minister's Office: Correspondence and Papers, 1951–1964 – TURKEY' have been rejected by the authorities.
12  Freedom of Information Requests to the Turkish State Archives, and also to the National Security Council, to reveal the minutes of the Turkish National Security High Council, have been rejected.
13  See R. Aldrich and R. Cormac. *The Black Door: Spies, Secret Intelligence, and British Prime Ministers* (London, 2016); D. C. Unger, *The Emergency State: America's Pursuit of Absolute Security at All Costs* (New York, 2012).
14  See A. Stein, 'Turkey's Evolving Syria Strategy', *Foreign Affairs*, 9 February 2015.
15  See E. Lin-Greenberg, 'Now That Turkey Shot Down a Russian Bomber, What Does Escalation Look Like?' *War on the Rocks*, 27 November 2015; cf. Putin calls jet's downing 'stab in the back'; 'Turkey says warning ignored', *CNN*, 25 November 2015.
16  'Turkish intelligence helped ship arms to Syrian Islamist rebel areas', *Reuters*, 21 May 2015.
17  'Turkey and Russia share military intelligence', *The Times*, 25 October 2016.

# Bibliography

## Primary Sources

### NATO Archives, Brussels

AC/19: Annual Review Committee Series
AC/24: Working Group on Information Policy Series
AC/35: Security Committee Series
AC/100: Defence Planning – Multilateral Discussions Series
C-M: Council Memoranda Series
MC: Military Committee Series
NAC/C1- C9: North Atlantic Council, 1st to 9th sessions Documents.
PO: Private Office of the Secretary General Fond
SGM: Standing Group Memoranda Series
SGWM: Standing Group Working Memoranda Series
SG: Standing Group Series

### Poland

#### *Archiwum Instytutu Pamięci Narodowej, Warsaw*

AIPN: 02386/130: Files on Turkish Intelligence Service
13: Plan on gathering information about 'SAMANTA' – codename of Turkish Secret Services (case conducted by civilian intelligence)
20: Report on Intelligence and Counterintelligence in Turkey, translated from Russian to Polish, report from KGB, 1970
35: People in charge of Turkish services, report from KGB, 1970, translated to Polish
46: Structures, Goals of Turkish security apparatus and police training, report from KGB, 1973
66: Intelligence situation in Turkey
91: Report about MIT, 1976
94: Turkish Section of Interpol, 1976
100: Turkish officers working undercover as diplomats

## Turkey

### Genelkurmay Askerî Tarih ve Stratejik Etüt. (ATASE) Daire Başkanlığı, Ankara

İDH: İkinci Dünya Harbi Evrakları

### Devlet Arşivleri Genel Müdürlüğü, Ankara

030.01: Başbakanlık Özel Kalem Müdürlüğü Evrakı
030.10: Başbakanlık Muamelât Genel Müdürlüğü Evrakı
030.18: Bakanlar Kurulu Kararları
490.01: Cumhuriyet Halk Partisi Evrakı

### Milli Kütüphane Başkanlığı, Ankara

Büyük Erkân-ı Harbiye 13. İstihbarat Şubesi
Erkanıharbiye Umumiye Riyaseti Karargahı İstihbarat Başkanlığı Raporları
Genelkurmay Başkanlığı XI.Şube
Jandarma Mecmuası
Ordu Dergisi
Silahlı Kuvvetler Dergisi
Topçu Mecmuası
Kara Kuvvetleri Dergisi

### Toplumsal Tarih Vakfı Bilgi-Belge Merkezi, İstanbul

Necmetttin Sahir Sılan Evrakları

### Türkiye Büyük Millet Meclisi, Ankara

TBMM Tutanakları: 8. Dönem, 4. Cilt, 37. Birleşim
TBMM Tutanakları: 10. Dönem, 5. Cilt, 40. Birleşim
TBMM Tutanakları: 10. Dönem, 10. Cilt, 36. Birleşim
TBMM Tutanakları: 9. Dönem, 4. Cilt, 31. Birleşim
TBMM Tutanakları: 9. Dönem, 25. Cilt, 9. Birleşim

## United Kingdom

### The National Archives, London

CAB21: Cabinet Office and predecessors: Registered Files (1916 to 1965)
DEFE60: Ministry of Defence: Joint Intelligence Bureau: Economic
and General Division, later Division of Joint Services and Economic

Intelligence: Intelligence Assessments, Reports, Memoranda and Surveys
FCO1: Australian Royal Commission into United Kingdom Nuclear Weapons Testing in Australia: Photocopies of documents made available to the Commission by the Foreign and Commonwealth Office
FO1110: Foreign Office and Foreign and Commonwealth Office: Information Research Department: General Correspondence
FO195: Foreign Office: Embassy and Consulates, Turkey (formerly Ottoman Empire): General Correspondence
FO371: Foreign Office: Political Departments: General Correspondence from 1906 to 1966
KV4: The Security Service: Policy (Pol F Series) Files
PREM11: Prime Minister's Office: Correspondence and Papers, 1951–1964
WO106: War Office: Directorate of Military Operations and Military Intelligence, and predecessors: Correspondence and Papers
WO201: War Office: Middle East Forces; Military Headquarters Papers, Second World War

## Documents Released under Freedom of Information Act, Ref. No: 0805-15

Group: FO, Class: 195, Piece: 2600, Folio: 212
Content: Year-1946 from British Embassy in Ankara, Soviet Union–Turkey Political Relations
Group: FO, Class: 195, Piece: 2611, Folio: 40, 41, 18, 3, 5, 6–12, 15, 16
Content: Year-1948 From British Embassy in Ankara, Intelligence Services

## Churchill Archives Centre, Cambridge

(AMEJ): Julian Amery Papers
(ELMT): The Papers of Air Marshal Sir Thomas Elmhirst
British Diplomatic Oral History Programme: Sir Anthony Parsons, interviewed by Jane Barder on 22 March 1996

# United States

## The Association for Diplomatic Studies and Training (ADST) Oral History Project:

Anthony D. Marshall, Interviewed Richard L. Jackson on 20 February 1998
Wilbur B. Chase, interviewed by Charles Stuart Kennedy on 24 July 1990

William M. Rountree, interviewed by Arthur L. Lowrie on 22 December 1989

## CIA:
CREST: 25-Year Program Archive
Declassified File Series

## Wilson Center International History Project Archives, Washington, DC
Bulgarian Cold War Research Group

## Eisenhower Presidential Library and Archives, Abilene, KS
John Foster Dulles Papers
Papers as President (Ann Whitman Files)
White House Office, National Security Council Staff: Papers, 1948–1961
White House Office, National Security Council Staff: Papers, 1953–1961
White House Office, Office of the Staff Secretary Records
White House Office, Office of the Staff Secretary, Records of Paul T. Carroll, Andrew J. Goodpaster, L. Arthur Minnich, and Christopher H. Russel, 1952–1961
White House, Office of the Special Assistant for National Security Affairs: Records, 1952–1961

## Library of Congress, Washington, DC
The Papers of Archibald Roosevelt
The Papers of John J. Ballentine

## National Archives and Records Administration, College Park, MD
RG59: State Department Central Files
State Department Decimal File Series

## Truman Presidential Library and Archives, Independence, MI
Dean Acheson Papers
George McGhee Papers
Psychological Strategy Board Files

## Printed Sources

Doğu bölgesindeki geçmiş isyanlar ve alınan dersler (Ankara, 1946)
Foreign Relations of the United States, Vol. V (1950)
İlter, E. Milli İstihbarat Teşkilatı Tarihçesi (Ankara, 2002)
Şenel, M. and T. Şenel, *Siyasi Polisin El Kitabı: Temel Güvenlik Konularımız İstihbarat, Karşı İstihbarat ve Propaganda* (Ankara, 1972)

# Secondary Sources

## Books

Aldrich, R. (ed.), *Espionage, Security and Intelligence in Britain, 1945-1970* (Manchester, 1998).
Aldrich, R. *GCHQ: The Uncensored Story of Britain's Most Secret Intelligence Agency* (London, 2010).
Aldrich, R. *The Hidden Hand: Britain, America and Cold War Secret Intelligence* (London, 2001).
Aldrich, R., R. Cormac, and M. S. Goodman, *Spying on the World: The Declassified Documents of the Joint Intelligence Committee, 1936-2013* (Edinburgh, 2014).
Altaylı, E. *Ruzi Nazar: CIA'nin Turk Casusu* (İstanbul, 2013).
Alvarez, D. J. *Bureaucracy and Cold War Diplomacy: The United States and Turkey 1943-1946* (Thessaloniki, 1980).
Andrew, C. *Secret Service: The Making of the British Intelligence Community* (London, 1985).
Andrew, C. *Defend the Realm: The Authorized History of MI5* (London, 2009).
Andrew, C. and V. Mitrokhin, *The Mitrokhin Archive II* (London, 2005).
Andrew, C. and V. Mitrokhin, *The World Was Going Our Way: The KGB and the Battle for the Third World* (London, 2005).
Andrew, C. and D. Dilks, *The Missing Dimension: Governments and Intelligence Communities in the Twentieth Century* (London, 1984).
Andrew, C. and O. Gordievsky, *KGB: The Inside Story of Its Foreign Operations from Lenin to Gorbachev* (London, 1990).
Andrew, C., R. Aldrich and W. Wark (ed.), *Secret Intelligence: A Reader* (London, 2010).

Andrew, C. et al. *The Mitrokhin Archive II: The KGB and the World* (London, 2005).
Antonius, G. *The Arab Awakening* (London, 1938).
Ashton, N. *Eisenhower, Macmillan and the Problem of Nasser: Anglo-American Relations and Arab Nationalism, 1955–59* (London, 1996).
Athanassopoulou, E. *Turkey-Anglo-American Security Interests, 1945–1952: The First Enlargement of Nato* (London, 1999).
Barkey, H. and G. Fuller, *Turkey's Kurdish Question* (Lanham, MD, 2000).
Bazzett, T. *Soldier Boy: At Play in the ASA* (Reed City, MI, 2008).
Blackwell, S. *British Military Intervention and the Struggle for Jordan: King Hussein, Nasser and the Middle East Crisis, 1955–1958* (London, 2013).
Berridge, G. R. *British Diplomacy in Turkey, 1583 to the Present: A Study in the Evolution of the Resident Embassy* (Leiden, 2009).
Berridge, G. R. *Diplomacy: Theory and Practice* (London, 2015).
Betts, R. K. *Nuclear Blackmail and Nuclear Balance* (Washington, DC, 1987).
Born, Hans, Ian Leigh, and Aidan Wills (eds.), *International Intelligence Cooperation and Accountability* (London, 2011).
Born, H. and M. Caparini, *Democratic Control of Intelligence Services: Containing Rogue Elephants* (Farnham, 2007).
Brugioni, D. *Eyes in the Sky: Eisenhower, the CIA, and Cold War Aerial Espionage* (Annapolis, MD, 2011).
Bruneau, T. C. and S. C. Boraz (ed.), *Reforming Intelligence: Obstacles to Democratic Control and Effectiveness* (Austin, TX, 2007).
Carruthers, L. S. *Winning Hearts and Minds: British Governments, the Media and Colonial Counter-Insurgency, 1944–1960* (Leicester, 1995).
Chaliand, G. *A People without a Country: The Kurds and Kurdistan* (London, 1980).
Chesterman, S. *Shared Secrets* (New South Wales, Australia, 2006).
Chipman, J. (ed.), *NATO's Southern Allies: Internal and External Challenges* (London, 1988).
Cohen, M. *Strategy and Politics in the Middle East, 1954–1960: Defending the Northern Tier* (London, 2004).
Cormac, R. *Confronting the Colonies: British Intelligence and Counterinsurgency* (Oxford, 2014).
Darling, A. B. *The Central Intelligence Agency: An Instrument of Government to 1950* (Pennsylvania, PA, 1990).
Davies, P. and K. C. Gustafson (eds.), *Intelligence Elsewhere: Spies and Espionage outside the Anglosphere* (Washington, DC, 2013).

Deringil, S. *Turkish Foreign Policy during the Second World War: An 'Active' Neutrality* (Cambridge, 2004).
Dimitrakis, P. *Failed Alliances of the Cold War* (London, 2012).
Eveland, W. C. *Ropes of Sand: America's Failure in the Middle East* (New York, 1980).
Eymür, M. *Analiz: bir MİT mensubu'nun anıları* (Istanbul, 1991).
Ganser, D. *NATO's Secret Armies: Operation Gladio and Terrorism in Western Europe* (London, 2005).
Gerolymatos, A. *Castles Made of Sand: A Century of Anglo-American Espionage and Intervention in the Middle East* (London, 2010).
Ghassemlou, A. R. *Kurdistan and the Kurds* (Prague, 1965).
Gibson, B. R. *Sold Out? US Foreign Policy, Iraq, the Kurds, and the Cold War* (New York: 2015).
Gingeras, R. *Heroin, Organized Crime, and the Making of Modern Turkey* (Oxford, 2014).
Gokay, B. Soviet Eastern Policy and Turkey, 1920–1991: Soviet Foreign Policy, Turkey and Communism (London, 2006).
Gonlubol, M. et al., Olaylarla Türk Dış Politikası, 9th edition (Ankara, 1996).
Goodman, M. S. Spying on the Nuclear Bear: Anglo-American Intelligence and the Soviet Bomb (Stanford, CA, 2007).
Grey, S. *The New Spymasters: Inside Espionage from the Cold War to Global Terror* (London, 2015).
Gunter, M. *The Kurds and the Future of Turkey* (London, 1997).
Gürses, M. and D. Romano, *Conflict, Democratization, and the Kurds in the Middle East* (New York, 2014).
Hale, W. *Turkish Foreign Policy since 1774* (London, 2012).
Harris, G. *The Origins of Communism in Turkey* (Stanford, CA, 1967).
Hasanli, J. *Stalin and the Turkish Crisis of the Cold War, 1945–1953* (Lanham, MD, 2011).
Hashimoto, C. (ed. by R. Cormac), *The Twilight of the British Empire: British Intelligence and Counter-Subversion in the Middle East, 1948–63* (Edinburgh, 2017).
Hennessy, P. *The Secret State: Whitehall and the Cold War* (London, 2003).
Heper, M. *The State and Kurds in Turkey: The Question of Assimilation* (London and New York, 2007).
Herman, M. *Intelligence Power in Peace and War* (Cambridge, 1996).
Herman, M. and H. Gwilym (ed.), *Intelligence in the Cold War: What Difference Did It Make?* (London, 2013).

Hiçyılmaz, E. *Teşkilât-ı Mahsusa'dan MİT'e* (Ankara, 1990).
Holmes, A. A. *Social Unrest and American Military Bases in Turkey and Germany since 1945* (Cambridge, 2014).
Hutton, L. *Looking beneath the Cloak: An Analysis of Intelligence Governance in South Africa* (Pretoria, 2007).
İnalcık, H. *The Origin of the Ottoman-Russian Rivalry and the Don-Volga Canal* (Ankara, 1947).
Jeffrey, K. *MI6: History of the Secret Intelligence Service 1909–1949* (London, 2010).
Johnson, L. K. (ed.), *Handbook of Intelligence Studies* (London, 2007).
Karpat, K. H. (ed.), *Turkey's Foreign Policy in Transition: 1950–1974* (Leiden, 1975).
Kayalı, H. *Arabs and Young Turks. Ottomanism, Arabism, and Islamism in the Ottoman Empire, 1908–1918* (Berkeley, CA, 1997).
Kragenbrook, P. and S. Speri (ed.), *The Kurds: A Contemporary Overview* (London, 1992).
Kuniholm, B. R. *The Origins of the Cold War in the Near East: Great Power Conflict and Diplomacy in Iran, Turkey, and Greece* (Princeton, NJ, 1980).
Kurzman, D. *Subversion of the Innocents: Patterns of Communist Penetration in Africa, the Middle East, and Asia* (New York, 1963).
Landau, J. M. *Radical Politics in Modern Turkey* (London, 2016).
Laqueur, W. *Communism and Nationalism in the Middle East* (London, 1956).
Laqueur, W. *The Soviet Union and the Middle East* (London, 1959).
Lawrence, Q. *Invisible Nation* (New York, 2008).
Lee, A. S. G. *Special Duties: Reminiscences of a Royal Air Force Staff Officer in the Balkans, Turkey and the Middle East* (London, 1946).
Lowenthal, M. *Intelligence: From Secrets to Policy* (London, 2011).
Marcus, A. *Blood and Belief: The PKK and the Kurdish Fight for Independence* (New York, 2007).
McDowell, D. *A Modern History of the Kurds* (London, 1997).
McGhee, G. C. *The Us-Turkish-Nato Middle East Connection: How the Truman Doctrine and Turkey's Nato Entry Contained the Soviets* (Basingstoke, 1990).
Mockaitis, T. R. *British Counterinsurgency in the Post-Imperial Era* (Manchester, 1995).
Moran, C. *Classified: Secrecy and the State in Modern Britain*(Cambridge, 2012).
Moran, C. and C. Murphy, *Intelligence Studies in Britain and the US: Historiography since 1945* (Edinburgh, 2013).

Newman, B. *Soviet Atomic Spies* (London, 1952).
Newsinger, J. *British Counterinsurgency* (London, 2016).
O'Brien, P. P. (ed.), *Technology and Naval Combat in the Twentieth Century and Beyond* (London, 2001).
Olson, R. *The Emergence of Kurdish Nationalism and the Sheikh Said Rebellion, 1880–1925* (Austin, TX, 1989).
Onslow, S. (ed.), *Cold War in Southern Africa: White Power, Black Liberation* (London, 2009).
Osborn, P. R. *Operation Pike: Britain versus the Soviet Union, 1939–1941* (Portsmouth, 2000).
Ovendale, R. *Britain, the United States, and the Transfer of Power in the Middle East, 1945–1962* (Leicester, 1996).
Özcan, N. A. *PKK: Kürtistan Isci Partisi, tarihi, ideolojisi ve yöntemi* (Ankara, 1999).
Özkan, T. *Milli İstihbarat Teşkilatı-MİT (Mit'in Gizli Tarihi)* (Istanbul, 2015).
Page, B. et.al. *Philby: The Spy Who Betrayed a Generation* (London, 1977).
Pelt, M. *Military Intervention and a Crisis Democracy in Turkey: The Menderes Era and Its Demise* (London, 2014).
Philby, K. *My Silent War: The Autobiography of Kim Philby* (London, 1989).
Porter, B. *The Origins of the Vigilant State: The London Metropolitan Police Special Branch before the First World War* (Woodbridge, 1987).
Prados, J. *Keepers of the Keys: A History of the National Security Council from Truman to Bush* (New York, 1991).
Ranelagh, J. *The Agency: The Rise and Fall of the CIA* (New York, 1986).
Rathmell, A. *Secret War in the Middle East: The Covert Struggle for Syria, 1949–1961* (London, 1995).
Reynolds, M. A. *The Ottoman-Russian Struggle for Eastern Anatolia and the Caucasus, 1908–1918: Identity, Ideology and the Geopolitics of World Order* (Princeton, NJ, 2003).
Rich, P. and I. Duyvesteyn, *The Routledge Handbook of Insurgency and Counterinsurgency* (London, 2012).
Richelson, J. *The US Intelligence Community* (New York, 1989).
Roman, P. J. *Eisenhower and the Missile Gap* (Ithaca, NY, 1995).
Rothkopf, D. *Running the World: The Inside Story of the National Security Council and the Architects of American Power* (New York, 2006).
Rovner, R. *Fixing the Facts: National Security and the Politics of Intelligence* (Ithaca, NY, 2011).
Rubin, B. M. *Istanbul Intrigues* (New York, 1992).

Shlaim, A. *The United States and the Berlin Blockade, 1948–1949: A Study in Crisis Decision-Making* (Berkeley, CA, 1983).

Schrecker, E. *Many Are the Crimes: McCarthyism in America* (Princeton, NJ, 1998).

Seale, P. *The Struggle for Syria: A Study of Post War Arab Politics 1945–1958* (Oxford, 1965).

Shulsky, A. N. and G. J. Schmitt, *Silent Warfare: Understanding the World of Intelligence*, 3rd ed. (Dulles, VA, 2002).

Söyler, M. *The Turkish Deep State: State Consolidation, Civil-Military Relations and Democracy* (London, 2015).

Stoddard, P. *The Ottoman Government and the Arabs, 1911 to 1918: A Preliminary Study of the Teşkilât-i Mahsusa* (Princeton, NJ, 1963).

Sudoplatov, P. et al. *Special Tasks: The Memoirs of an Unwanted Witness, a Soviet Spymaster* (Boston, MA, 1995).

Tamkin, N. *Britain, Turkey, and the Soviet Union, 1940–45: Strategy, Diplomacy, and Intelligence in the Eastern Mediterranean* (London, 2009).

Tamkoç, M. *The Warrior Diplomats: Guardians of the National Security and Modernization of Turkey* (Salt Lake, UT, 1976).

Tully, A. *The Central Intelligence Agency: The Inside Story* (London, 1962).

Türkkaya A. *Turkish Foreign Policy, 1939–1945* (Ankara, 1965).

Ulus, Ö. M. *The Army and the Radical Left in Turkey: Military Coups, Socialist Revolution and Kemalism* (London, 2010).

Uzer, U. *Identity and Turkish Foreign Policy: The Kemalist Influence in Cyprus and the Caucasus* (London, 2010).

Walsh, J. *The International Politics of Intelligence Sharing* (New York, 2010).

Weber, F. G. *The Evasive Neutral: Germany, Britain, and the Quest for a Turkish Alliance in the Second World War* (Columbia, MI, 1979).

Weisband, E. *Turkish Foreign Policy 1943–1945: Small State Diplomacy and Great Power Politics* (Princeton, NJ, 1973).

Westad, O. A. *The Global Cold War: Third World Interventions and the Making of Our Times* (Cambridge, 2005).

Wilford, H. *America's Great Game* (New York, 2013).

Yilmaz, Ş. *Turkish-American Relations, 1800–1952: Between the Stars, Stripes and the Crescent* (London, 2015).

Yesilbursa, B. K. *The Baghdad Pact: Anglo-American Defence Policies in the Middle East, 1950–59* (London, 2005).

Zeine, N. *The Emergence of Arab nationalism: With a Background Study of Arab-Turkish Relations in the Near East* (Delmar, NY, 1973).

Zhelyazkova, A. (ed.), *Between Adaptation and Nostalgia: The Bulgarian Turks in Turkey* (Sofia, 1998).

Zubok, V. *A Failed Empire: The Soviet Union in the Cold War from Stalin to Gorbachev* (Chapel Hill, NC, 2007).

## Journal Articles

Aldrich, R. '"Grow Your Own": Cold War Intelligence and History Supermarkets', *Intelligence and National Security*, 17:1 (2002), 135–152.

Aldrich, R. 'Transatlantic Intelligence and Security Cooperation', *International Affairs*, 80:4 (2004), 731–753.

Aldrich, R. and J. Kasuku, 'Escaping from American Intelligence: Culture, Ethnocentrism and the Anglosphere', *International Affairs*, 88:5 (2012), 1009–1028.

Alvarez, D. 'No Immunity: Signals Intelligence and the European Neutrals, 1939–45', *Intelligence and National Security*, 12:2 (1997), 22–43.

Alvarez, D. 'American Clandestine Intelligence in Early Postwar Europe', *Journal of Intelligence History*, 4:1 (2004), 7–24.

Arditti, R. 'Security Intelligence in the Middle East (SIME): Joint Security Intelligence Operations in the Middle East, c. 1939–58', *Intelligence and National Security*, 31:3 (2016), 369–396.

Ashton, N. J. '"A Great New Venture"?-Anglo-American Cooperation in the Middle East and the Response to the Iraqi Revolution July 1958', *Diplomacy and Statecraft*, 4:1 (1993), 59–89.

Aybay, R. 'Milli Güvenlik Kavramı ve Milli Güvenlik Kurulu', *Ankara Üniversitesi SBF Dergisi*, 33:01 (1978), 59–82.

Aydin, M. 'Determinants of Turkish Foreign Policy: Changing Patterns and Conjectures during the Cold War', *Middle Eastern Studies*, 36:1 (2000), 103–139.

Bar-Joseph, U. 'The Politicization of Intelligence: A Comparative Study', *International Journal of Intelligence and Counterintelligence*, 26:2 (2013), 347–348.

Baxter, C. 'Forgeries and Spies: The Foreign Office and the "Cicero" Case', *Intelligence and National Security*, 23:6 (2008), 807–826.

Bezci, E. 'Turkish Intelligence Diplomacy during the Second World War', *Journal of Intelligence History*, 15:2 (2016), 80–95.

Bezci, E. and G. G. Öztan, 'Anatomy of the Turkish Emergency State: A Continuous Reflection of Turkish Raison d'état between 1980 and 2002', *Middle East Critique*, 25:2 (2016), 163–179.

Bilgin, M. S. and S. Morewood, 'Turkey's Reliance on Britain: British Political and Diplomatic Support for Turkey against Soviet Demands, 1943–47', *Middle Eastern Studies*, 40:2 (2004), 24–57.

Blackwell, S. 'A Desert Squall: Anglo-American Planning for Military Intervention in Iraq, July 1958–August 1959', *Middle Eastern Studies*, 35:3 (1999), 1–18.

Blackwell, S. 'Britain, the United States and the Syrian Crisis, 1957', *Diplomacy and Statecraft*, 11:3 (2000), 139–158.

Bock, R. 'Anglo-Soviet Intelligence Cooperation, 1941–45: Normative Insights from the Dyadic Democratic Peace Literature', *Intelligence and National Security*, 30:6 (2015), 890–912.

Brown, J. N. and A. Farrington, 'Democracy and the Depth of Intelligence Sharing: Why Regime Type Hardly Matters', *Intelligence and National Security*, 32:1 (2017), 68–84.

Carothers, T. 'The End of the Transition Paradigm', *Journal of Democracy*, 13:1 (2002), 5–21.

Cizre, Ü. 'Demythologyzing the National Security Concept: The Case of Turkey', *The Middle East Journal*, 57:2 (2003), 213–229.

Cohen, M. 'From "Cold" to "Hot" War: Allied Strategic and Military Interests in the Middle East after the Second World War', *Middle Eastern Studies*, 43:5 (2007), 725–748.

Cormac, R. 'The Pinprick Approach: Whitehall's Top-Secret Anti-Communist Committee and the Evolution of British Covert Action Strategy', *Journal of Cold War Studies*, 16:3 (2014), 5–28.

Cormac, R. 'Disruption and Deniable Interventionism: Explaining the Appeal of Covert Action and Special Forces in Contemporary British Policy', *International Relations* (2016): 0047117816659532.

Cossaboom, R. and G. Leiser, 'Adana Station 1943–45: Prelude to the Post-War American Military Presence in Turkey', *Middle Eastern Studies*, 34:1 (1998), 73–86.

Criss, N. B. 'Strategic Nuclear Missiles in Turkey: The Jupiter Affairs 1959–1963', *Journal of Strategic Studies*, 20:3 (1997), 97–122.

Curtright, L. 'Great Britain, the Balkans, and Turkey in the Autumn of 1939', *The International History Review*, 10:3 (1988), 433–455.

Davies, P. 'From Special Operations to Special Political Action: The "Rump SOE" and SIS Post-War Covert Action Capability 1945-1977', *Intelligence and National Security*, 15:3 (2000), 55-76.

Davies, P. 'Spies as Informants: Triangulation and the Interpretation of Elite Interview Data in the Study of the Intelligence and Security Services', *Politics*, 21:1 (2001), 73-80.

Davies, P. 'Intelligence Culture and Intelligence Failure in Britain and the United States', *Cambridge Review of International Affairs*, 17:3 (2004), 495-520.

Dovey, H. O. 'The Middle East Intelligence Centre', *Intelligence and National Security*, 4:4 (1989), 800-812.

Dovey, H. O. 'The Intelligence War in Turkey', *Intelligence and National Security*, 9:1 (1994), 59-87.

Dylan, H. 'Britain and the Missile Gap: British Estimates on the Soviet Ballistic Missile Threat, 1957-61', *Intelligence and National Security*, 23:6 (2008), 777-806.

Dylan, H. 'The Joint Intelligence Bureau: (Not So) Secret Intelligence for the Post-War World', *Intelligence and National Security*, 27:1 (2012), 27-45.

Ekinci, N. 'Kurtuluş Savaşında İstanbul ve Anadolu'daki Türk ve Düşman Gizli Faaliyetleri', *Ankara Üniversitesi Türk İnkılap Tarihi Enstitüsü Atatürk Yolu Dergisi*, 14 (1994), 167-184.

Ergil, D. 'The Kurdish Question in Turkey', *Journal of Democracy*, 11:3 (2000), 122-135.

Ferris, J. 'Coming in from the Cold War: The Historiography of American Intelligence, 1945-1990', *Diplomatic History*, 19:1 (1995), 87-115.

Gaddis, J. L. 'Intelligence, Espionage, and Cold War Origins', *Diplomatic History*, 13:2 (1989), 191-212.

Gingeras, R. 'Last Rites for a "Pure Bandit": Clandestine Service, Historiography and the Origins of the Turkish "Deep State"', *Past and Present*, 206:1 (2010), 151-174.

Gönlübol, M. 'A Short Appraisal of the Foreign Policy of the Turkish Republic (1923-1973)', *Turkish Yearbook of International Relations*, 14 (1974), 1-19.

Goodman, M. S. 'Learning to Walk: The Origins of the UK's Joint Intelligence Committee', *International Journal of Intelligence and Counterintelligence*, 21:1 (2007), 40-56.

Gries, D. D. 'Opening Up Secret Intelligence', *Orbis*, 37:3 (1993), 365-372.

Güney, A. 'Anti-Americanism in Turkey: Past and Present', *Middle Eastern Studies*, 44:3 (2008), 471-487.

Gunn, C. 'The 1960 Coup in Turkey: A US Intelligence Failure or a Successful Intervention?', *Journal of Cold War Studies*, 17:2 (2015), 103–139.

Gunter, M. 'Foreign Influences on the Kurdish Insurgency in Iraq', *Conflict Quarterly*, 12:4 (1992), 5–24.

Gunter, M. 'United States-Turkish Intelligence Liaison since World War II', *Journal of Intelligence History*, 3:1 (2003), 33–46.

Hashimoto, C. 'Fighting the Cold War or Post-Colonialism? Britain in the Middle East from 1945 to 1958: Looking through the Records of the British Security Service', *The International History Review*, 36:1 (2014): 19–44.

Hashimoto, C. and E. Bezci, 'Do the Kurds Have 'No Friends but the Mountains'? Turkey's Secret War against Communists, Soviets and the Kurds', *Middle Eastern Studies*, 52:4 (2016), 640–655.

Hastedt, G. P. 'Towards the Comparative Study of Intelligence', *Journal of Conflict Studies*, 11:3 (1991), 55–72.

Hatzivassilliou, E. 'Images of the Adversary: NATO Assessments of the Soviet Union, 1950–1964', *Journal of Cold War Studies*, 11:2 (2009), 89–116.

Hinnebusch, R. 'Modern Syrian Politics', *History Compass*, 6:1 (2008), 263–285.

Hobson, J. M. 'Reconstructing International Relations through World History: Oriental Globalization and the Global–Dialogic Conception of Inter-Civilizational Relations', *International Politics*, 44:4 (2007), 414–430.

Hobson, J. M. and George Lawson, 'What Is History in International Relations?', *Millennium*, 37:2 (2008), 415–435.

Hulnick, A. S. 'Openness: Being Public about Secret Intelligence', *International Journal of Intelligence and Counterintelligence*, 12:4 (1999), 463–483.

Hurd, I. 'Law and Practice of Diplomacy', *International Journal*, 66:3 (2011), 581–596.

İnanç, G. and Y. Şuhnaz, 'Gunboat Diplomacy: Turkey, USA and the Advent of the Cold War', *Middle Eastern Studies*, 48:3 (2012), 401–411.

Jeffery, K. 'Intelligence and Counter-Insurgency Operations: Some Reflections on the British Experience', *Intelligence and National Security*, 2:1 (1987), 118–149.

Johnson, L. K. 'On Drawing a Bright Line for Covert Operations', *The American Journal of International Law*, 86:2 (1992), 284–309.

Johnson, L. K. 'Preface to a Theory of Strategic Intelligence', *International Journal of Intelligence and Counterintelligence*, 16:4 (2003), 638–663.

Jones, M. 'The 'preferred plan': The Anglo-American Working Group Report on Covert Action in Syria, 1957; *Intelligence and National Security*, 19:3 (2004), 401–415.

Jung, D. 'Turkey and the Arab World: Historical Narratives and New Political Realities; *Mediterranean Politics*, 10:1 (2005), 1–17.

Karakoç, E. 'Atatürk'ün Hatay Davası; *Bilig*, 50 (2009), 97–118.

Karaosmanoğlu, A. L. 'The Evolution of the National Security Culture and the Military in Turkey; *Journal of International Affair*, 54:1 (2000), 199–216.

Karber, P. A. and J. A. Combs, 'The United States, NATO, and the Soviet Threat to Western Europe: Military Estimates and Policy Options, 1945–1963; *Diplomatic History*, 22:3 (1998), 399–429.

Kelly, S. 'A Succession of Crises: SOE in the Middle East, 1940–45; *Intelligence and National Security*, 20:1 (2005), 121–146.

Kilcullen, D. 'Counter-Insurgency Redux; *Survival*, 48:4 (2006), 111–130.

Kirisci, K. 'Refugees of Turkish Origin: "Coerced Immigrants" to Turkey since 1945; *International Migration*, 34:3 (1996), 385–412.

Koelle, P. B. 'The Inevitability of the 1971 Turkish Military Intervention; *Journal of South Asian and Middle Eastern Studies*, 24:1 (2000), 38–56.

Krasztev, P. 'Understated, Overexposed. Turks in Bulgaria-Immigrants in Turkey; *Balkanologie: Revue d'études pluridisciplinaires*, 5:1–2 (2008), 1–23.

Lander, S. 'International Intelligence Cooperation: An Inside Perspective; *Cambridge Review of International Affairs*, 17:3 (2004), 481–493.

Lefebvre, S. 'The Difficulties and Dilemmas of International Intelligence Cooperation; *International Journal of Intelligence and Counterintelligence*, 16:4 (2003), 527–542.

Leffler, M. P. 'Strategy, Diplomacy, and the Cold War: The United States, Turkey, and Nato, 1945–1952; *The Journal of American History*, 71 (1985), 807–825.

Little, D. 'Cold War and Covert Action: The United States and Syria, 1945–1958; *Middle East Journal*, 44:1 (1990), 51–75.

Little, D. 'The United States and the Kurds: A Cold War Story; *Journal of Cold War Studies*, 12:4 (2010), 63–98.

Lucas, S. and A. Morey, 'The Hidden "Alliance": The CIA and MI6 before and after Suez; *Intelligence and National Security*, 15:2 (2000), 95–120.

Marzari, F. 'Western-Soviet Rivalry in Turkey, 1939–I; *Middle Eastern Studies*, 7:1 (1971), 201–220.

Matei, F. C. and T. C. Bruneau, 'Policy Makers and Intelligence Reform in the New Democracies; *International Journal of Intelligence and Counterintelligence*, 24:4 (2011), 656–691.

Millman, B. 'Toward War with Russia: British Naval and Air Planning for Conflict in the Near East, 1939–40', *Journal of Contemporary History*, 29:2 (1994), 261–283.

Millman, B. 'Turkish Foreign and Strategic Policy 1934–42', *Middle Eastern Studies*, 31:3 (1995), 483–508.

Mufti, M. 'Daring and Caution in Turkish Foreign Policy', *Middle East Journal*, 52:1 (1998), 32–50.

Murphy, P. 'Intelligence and Decolonization: The Life and Death of the Federal Intelligence and Security Bureau, 1954–63', *The Journal of Imperial and Commonwealth History*, 29:2 (2001), 101–130.

Norris, R. S., W. Arkin and W. Burr, 'Where They Were', *Bulletin of the Atomic Scientists* (November/December 1999), 26–35.

Noyon, J. 'Bridge over Troubled Regions', *Washington Quarterly*, 7:3 (1984), 77–85.

Ögel, Ş. Â. 'Millî Emniyet Hizmeti Nasıl Kuruldu?', *Türk Kültürü*, 128 (1973), 605–607.

Özdemir, E. and A. F. Sendil, 'The Turkish Left as an Image between Reality and Perception in the Cold War: Approach of Democrat Party towards Leftist Movements', *Cumhuriyet Tarihi Arastirmalari Dergisi*, 12:23 (2016), 337–366.

Özlü, H. 'Arşiv Belgelerine Göre, İkinci Dünya Savaşı'nda İzmir ve Trakya'nın Savunmasına Yönelik Türk- İngiliz Heyetlerinin Görüşmeleri ve Alınan Önlemler', *Çağdaş Türkiye Tarihi Araştırmaları Dergisi*, 10:23 (2011), 233–253.

Park, B. 'Turkey's Deep State: Ergenekon and the Threat to Democratisation in the Republic', *The RUSI Journal*, 153:5 (2008), 54–59.

Pearson, I. 'The Syrian Crisis of 1957, the Anglo-American "Special Relationship," and the 1958 Landings in Jordan and Lebanon', *Middle Eastern Studies*, 43:1 (2007), 54–64.

Petkova, L. 'The Ethnic Turks in Bulgaria: Social Integration and Impact on Bulgarian-Turkish Relations, 1947–2000', *The Global Review of Ethnopolitics*, 1:4 (2002), 42–59.

Poteat, E. 'The Use and Abuse of Intelligence: An Intelligence Provider's Perspective', *Diplomacy and Statecraft*, 11:2 (2000), 1–16.

Reveron, D. 'Old Allies, New Friends: Intelligence-Sharing in the War on Terror', *Orbis*, 50:3 (2006), 453–468.

Reynolds, M. A. 'Abdürrezzak Bedirhan: Ottoman Kurd and Russophile in the Twilight of Empire', *Kritika: Explorations in Russian and Eurasian History*, 12:2 (2011), 411–450.

Richelson, J. 'The Calculus of Intelligence Cooperation', *International Journal of Intelligence and Counter Intelligence*, 4:3 (1990), 307–327.
Roberts, G. 'Moscow's Cold War on the Periphery: Soviet Policy in Greece, Iran, and Turkey, 1943–8', *Journal of Contemporary History*, 46 (2011), 58–81.
Rovner, J. 'Is Politicization Ever a Good Thing?', *Intelligence and National Security*, 28:1 (2013), 55–67.
Rubin, M. 'A Comedy of Errors: American-Turkish Diplomacy and the Iraq War', *Turkish Policy Quarterly*, 4:1 (2005), 120–130.
Rudner, M. 'Hunters and Gatherers: The Intelligence Coalition against Islamic Terrorism', *International Journal of Intelligence and Counterintelligence*, 17:2 (2004), 193–230.
Rühl, L. 'Turkey, between Europe and the East', *Europa-Archiv*, 47:11 (1992), 295–302.
Sanjian, A. K. 'The Sanjak of Alexandretta (Hatay): Its Impact on Turkish-Syrian Relations (1939–1956)', *Middle East Journal*, 10:4 (1956), 379–384.
Sahin, H. 'Reading the Memoirs: Some Notes on Turkish Soldiers' Political Thoughts', *Mediterranean Quarterly*, 27:2 (2016), 28–46.
Scott, L. 'Secret Intelligence, Covert Action and Clandestine Diplomacy', *Intelligence and National Security*, 19:2 (2004), 322–341.
Seagle, A. N. 'Intelligence Sharing Practices within NATO: An English School Perspective', *International Journal of Intelligence and Counterintelligence*, 28:3 (2015), 557–577.
Sims, J. 'Foreign Intelligence Liaison: Devils, Deals, and Details', *International Journal of Intelligence and Counterintelligence*, 19:2 (2006), 195–217.
Stone, D. R. 'Soviet Arms Exports in the 1920s', *Journal of Contemporary History*, 48 (2013), 57–77.
Strachan-Morris, D. 'Threat and Risk: What Is the Difference and Why Does It Matter?', *Intelligence and National Security*, 27:2 (2012), 172–186.
Svendsen, A. 'Connecting Intelligence and Theory: Intelligence Liaison and International Relations', *Intelligence and National Security*, 24:5 (2009), 700–729.
Tachau, F. 'Turkish Foreign Policy: Between East and West', *Middle East Review*, 17:3 (1985), 21–26.
Tamkin, N. 'Diplomatic Sigint and the British Official Mind during the Second World War: Soviet Claims on Turkey, 1940–45', *Intelligence and National Security*, 23:6 (2008), 749–766.
Totrov, Y. 'Western Intelligence Operations in Eastern Europe, 1945–1954', *Journal of Intelligence History*, 5:1 (2005), 71–80.

Türkmen, Z. 'Özdemir Bey'in Musul Harekâtı ve İngilizlerin Karşı Tedbirleri (1921-1923)', *Atatürk Araştırma Merkezi Dergisi*, 17 (2001), 49-80.

Ulunian, A. 'Soviet Cold War Perceptions of Turkey and Greece, 1945-58', *Cold War History*, 3:2 (2003), 35-52.

Van Puyvelde, D. and S. Curtis, 'Standing on the Shoulders of Giants': Diversity and Scholarship in Intelligence Studies', *Intelligence and National Security*, 31:7 (2016), 1040-1054.

Warhola, J. W. and O. Boteva, 'The Turkish Minority in Contemporary Bulgaria', *Nationalities Papers*, 31:3 (2003), 255-279.

Warner, M. 'Salvage and Liquidation: The Creation of the Central Intelligence Group', *Studies in Intelligence*, 39:5 (1996), 111-120.

Watt, D. C. 'Intelligence and the Historian: A Comment on John Gaddis's "Intelligence, Espionage, and Cold War Origins"', *Diplomatic History*, 14:2 (1990), 199-204.

Welch, M. 'AFTAC Celebrates 50 Years of Long Range Detection', *The AFTAC Monitor* (October 1997), 8-32.

Westerfield, H. B. 'America and the World of Intelligence Liaison', *Intelligence and National Security*, 11:3 (1996), 523-560.

Williams, M. 'Mussolini's Secret War in the Mediterranean and the Middle East: Italian Intelligence and the British Response', *Intelligence and National Security*, 2:6 (2007), 881-904.

Worral, R. J. 'Coping with a Coup d'Etat: British Policy towards Post-Revolutionary Iraq, 1958-63', *Contemporary British History*, 21:2 (2007), 173-199.

Yavuz, M. H. 'A Preamble to the Kurdish Question: The Politics of Kurdish Identity', *Journal of Muslim Minority Affairs*, 18:1 (1998), 9-18.

Yeğen, M. 'The Turkish State Discourse and the Exclusion of Kurdish Identity', *Middle Eastern Studies*, 32:2 (1996), 216-229.

Yeğen, M. '"Prospective-Turks" or "Pseudo-Citizens": Kurds in Turkey', *The Middle East Journal*, 63:4 (2009), 597-615.

Yeşilbursa, B. K. 'Turkey's Participation in the Middle East Command and Its Admission to NATO, 1950-52', *Middle Eastern Studies*, 35:4 (1999), 70-102.

Yeşilbursa, B. K. 'The "Revolution" of 27 May 1960 in Turkey: British Policy towards Turkey', *Middle Eastern Studies*, 41:1 (2005), 121-151.

Yiğit, Y. 'The Teşkilat-ı Mahsusa and World War I', *Middle East Critique*, 23:2 (2014), 157-174.

Yılmaz, Ş. 'Turkey's Quest for NATO Membership: The Institutionalization of the Turkish-American Alliance', *Southeast European and Black Sea Studies*, 12:4 (2012), 481-495.

Zabetakis, S. G. and J. F. Peterson, 'Diyarbakir Radar', *Studies in Intelligence*, 8:4 (1964), 41–47.
Zubok, V. 'Spy vs. Spy: The KGB vs. the CIA, 1960–1962', *Cold War International History Project Bulletin*, 4 (1994), 22–33.

## Unpublished Theses

Aslan, Ö. *U.S. Involvement in Military Coups d'état in Turkey and Pakistan during the Cold War: Between Conspiracy and Reality*, unpublished thesis (Bilkent University, 2016).
Davey, G. *Intelligence and British Decolonisation: The Development of an Imperial Intelligence System in the Late Colonial Period 1944–1966*, unpublished thesis (King's College London, 2015).
Hashimoto, C. *British Intelligence, Counter-Subversion, and "Informal Empire" in the Middle East, 1949–63*, unpublished thesis (Aberystwyth University, 2014).
Odinga, S. O. *Looking for Leverage: Strategic Resources, Contentious Bargaining, and US-African Security Cooperation*, unpublished thesis (City University of New York, 2016).
Sever, A. *Cold Warrior of the Middle East? Turkey, the Cold War and the Middle East, 1951–1958*, unpublished thesis (University of Reading, 1994).
M. A. van den Berg. *The Intelligence Regime in South Africa (1994–2014): An Analytical Perspective*, unpublished thesis (North-West University, 2014).

## Newspapers, Magazines and Blogs

*CNN*
*Foreign Affairs*
*Milliyet*
*New York Times*
*Reuters*
*The Times*
*War on the Rocks*

# Index

Abwehr 6, 75, 82, 89
Acheson, Dean 100-1
AFTAC 163
aid: economic 7, 138, 143, 256, 168, 257, 259; Marshall 98; military 6, 85, 87, 124, 143, 224, 256-7, 262; technical 84, 89; UK 78, 89; US 138
Akhmedov, İsmail 78
Albania 39, 72, 141, 257
Anglo-French-Turkish treaty 72, 73, 78, 257
Arab League 219, 222
Aras, Tevfik Rüştü 70
ASA 12, 38, 165
Atatürk, Mustafa Kemal 42, 51, 65-8, 177
Atomic Energy Commission 159-63

Ba'ath Party 222-3, 224, 232
Balkans: espionage missions 123; Second World War 72-3, 80, 82-5, 88, 90; security 99; students 141; territory 146, 211
Barzani, Mustafa 182, 185-6, 188, 190-1
Beria, Lavrenti 73, 178
British Ambassador: Ankara in 47, 76, 80, 226; Baghdad in 111; Washington in 124; Tehran in 125
Bulgaria: intelligence service 180; missiles 149; note 150; subversive activities in 151; Turkish minority in 146-7, 150, 214; uranium 148; see emigres
Burrows, Bernard 47

Carım, Fuat 48
Caucasus 73, 85, 116, 121, 123, 142, 148, 200-1, 262

CENTO: counter-subversion office 262; military committee 111, 123-4, 263; security organization 109-10
Central Intelligence Agency (CIA): agents 217; in Ankara 145; in İstanbul 145, 155, 200; MAH with 145-6, 199; spy flights 139, 154-5
Chamberlain, Neville 71
Chastelain, Gardyne de 81
Churchill, Winston 41, 78, 79, 80, 157
Cold War: alliance 21, 240; early 147, 216, 245
Comintern 40, 177
Committee for State Security (KGB) 21, 102-4, 141, 182
Committee of Union and Progress 65-6
Communism: CIA 198; Kurdish nationalism 202; Turkey 66, 176-7, 180-1, 185, 187; region 194
Communist Party of Turkey (TKP) 176-9; see Communism
CORONA mission 15
COSMIC system 105, 108-9
coup: communist 225; Iraq 112, 227, 237, 239; Syria 216, 217, 223, 229; Turkey 11, 51, 153, 156, 163, 243-6, 255-61
covert action: Bulgaria 214; Syria 150, 216, 228, 255; Middle East 231, 246, 263

defector 33, 102, 200; see refugee
Democrat Party 160, 229, 242
Dodecanese Islands 72-4, 82
Dulles, Allen 155
Dulles, John Foster 124, 139, 232, 234-5, 238

Eden, Anthony 70
Egypt 7, 76, 219, 226, 227, 235, 238, 260
Eisenhower, Dwight 110, 152, 154–6, 230–4, 244, 255–6
emigres 137, 141, 147, 151, 199, 200, 214
Erim, Said 82
European Kurdish Students Association (EKSA) 185, 193

First World War 41, 43, 79, 82–3, 105, 116
France 63–5, 68–72, 102, 220, 223, 227, 257
Fuchs, Klaus 137

Gaulle, Charles de 155
Gluech, Paul Karl 82; see Abwehr
Göktan, Cemal 47
Gorshkov, Sergey 121
Government Communications Headquarters (GCHQ): bases in Turkey 158, 266; intelligence 6, 38, 41–2, 77; see SIGINT
Griddle report 98
guerrilla 49, 107, 178, 212–13; see stay-behind networks
Gürsel, Cemal 257

Harrington, Charles 66
Hatay 68, 71, 212, 217, 221, 224, 231, 245, 264
Hitler, Adolf 74, 78, 80, 82, 90
Hoxha, Enver 39

Incirlik base 83, 154, 155, 157, 239; see TUSLOG
İnönü, İsmet 71, 74, 76, 79, 80, 183, 191
intelligence: definition 31, 33; diplomacy 11, 99, 120, 166, 186, 216
Iran: policy 74, 80, 109, 111, 124–7, 144, 150, 178, 181–90; Shah of

Iran 240; Turco-Iranian Bureau 191
IRD 195–8
Israel 9, 175, 217, 222, 225, 227, 235
Italy 72–4

Johnson, Lyndon 2
Joint Intelligence Committee (JIC) 11, 33, 42, 53–5, 110, 125
Joint United States Military Mission for Aid to Turkey(JUSMATT) 144, 158, 160
Jordan 219, 235, 237, 239, 240

Kapustin Yar 152, 165
Karasapan, Celal Tevfık 70
Khrushchev, Nikita 121, 182, 236–7
Knatchbull-Hugessenn, Hughe 80, 86; see British Ambassador
Köprülü, Fuat 99, 100, 158, 179
Korur, Nuri Refet 162–3
Kurdish Democratic Party (KDP) 182–3
Kurds: CENTO 126, 129, 190, 193; CIA 192; Soviet 21, 74, 181, 184, 187; Syria 189; Turkey 183, 185, 187

Lebanon 65, 225, 237–40, 264

Macmillan, Harold 124, 125, 234
MAH: apprehended by 103; CIA 145–6, 199, 212; contacts 200; human agents 183; IRD 196–8; smuggle 149; prevented by 189; report by 178; Turkish intelligence 13, 15, 33–4, 41–9
Main Intelligence Agency (GRU) 102–3, 193; see Committee for State Security (KGB)
Mayatepek, Hüveyda 162
McGhee, George 99–100
Menderes, Adnan: government 144, 156, 159, 196, 200, 238, 243–6; overthrown 185; prime minister 155, 159, 162, 194, 216, 227, 235

Menderes, Ethem 184, 243–4
Menemencioğlu, Numan 86–8
Middle East: British Policy 114, 199; Eisenhower doctrine 231; global war 127; Kurdish movement 186; oil 217; operations 75; OSS 82; RAF HQ 86–8; rivalry 217, 245; SOE 89; Soviet 175, 181–2, 234; Turkish Policy 99, 229, 235, 239, 242, 246, 256; US Policy 227, 237–8; Western Intervention 230
Mirza, Iskender 124
MM 66–7
Molotov, Vyacheslav 72, 78, 258
Montreux Convention 71, 121
Mosul 68, 178, 187, 215, 241
Mussolini, Benito 72

Nasser, Gamal Abdul 7, 111, 228, 231, 233, 236, 238, 260, 265
National Security Agency (NSA) 12, 23, 54, 139, 152, 165
National Security Council 11, 51, 54, 143, 154, 199, 255
Nazi 78, 80, 81, 147, 178, 257
North Atlantic Treaty Organization (NATO): Information Service 195; intelligence 102, 113–17, 148–9; military planning 102, 106; Security Committee 105, 107–8; SHAPE 143; Special Committee 17, 19; Standing Group 105, 119, 122, 263
nuclear; attack 139, 155, 157; missile 139, 261; radioisotopes 160; research 159, 158, 162; Soviet programme 139, 145, 148–51, 163, 166–7, 213; weapons 120, 127, 129, 139–40, 151, 155

Office of Strategic Services (OSS) 35, 37, 81–3
Öğel, Şükrü Ali 15, 55, 70, 71
Okday, İsmail 82

Operation OVERFLIGHT 154
Operation Straggle 22, 225–9, 231, 264
Orbay, Kazım 85–6, 178
Özdemir Bey 69, 245

Penkovsky, Oleg 103, 193; see Main Intelligence Agency (GRU)
People's Commissariat for Internal Affairs (NKVD) 104, 137, 178
Philby, Kim 141, 142
Power, Gary 156
propaganda: British 196; centres 183, 193, 200; Cominform 195; communist 173, 195–7; foreign 180; MAH 198; method 70, 81, 194, 200, 220, 227, 237, 242; Soviet 184, 186, 190, 192, 202, 228; see psychological warfare
Psychological Strategy Board (PSB) 199
psychological warfare 33, 186, 192, 195, 198–201, 266

Qasim, Abd-ul Karim 112, 189
Quwatli, Shukri 220–4

refugee 33, 108, 191, 232; see emigres
Republican People's Party (CHP) 44, 46, 197, 242
Roosevelt, Archibald 186, 200
Roosevelt, Franklin 79

sabotage 46, 66, 80–1, 151, 212, 231
Said, Nuri al 228, 261
Saka, Hasan 220
San Francisco Conference 89, 183, 218–19, 258
Saraçoğlu, Şükrü 72–7, 258
Second World War 63, 77, 89, 105, 115, 182, 193, 212
Secret Intelligence Service (MI6) 141–2, 149, 212–13, 259
Security Service (MI5) 101, 104–7, 110–12, 135, 148, 180

# Index

SIGINT: activities 12, 33, 45, 50, 76, 86, 151; bases 38, 51, 90, 167, 259, 266; posts 6, 63, 86–7, 165
Sixth fleet 114–15, 122
SOFA 152–3, 156, 166–7
Soviet Union: agents 21, 68, 104, 111, 137, 188, 190; intelligence 78, 104, 137, 175, 193; military 72, 113, 141, 187, 241, 258; propaganda 47, 184, 195, 202, 228; supported 22, 118; weapon 119, 166
Soyoğuz, Remzi 83–5
Special Operations Executive (SOE) 40, 80–1
Stalin, Joseph 98, 140
stay-behind networks 19, 80–1, 107, 212, 243
Suez crisis 128, 199, 212, 227–9, 237, 245
Syria: covert action 216; diplomatic crisis 226; CIA 230; French mandate 69, 212, 219; intelligence 220, 231; Soviet Union 227; Turkish policy 217–18, 224, 229, 234, 240

Tito, Joseph Broz 88
Truman, Harry: 36–7, 55, 217, 259; doctrine 98
Turkey: covert operation 70, 211–12; diplomatic codes 75; economy 143, 155, 180; eastern provinces 72, 178, 241, 258; foreign policy 68, 82, 99, 197, 218; influence 150, 211; NATO 102, 106, 108–9, 119, 152; secret intelligence 76, 213, 239; security 100, 108, 116, 121
Turkish General Staff (TGS): building 107–8; informed 148, 178; intelligence 42, 44, 50, 76, 117; liaison 153; national security 53, 83–6; NATO staff 119, 121, 123; nuclear energy 164
Turkish Straits: military positions 104, 165; Soviet activities 107, 121–2, 178–9, 258; see Montreux Convention
TUSLOG 38, 42, 154, 155, 157, 165, 167

U-2 117, 154–8, 164, 243, 261
Ulusan, Aziz 107–8
United Arab Republic 235, 237, 240
United Kingdom: CENTO 110–12, 123–6; cooperation 81–4; consulate in Istanbul 149; decipher 73; embassy 80–1, 162, 188–9, 196, 242; intelligence 53, 63–4, 75–6, 88, 109; interception 80; interests 89; NATO 114–15; occupation 69; spyflight 117; support 70, 74, 142, 157; threat 54
United Nations (UN): discussions 89, 125, 183, 211, 218, 225–7; General Assembly 236; Security Council 226
United States: CENTO 124, 241; intelligence needs 63; intelligence sharing 18, 21, 152; relations with Turkey 79, 81, 99, 143, 159, 217; Kurdish question 186, 202; National Intelligence Estimate 16, 37, 55; Soviet agents in 137
uranium 139, 148, 166, 214; see nuclear
Ürgüplü, Suat Hayri 144–5, 231, 238–9

Von Papen, Franz 74, 79

Warren, Fletcher 144, 157, 216–17, 230–1, 240, 243, 257, 261
Wavel, Archibald 79

Yalta conference 98
Yamut, Nuri 120–1
Yugoslavia 78, 82, 88

Zaim, Husni 217, 223–4
Zorlu, Fatin Rüştü 139, 240, 244

www.ingramcontent.com/pod-product-compliance
Lightning Source LLC
Chambersburg PA
CBHW070018010526
44117CB00011B/1625